BEAT THE MENOPAUSE
WITHOUT HRT

About the Authors:

Maryon Stewart studied preventive dentistry and nutrition at the Royal Dental Hospital in London and worked as a counsellor with nutritional doctors in England for four years. At the beginning of 1984 she set up the PMT Advisory Service which has subsequently helped thousands of women world-wide. In 1987 she launched the Women's Nutritional Advisory Service which now provides broader help to women of all ages.

Maryon Stewart is the author of the bestselling books *Beat PMS Through Diet*, now in its third edition, and *Beat Sugar Craving*. She is the co-author of *The Vitality Diet, Beat IBS Through Diet* and *The PMT Cookbook*. She has had her own weekly radio programme on health and nutrition, she has co-written several medical papers and has written articles for many glossy magazines and for the *Daily Mirror*. She has also appeared on several popular TV magazine shows. She has contributed regularly to 'Capital Woman', has done a series of programmes for Yorkshire TV's 'Help Yourself' programmes and has helped Anglia TV with their 'Bodyworks' series. Maryon has written her own regular page in the magazine *House & Garden* and she now writes regularly for *Healthy Eating* magazine. She frequently lectures to both the public and the medical profession. She is married to Dr Alan Stewart and they live in Lewes, Sussex, with their four children.

Dr Alan Stewart qualified as a doctor at Guy's Hospital, London, in 1976 and spent five years specialising in hospital medicine. He is a member of the Royal College of Physicians. He worked at the British Homeopathic Hospital in London and qualified as a Member of the Faculty of Homeopathy. For the last twelve years he has specialised in nutritional medicine and was a founding member of the British Society for Nutritional Medicine. He is medical advisor to the Women's Nutritional Advisory Service and is actively involved in educating other doctors on the subject of nutrition.

He is the author of several bestselling books, has written medical papers and many articles in both the medical and popular press and has frequently appeared on radio and television.

Cartoons by Mik Brown.

BEAT THE MENOPAUSE WITHOUT HRT

Maryon Stewart

with contributions from
Dr Alan Stewart

HEADLINE

To my mother, Rosa,
with eternal love

First published in 1995
by HEADLINE BOOK PUBLISHING

10 9 8 7 6 5 4 3 2 1

ISBN 0 7472 7840 7

Typeset by
Letterpart Limited, Reigate, Surrey

Printed and bound in Great Britain by
Mackays of Chatham plc, Chatham, Kent

HEADLINE BOOK PUBLISHING
A division of Hodder Headline PLC
338 Euston Road
London NW1 3BH

Contents

May you live all the days of your Life

Jonathan Swift (1667–1745)

Important Note

There are many fairly technical terms used to describe the phases of the menopause and its associated conditions. While many of the terms are explained in the text, you will find a Dictionary of Terms on page 285. It is important to have a good understanding of the text, so do look words up even if you are only vaguely unsure of their meaning.

If after reading this book you feel you would rather have a programme individually devised for you, you are welcome to contact the Women's Nutritional Advisory Service for help. You will find details on page 283.

Acknowledgements

I should first sincerely like to thank the many researchers who have gone before me, and as a result made my path so much easier to tread. In particular, thanks are due to Dr John Studd, Dr Malcolm Whitehead, the psychologist Myra Hunter, and to Dr Morris Notelovitz in Florida and Dr Lorraine Dennerstein in Australia whose work has been particularly instructive.

Special thanks are due both to Dr Alan Stewart and Dr Guy Abraham for their advice and support over the years. Without their technical support we would not have been able to provide such valuable help to so many women, and education on the nutritional approach to health to so many doctors and health-care professionals.

I should like to express deep gratitude to the wonderful patients who have volunteered to share their case-histories with us in this book in a quest to help others with similar suffering. Their willingness to divulge intimate details so frankly, especially before they knew that I was intending to change their names, is highly appreciated.

I am very grateful to *Woman's Realm* for allowing us to conduct a survey of their readers and to Kimberly-Clark and Efamol for providing the funds for the analysis of both this and the GP survey.

Next I must thank my dedicated team at the Women's Nutritional Advisory Service, who have jointly helped to make this book possible. In particular thanks are due to Cheryl Griffiths for her wonderfully calm coordination skills, Jayne Tooke who even continued with the data entry when she went into premature labour, and to Jenny and Annie for their typing skills. Thanks also to Joanne Rooke for her help with some of the delicious recipes, and to our extended team at the Hale Clinic in London and at our clinics in Sussex.

I am very grateful for advice I received from Deryn Bell on osteopathy, Paul Lundberg on acupuncture and acupressure, Julian Barker on herbal medicine and Helen Keighley of the YMCA on exercise.

As always I am indebted to Lavinia Trevor, my agent, whose fancy footwork helped to make this book possible, to Sue Fleming for her expert editing and to Anna Powell at Headline for her support and enthusiasm.

Last I thank my husband, Alan, for his support with both the technical side of the book and on the home front, and our four dear children – Phoebe, Chesney, Hester and Simeon – for allowing me the time out to get the words on the page, and for providing cuddles, back-rubs and refreshments on request, even if I did have to bribe them!

Maryon Stewart
Sussex, 1994

Foreword

The menopause is something which must come to every woman, and this 'change of life' unfortunately brings with it a number of problems. The readjustments that take place within the body at this time can cause hot flushes, sleeplessness and irritability amongst many symptoms, and can lead the way to other conditions, not least osteoporosis, the fragile bone disease to which so many women over fifty fall victim.

Up until very recently it seemed as though the medical establishment was blind to the problems of women of that certain age, and our mothers and grandmothers would have had to suffer in silence. With the advent of hormone replacement therapy (HRT), however, everything appeared to be solved, and women felt they could look forward to a middle and old age free of all the symptoms they anticipated with dread. At last the spectre of the menopause had been banished from their futures.

But had it? Well, no, for some women the spectre remained. Just as every woman has a different reaction to the hormonal upheavals that take place in the body during the menopause, so women had different reactions to the various constituents of the pills or patches of HRT. Some experienced symptoms even worse than those of the menopause they were trying to evade; many others disliked the idea of chemical interference anyway; but even more women were actually unable to take HRT – for a variety of health reasons, some quite serious – in my case the risk associated with breast cancer.

It was then that the cavalry arrived, in the shape of the Women's Nutritional Advisory Service and in the person of Maryon Stewart. Having spent a dozen or so years studying the effects of the pre-menstrual syndrome (PMS) on women, she knew that a natural rather than a chemical approach was the answer, and realized that the same principles could be applied to the problems involved in the menopause. It could be faced through means other than HRT.

Her emphasis on weight-bearing exercise and a more active lifestyle, plenty of relaxation, sensible nutritional supplementation and on eating good natural foods makes for a healthy framework for living that could last well beyond the years of the menopause. *Beat the Menopause without HRT* is a book that every woman should buy, read and follow. The rest of their lives could depend on it.

Diana Moran
London, 1994

Introduction

At the time of the menopause the leisure and pleasure years should stretch joyously before you. Now that women are living longer than ever before, there are golden opportunities to indulge in all the leisure pursuits that may have taken your fancy and achieve some of the goals that were just dreams when family and work commitments took a priority. When the family are old enough to be independent and the financial commitments have dwindled, in theory there should be no stopping you so long as you are in good health.

However, for at least three-quarters of all women, the menopause brings with it rapid changes and unwanted symptoms which, in many cases, are life-disrupting and produce utter misery. Being reduced to a hot, red, anxious, introverted wreck, struggling to keep a grip on life at the very time when it should be at its peak, is a bitter pill to swallow.

Until recently the menopause has been shrouded in secrecy, a near taboo subject that was hardly discussed in public. Who wants to admit that they are 'at the beginning of the end' and having a rough time? As we live longer, it stands to reason that we shall survive experiences that perhaps previous generations did not encounter. How should we cope with this? Who should we turn to for answers, when the medical profession are perhaps not fully equipped to deal with them? The menopause can be and has been for many women both a frightening and an isolating experience.

In a sense, we are pioneers, and there are lots of thus far unanswered questions which I shall address in this book. Here you will find the myths of menopause uncovered and the pros and cons of HRT unveiled. You will learn about the hormonal changes that occur at the time of the menopause and why they rob you of your confidence, your 'cool' and your libido. After reading Parts One and Two you will be able to stand back and make some informed choices for yourself, feeling secure about your new knowledge and the fact that you are in control of your body.

For those who can or wish to take Hormone Replacement Therapy (HRT) a rapid solution may be in sight. However, for those who cannot tolerate HRT, either for medical reasons or because of the many side-effects, or for those who do not wish to take it, the medical profession has little to offer to allay symptoms and to help prevent the silent bone-thinning disease, osteoporosis.

All in all, I estimate that there are up to 50 per cent of women for whom HRT is not an option in the long term. A large proportion of women do not take hormones as a solution to their menopausal symptoms. Estimates of usage in countries like Italy, France, Germany, Denmark, South Australia, the UK and the USA, range from 3 per cent in Italy to 32 per cent in California. Many women who begin using hormone therapy abandon it within a few months: according to one study the average duration of therapy is nine months and of those who start treatment, up to two-thirds will abandon it within one year. It therefore follows that there has to be an alternative.

At the Women's Nutritional Advisory Service, over the past ten years, we have pioneered a scientifically based natural approach to overcoming menopausal symptoms which also helps to prevent osteoporosis. Designed either for those women who cannot or do not wish to take HRT, it's an effective programme which combines dietary changes, simple exercise, plenty of relaxation and specific nutritional supplements. As well as helping with the short-term menopause symptoms, patients report that the programme also improves their general well-being and, as a result, improves their quality of life in the long term. It therefore follows that the natural approach can also be used by women taking HRT as it is perfectly compatible and may also reach the parts that HRT does not.

Menopause Symptom Questionnaire

Do you suffer from any of the following? Please ensure each symptom is only ticked *once*.

MOLLY	*How many times per month	None	Mild	Moderate	Severe
1 Hot/cold flushes*	TOO MANY TO COUNT				✓
2 Facial/body flushing*					✓
3 Nightsweats*					✓
4 Palpitations*			✓		
5 Panic attacks*			✓		
6 Generalised aches and pains				✓	
7 Depression			✓		
8 Perspiration			✓		
9 Numbness/skin tingling in arms and legs		✓			
10 Headaches				✓	
11 Backache				✓	
12 Fatigue				✓	
13 Irritability				✓	
14 Anxiety				✓	
15 Nervousness				✓	
16 Loss of confidence					✓
17 Insomnia					✓
18 Giddiness/dizziness		✓			
19 Difficulty/frequency in passing water				✓	
20 Water retention					✓

21	Bloated abdomen			
22	Constipation	✓		
23	Itchy vagina		✓	
24	Dry vagina		✓	
25	Painful intercourse			
26	Decreased sex drive			
27	Loss of concentration			✓
28	Confusion/Loss of vitality			✓

Have you noticed since the onset of the menopause:

1 Loss of height   Yes/No

2 Difficulty in bending   Yes/No

3 Increased curvature of back   Yes/No

Are any of the above symptoms cyclic? (i.e. come in cycles, for example on a monthly basis)   I HAVE NOT NOTICED

Have you gained weight since you started the menopause?   Yes/No   If yes, how much   7-10 lb

Do you have any other menopausal symptoms not mentioned above?

How long have you had menopausal symptoms?   18 MONTHS

Did you suffer from pre-menstrual tension prior to the menopause?   Yes/No   If yes, for how long?

xv

Follow-up Menopause Questionnaire

Do you suffer from any of the following? Please ensure each symptom is only ticked *once*.

MOLLY	*How many times per month	None	Mild	Moderate	Severe
1 Hot/cold flushes*	1-3 PER DAY		✓		
2 Facial/body flushing*			✓		
3 Nightsweats*		✓			
4 Palpitations*		✓			
5 Panic attacks*		✓			
6 Generalised aches and pains		✓			
7 Depression		✓			
8 Perspiration		✓			
9 Numbness/skin tingling in arms and legs		✓			
10 Headaches		✓			
11 Backache		✓			
12 Fatigue			✓		
13 Irritability			✓		
14 Anxiety		✓			
15 Nervousness		✓			
16 Loss of confidence		✓			
17 Insomnia		✓			
18 Giddiness/dizziness		✓			
19 Difficulty/frequency in passing water		✓			
20 Water retention		✓			

21 Bloated abdomen	✓		
22 Constipation	✓		
23 Itchy vagina	✓		
24 Dry vagina	✓		
25 Painful intercourse			
26 Decreased sex drive			
27 Loss of concentration		✓	
28 Confusion/Loss of vitality	✓		

Are any of the above symptoms cyclic? (i.e. come in cycles, for example on a monthly basis) _____

I DON'T KNOW, NONE ARE BAD ENOUGH TO BE A PROBLEM

xvii

Whether you can grasp the thought of it or not, there is no need to go on suffering with symptoms unnecessarily. By following the programme laid out in this book you will not only overcome your menopause symptoms in the short term, but you will notice that common symptoms like fatigue, headaches, constipation, bloating, insomnia and general aches and pains may also improve.

Molly's Story

Molly was a forty-nine-year-old mother of two from Potters Bar in Hertfordshire. When she approached the WNAS for help she was taking prescribed hormones and was experiencing severe PMS symptoms as a side-effect.

'As my periods diminished the hot flushes began. By the time my periods stopped altogether I was experiencing horrendous night-sweats, at least two or three times per night, with never a night off. I also suffered tingling and numbness in my arms and legs, loss of confidence, vitality and ability to concentrate. I became aggressive, had water retention, breast tenderness, fatigue, aching legs, was hypersensitive to music and light, had alternating bouts of constipation and diarrhoea, plus flatulence, migraine, depression and itchy skin that had bothered me for years.

'My doctor prescribed Prempak-C which seemed OK at first but after approximately three months I was experiencing headaches and progressively heavier bleeding, so much so that even two night-time sanitary towels together would not cope with the flow.

'After six months my doctor changed my hormone preparation to Syntex Menophase, which again was fine at the start. After a few months I began experiencing cramps for two days and nights each month, and severe PMS, worse than anything I had ever known before. I felt so wretched before my monthly bleed that I did not want to go out or see anyone. For this my doctor then prescribed progesterone pessaries. I used one each morning for three days, but these made me feel as if I was enveloped in a net shroud so that I felt completely detached from what was happening around me. I also gained about ten pounds in weight while on the HRT.

'My attitude to my family changed. I became very grudging, not wanting to do anything for anyone. A resentful attitude pervaded everything I did. I was very bad-tempered with my husband and generally unhappy. I often wrote myself notes to remind me of things to nag him about when he came home from work.

'I reached rock bottom one evening when I was tired and hungry while cooking dinner. My husband insisted on questioning me despite my telling him to leave me alone until after I had eaten. He persisted, saying he needed an immediate answer. I picked up a sharp pointed kitchen knife and thrust it at his abdomen. Fortunately for both of us it was winter and the knife did not seriously penetrate his layers of clothing.

'I was relieved to learn about the work of the WNAS while watching a lunchtime television programme and subsequently enrolled on their postal and telephone services. Initially I bought the book *Beat PMS through Diet* and began to follow its recommendations. Once I had completed my questionnaire and diet diary sent to me by the WNAS they wrote a programme for me which I immediately began to follow. I reduced my intake of wheat, sugar, salt, tea, coffee, alcohol, chocolate and spicy food. On the third day withdrawal symptoms started, mainly headaches, and lasted for four days. After this my symptoms began lifting and I knew I was heading in the right direction. I also took the supplements Gynovite Plus and vitamin E, and followed a moderate weight-bearing exercise programme. That was four years ago. Now I am more stable and things do not bug me like they used to. I was told that I was a much nicer person than I had been for years within three months of starting the programme. I really think that if I had not followed the WNAS programme I would now be in Holloway Prison serving a sentence for murder!'

Molly and the many other case-histories who have kindly agreed to appear in this book will assure you that you are not suffering alone and will give you confidence that the end of your symptoms is in sight. Realistically, you need to invest the next four to six months in helping yourself back to good health. According to our research, the degree to which you follow the recommendations is directly related to the rate at which you will recover. Once you have read through the book and worked out the programme to follow, the message is to stick to it like superglue!

If you feel you can't manage alone and would like some extra help or advice, then you will find the address of the WNAS on page 283. It's never too early to improve your general health and to work towards preventing osteoporosis. So as you approach menopausal age, even if you are symptom-free, work out a diet that you would find enjoyable, using the guidelines given later in this book, together with a moderate exercise and nutritional supplement regime. If you start in time you might even sail through your menopause without really noticing it!

Whether you are approaching the menopause, currently in the throes of it or have just emerged from it, you will need to read the first parts of the book and then go on to work out your tailor-made programme from the guidelines in Parts Three and Four. You will also find daily menus and delicious recipes to try there, as well as notes on the nutritional content of food: this will help you choose the foods you like, knowing that they are rich in the essential vitamins and minerals.

Finding the programme that your body thrives on is a voyage of discovery that need only be made once. It's a voyage that both you and your family will undoubtedly be glad you undertook.

Good luck and bon voyage.

Part One

THE REALITIES
OF THE MENOPAUSE

One

You and the Menopause

The word menopause does not mean it's the beginning of the end or a pause between men! Simply translated, it actually means the end of the monthly fertility cycle. The term was coined by a French physician called Gardanne, who referred to it in 1812 as *menepausie* and subsequently shortened it to *menopause* in 1821. The word menopause comes from the Greek *meno*, meaning 'month', and *pausis*, which means 'ending' or, more literally, 'a pause in a life-cycle'.

Throughout the years, this 'pause' has been vilified, misunderstood, dreaded . . . But now, fortunately for all of us, we have a much better understanding of the workings of the body, and the ways in which we can influence our brain chemicals and hormones by improving our nutritional state. Although hormone replacement is still a favourite first-line therapy in some quarters, there are now other proven approaches to overcoming menopausal symptoms and preventing osteoporosis. As modern women, who have an equal voice in society, we now have a choice.

What your mother didn't tell you

We were taught about contraception at school and given information about having children. During pregnancy we were bombarded with information and choices about where and how to have our babies. Our mothers and their friends gave advice at every available opportunity, hoping to pass on their wisdom and make life easier for us. So why is it that we are all in the dark about the menopause? The menopause is a natural event, after all, not a disease, and it affects one-half of the world's population!

3

In the UK alone over thirteen million women are over forty and it's estimated that this will increase by a further one and a half million by the year 2001. In the USA statistics show that between forty and fifty million women will pass through the 'change of life' by the year 2000. Here in the UK and also in Australia, according to Theresa Gorman MP, one-third of the hospital beds are occupied by women who have a menopausal-related problem. That must signify that the menopause and osteoporosis, the bone-thinning disease that affects one out of every three women, are causing serious problems, which are not being sufficiently addressed in preventive terms.

Many of our mothers' generation would not have been brought up on free communication. Before the 1960s, most women only spoke about their most personal and intimate problems behind closed doors. The average Victorian woman's expectation was to keep reproducing almost until she died. The average age expectancy was approximately fifty-five years, so there was therefore little need for society to make preparations to see women through the menopause and beyond.

Now that we live far longer than previous generations – the average lifespan for a woman is currently eighty-three – it means that at the time of the menopause we still have on average 40 per cent of our lives left to live. This completely takes care of the myth that by the start of the menopause we are already in God's waiting-room!

On the whole, women do not sit at home any more producing large families and waiting on their nearest and dearest. They have careers, pursue hobbies and are expected to remain productive members of society well into their sixties and even their seventies. Women of fifty in the 1990s simply don't look like women of a similar age fifty years ago. We not only look younger, we feel younger, which may be why the menopause often takes us by surprise. I've often heard women say 'I'm not old enough to be menopausal', but that is largely due to their preconceived ideas. In the recent survey we conducted on menopausal women, the youngest to start her menopause was only twenty-three years old! Admittedly that is abnormally

4

young because the average age is fifty, but it can happen at any time. We just have to prepare ourselves mentally and make sure that we are in the best possible shape.

Our expectations and perception of ourselves have also changed dramatically. These days, women in their forties and fifties are not on the social scrap-heap. It is quite acceptable for women of menopausal age to keep up with fashion trends if they so desire and to actively work to maintain their youthful appearance. There is even the extreme option of having faces lifted, breasts enlarged, and other little discreet tucks, purses permitting, all of which are procedures that didn't even occur in the wildest dreams of past generations. In the 1990s, thanks to Emily Pankhurst and her colleagues, women sit in boardrooms, they stand for parliament, they perform operations, they climb mountains and compete with men on a day-to-day basis. They do not expect to retire into the woodwork from the time of their first hot flush or expect to take a two-year sabbatical to have their menopause in peace.

Thankfully, medical science has moved on tremendously in the lifetime of our generation. We are far more enlightened about the causes of potentially fatal conditions like heart disease, cancer and indeed osteoporosis, and we are beginning to understand how we can prevent these diseases from taking over and bringing an abrupt end to our lives.

It is all a question of perception. Your expectations of your menopause may well influence the kind of menopause you experience. With this in mind, in 1994 we conducted a survey of 500 women who had recently experienced their menopause to examine their attitudes, hope and fears about the menopause as it approached.

Survey results

80 per cent of women reported that they were delighted that their periods had stopped. This was by far the most agreed-upon factor.

45 per cent looked forward to more leisure time.

40 per cent said they were afraid that their physical appearance

would disintegrate quickly once into their menopause.

37 per cent felt that the menopause signalled the start of old age! Whereas 33 per cent thought it was right 'to grow old gracefully' and 19 per cent were willing to trade youth for wisdom.

35 per cent were pleased they no longer needed to use contraception.

32 per cent felt positive about the start of a new era, and 28 per cent felt pleased that they could look forward to pursuing their own goals.

17 per cent dreaded their menopause, 8 per cent found it difficult to come to terms with no longer being fertile.

While 17 per cent wondered if their partner would now prefer a younger woman, 14 per cent felt sexually liberated!

The *Woman's Realm* survey

For many years the Women's Nutritional Advisory Service had been approached by women for advice about diet and lifestyle around the time of the menopause. In the early 1980s we felt that there was not really enough information to give much solid and useful advice to many of these women.

Gradually our opinion has changed and for several good reasons. First, the value of hormone replacement therapy has become much better defined. Its benefits and risks are now quite well-understood although there remain some important unanswered questions, and we know also what it is good for and what it is not so good for. It is clear that for some women it is not answer enough and in the UK in particular there is a degree of reluctance to use HRT by both doctors and the public.

Second, the last ten years has seen the publication of many scientific papers documenting the relationship between nutrition and hormone function. Could this explain the enormous variation in hormone levels within the normal female population and the great individual variation in response to some hormone treatments for menopausal-related and other symptoms?

Finally our own experience and that of others in treating

women with premenstrual syndrome led us to conclude that diet and lifestyle had a major impact on both the physical and mental symptoms of these women. Some of them began to come back saying 'You helped me with my PMS. Now that I am approaching the menopause, what can I do to help control my own symptoms?' Gradually, from listening to these women, understanding their symptoms and advising them along lines similar to those that had helped them with their premenstrual problems, we were able to see that dietary and lifestyle factors could also be important in the menopause.

We wanted to know more. Over the years tens of thousands of women have contacted us about PMS, but because of our caution our contact with women around the time of the menopause was rather limited. We knew, like most research scientists, that if you really want to know what is going on you will have to collect information from hundreds of women. The reason for this is that around the time of the menopause there are many factors to be considered. These include age at the time of the menopause (strictly speaking the date of the last natural period), gynaecological history, especially if there has been a hysterectomy, dietary factors, the influence of stress, the role that their partner might play and so on.

We were very pleased when Gill Cox at *Woman's Realm* agreed to help us by publishing a questionnaire for women at the time of the menopause. Kimberly-Clark helped with funding to analyse the results of the survey and kindly offered all the respondents a sample of their panty-liners. Efamol also kindly financially supported our research into the menopause.

We have been enormously helped by this survey which has brought forward our understanding of menopausal symptoms and their relationship to dietary and lifestyle factors. The results of this survey are to be found in the relevant chapters throughout this book and especially in the following three.

The response to the survey was excellent. After it appeared in a February issue we soon had the 500 replies we had hoped for and set about analysing the findings. (A further 200 were also received but we haven't as yet had time to look at these.) Each woman was asked more than thirty questions, many with several subsections, so that in all we had nearly a hundred pieces of information from each woman.

Of the first 500 replies, only 418 revealed their age! Who did they think we were going to tell? Their average age at the time of their last period was forty-six years; the youngest was twenty-three and the oldest fifty-seven. This sample had experienced their menopause some four years earlier than the general population.

AGE AT THE TIME OF THE MENOPAUSE

Age in years	23–30	31–40	41–45	46–50	51–55	56–
% of women in survey	1	16	27	40	15	1

TIME SINCE THEIR LAST PERIOD

Time since last period	Under 4 months	4–6 months	7–12 months	13–24 months	25–48 months	49–72 months	73–120 months	121–372 months
% of women	22	5	6	15	14	12	13	13

The average time since the last period was four years and eight months or fifty-six months.

CHANGES IN PERIODS
40.4 per cent commented that their periods became irregular as they approached the menopause. Furthermore, 44 per cent marked the questionnaire to say that their periods had become heavier, 17 per cent to say that they had become lighter and 39 per cent that there had been no change with this aspect of their periods.

HYSTERECTOMY
Of the 500 women, 119 (23.8 per cent) had previously had a hysterectomy, but oddly enough over one-third were not sure whether their ovaries were intact or not! You can bet their bodies knew.

RELATIONSHIP BETWEEN AGE AND SYMPTOMS

Though we looked at twelve different symptoms, only hot flushes showed any relationship. The younger women were at the time of the menopause, the more likely they were to be troubled by hot flushes. It would thus seem that the younger you are at the time of the change, the less easily it was tolerated. But this is not quite true, as hot flushes were the only symptom to show this pattern; no other symptom was influenced by age. This was our first clear indication that there was something more than just a change in hormones involved. This is a view increasingly supported by other researchers.

Two

The Facts of the Menopause

The menopause is not known as the 'change of life' for nothing. But exactly what changes can we expect? It is important to develop an understanding of the phases of change and the different symptoms and problems associated with them, if you are going to stay in control during your menopause. Once you have got to grips with exactly what it all entails, you will be in a better position to make a fully informed decision about treatment.

Medical terms defined
Certain words are in common general, medical and scientific usage and we need to know clearly what they mean.

MENOPAUSE
The word menopause only actually refers to the time at which the last natural period takes place. It is a date, not several months or years. Often it can only be ascertained for certain when there has been no natural period for one year. So in fact many women have their menopause without even knowing it!

PERIMENOPAUSE
The perimenopause refers to the time around the menopause, more usually the time leading up to the menopause.

POSTMENOPAUSE
The postmenopause refers to the time after the menopause. As the changes in hormone function are not sudden but gradual, and fluctuate over months or even over several years, it is often more scientific to say that a woman is either experiencing her

perimenopause, or postmenopause, rather than saying that she is actually menopausal.

MENARCHE

The menarche is the term that simply refers to the onset of periods. Like menopause, it is a date and not a long period of time.

MENSTRUATION

Menstruation is another word for monthly period, which is the approximately monthly loss of blood due to the shedding of the lining of the womb. This normally occurs each month if the woman has not become pregnant. Women who are taking HRT or the oral contraceptive pill do not, strictly speaking, have periods; they have a withdrawal bleed.

WITHDRAWAL BLEED

This is the bleed that occurs when the lining of the womb is lost as a result of stopping the administration of the female sex hormone oestrogen. This is a dependable response by the womb, and will almost always occur unless the woman is pregnant.

OESTROGEN

Oestrogen is one of the two female sex hormones. Its main functions are to encourage the development of female characteristics. It is mainly produced by the ovaries under the influence of the pituitary.

PROGESTERONE

This is the second female sex hormone. Its main function is to stimulate the growth of the lining of the womb. It does this in order to prepare the womb to receive a fertilized egg. It also modifies some of the functions of oestrogen.

TESTOSTERONE

Testosterone is the male sex hormone, which is also found in small amounts in women.

The normal menstrual cycle

Approximately each month the ovaries produce an egg ready for fertilization. This happens under the stimulus and direction of hormones produced by the pituitary gland which is situated at the base of the brain, a few inches behind our eyes. It produces many hormones to control the thyroid gland in the neck, the adrenal glands in the abdomen and the ovaries. It has been likened to the conductor of a hormonal orchestra. It controls hormone output by these glands on a day-to-day and even minute-to-minute basis. The ovary for its part provides two main elements: the eggs which come pre-formed as Graafian follicles (named after their discoverer), and the theca or substance of the ovary in which the tiny follicles are embedded and which is responsible for the production of the female sex hormones, oestrogen and progesterone.

The ovary has a limited supply of eggs all of which were formed in the womb before your own birth – hence the importance of your mother's health and diet during pregnancy. Each month several follicles are stimulated to develop by a hormone from the pituitary called, appropriately, follicle stimulating hormone or FSH. Usually one follicle, occasionally more, matures to a point where an egg is released, an event that normally takes place in the middle of the cycle. The egg is released as a result of a small rise in FSH, and a very large surge of a second hormone from the pituitary called luteinizing hormone, or LH.

In the first part of the cycle the ovaries are also busy producing oestrogen which encourages the lining of the womb to thicken so that it might be ready should fertilization take place. Oestrogen levels continue at a more moderate level after ovulation and are joined by the second female sex hormone, progesterone. This is produced by the follicle in the ovary after the egg has been released and reaches a substantial peak around day twenty-one of the cycle. It then falls away unless fertilization takes place; and the rapid fall in the level of progesterone causes the lining of the womb to be shed and a period results.

So these two key hormones from the pituitary, FSH and LH,

12

dictate the events in the ovary in terms of whether ovulation will take place or not and how much of the hormones oestrogen and progesterone will be in circulation.

So what happens at the menopause?

The normal menopause

For most women ovulation is a regular event between the ages of twenty and forty. From approximately the age of forty onward the supply of Graafian follicles begins to run out. There may be cycles in which the level of oestrogen is slightly reduced. The pituitary senses this and increases its release of FSH to stimulate the tiring ovary more. The follicles may mature more irregularly, often more slowly, so that the time between cycles becomes longer or shorter. Progesterone levels will fall as ovulation does not always occur.

The second hormone from the pituitary gland, LH, also rises a little later on. As oestrogen levels fall to very low levels the lining of the womb loses its main source of stimulation and periods cease. Levels of FSH and LH remain high for several years, as they continue to live in hope, before they finally get the message and subsequently fall away.

The last actual period denotes the date of the menopause itself. This can only be determined with hindsight, usually after there have been no periods for at least six months in a woman of suitable age, with typical symptoms or with hormonal evidence of the menopause. The commonest test is to measure FSH, LH and oestrogen levels in the blood.

During the run-up to the menopause there is considerable instability, with all these hormonal changes occurring. Not surprisingly this is the time when symptoms can be most troublesome, especially if you are already a sufferer of premenstrual syndrome.

Mary's Story

Mary is a forty-nine-year-old woman who worked full-time as a personal assistant to a managing director. Her job was fairly demanding and she also had a home and family to look after.

'My symptoms became noticeable after I had some tests for recurrent abdominal pain and exhaustion. I suddenly became aware that I was very tense at work, almost to the point of not being able to answer the telephone, or concentrate on anything. This would happen every two hours. I had waves of tension at night with sweating, my periods became heavier and irregular and my legs ached. I had no stamina, so much so I sometimes had to lie down at work as I felt as if I could not "put another foot forward".

'I managed to cope over Christmas. My doctor put me on Primulot N, a progesterone supplement, and iron tablets to replace iron lost during exceedingly heavy periods. I was not at all happy about taking the hormone pills but I was assured that it was a mild dose. My symptoms became worse. I would have sudden profuse sweating, I couldn't concentrate and I would feel tense and very shaky inside. I also experienced mood swings where I would suddenly feel tearful and low. My confidence was affected to the point that at times I did not want to drive the car or go shopping in case I felt ill.

'My doctor was at a loss to know what to do with me. "Try relaxation," she said, "It is not the menopause as your hormone levels are still normal." I was beginning to despair – was I going mad? The menopause books did not highlight symptoms like mine. I decided that I had to get back to basics – you are what you eat – and I happened to read about the work of the WNAS.

'I made an appointment to which my husband drove me. What a relief to meet Maryon Stewart, who after taking a good long case-history suggested that my symptoms may be due to low blood-sugar levels, influenced by the hormonal changes around the time of the perimenopause. She worked out a programme for me and suggested that I eat wholesome food, little and often. At last somebody understood my symptoms and was offering help.

'I filled in the menopause diary from the WNAS every day, grading my symptoms, which I found very useful. Basically my programme consisted initially of a wheat-free diet, supplements, a weekly massage, relaxation, a gradual increase in exercise and some acupuncture.

'My husband, son and boss have been most supportive. As we were not busy at work I was able to cut down my days to four instead of five, which I feel has aided my recovery. I noticed a change almost immediately following the WNAS advice. Gradually over the weeks and months the symptoms reduced. A year later, I can say that I am much better. I have regained my confidence, my stamina has returned and I am back to working five days per week. I can swim forty lengths at a time now, which I couldn't even have contemplated before.

'This experience has certainly made me re-assess my life and lifestyle and I now know that health is everything. My GP wants me to take HRT, but while I am feeling well I see no need to rock the boat and risk getting side-effects and gaining weight. I am hoping that as a result of my increased well-being and degree of fitness I will sail through the next stages of the menopause with ease, or at least with as little fuss as possible!'

After the menopause

By now you might think that a woman's hormones have left the equivalent of the Garden of Eden to enter the Wilderness. But where there is life there is hope!

Levels of oestrogen and other hormones do not fall away to nothing. Small but significant amounts of oestrogen are produced by the conversion of normal amounts of androgens (male sex hormones) that are still circulating in the blood-stream. These are produced by the adrenal glands, near the kidneys, and from the remaining part of the ovary. They are then converted into weak oestrogen hormones by chemical reactions in fat tissue, the skin and the adrenal glands themselves. Though these levels are low they are not insignificant.

Postmenopausal women who develop cancer of the lining of the womb have relatively high levels of oestrogens circulating in their body. As you can imagine, the more fat tissue you have the more of these residual oestrogens can be formed. So obesity is undoubtedly a risk factor for cancer of the uterus.

In the postmenopause the levels of FSH and LH eventually fall away; and with this stage comes a relatively stable hormonal situation with symptoms usually becoming less, but with a rise in the risk of conditions such as heart disease and osteoporosis. These risks are in part due to the fall in oestrogen and in part due to age, diet and other factors.

Is menopause primarily hormonal?

The view widely held until recently is that virtually all the symptoms of the menopause could be explained on the basis of a failure by the ovaries. Such a view was strongly supported by the experience and testimony of many women who had taken HRT and experienced dramatic relief from many or all of their symptoms. While there is indeed a strong relationship between *some* of the symptoms of the menopause and the falling levels of the hormone oestrogen, because we are extremely complex animals, it stands to reason that there are some other biological mechanisms at play. These should not only be considered but should also open the door to alternative and more natural solutions to HRT. This is the aim of this book.

Three

The Menopause is Here

When the first intimations of the menopause are experienced, they often bring with them a set of new symptoms that have never been experienced before. The menopause may well coincide with a number of other health factors, and the degree of severity may well be associated with the timing of the symptoms and whether you have experienced a hysterectomy.

Timing

There is a substantial variation in the timing of the menopause. For the majority of women their last natural period will be somewhere between the ages of forty-five and fifty-five, with an average in the UK of fifty point seven eight years, compared with the average age of onset in the US which is currently forty-nine point eight years. Interestingly, there has been little change in the time of onset of symptoms over the last hundred years and even in the Middle Ages fifty years was about the norm. The age at the onset of the menopause varies between cultures. Black women, for example, tend to experience an earlier menopause than white women in the US, and it can be nearly ten years earlier in malnourished women from developing countries. Nutrition, chronic infection and chronic illness in developing countries are factors that need to be taken into consideration.

Just why is there such a divergence in the Western population? Several studies have been conducted to look at what determines the age of the menopause. By far the biggest determinant of an early menopause is smoking: the more you smoke, the sooner your periods cease. This looks like a toxic effect of something in cigarettes and is yet another reason to stop or cut down if one were needed. Heavy smokers can reach the menopause two years earlier than their non-smoking counterparts.

Other factors that have been linked to a slightly earlier menopause are never having had children, possibly being short or underweight and possibly finishing your last pregnancy before the age of twenty-eight. These effects appear small.

Just because your periods began early does not mean that you will escape your periods earlier. It was once thought that an early start to periods meant that the menopause would be later, but even this theory was soon discounted.

As the cessation of menstruation is mainly determined by the ovaries running out of eggs, it would not be surprising if the factors present at the time your eggs were being formed are relevant. As this takes place before you were born, perhaps what was going on during your mother's pregnancy needs to be considered. Astonishingly, when the ovaries are developing some five to seven million follicles are formed by the fifth month of pregnancy. By the time the baby is born this has fallen to around two million and continues to fall thereafter. Mother Nature is already sorting out the wheat from the chaff.

It is now known that the female offspring of smokers are more likely to have difficulty getting pregnant, perhaps because their ovaries have taken a knock. Low birth-weight, being premature or severe illness of the mother during pregnancy might also be factors. We will have to see what future research reveals. Nutrition may well be found to be a factor, too, as smoking adversely affects the levels of many nutrients. Smokers tend to eat less well than non-smokers and, as we shall see, there are a number of essential nutrients that influence hormone metabolism, hormone problems and the function of the ovaries.

The story doesn't end there. During the perimenopause, the run-up to the last actual period, the rate of follicle loss increases in line with the rise in the level of pituitary hormones. It might just be possible that anything that increased the sensitivity of the ovary to respond to these stimulating hormones, such as the balance of certain nutrients, would help to delay the final day. See chapter 11.

Finally there are a few unfortunate women who will experience the menopause at a young age, before they are forty. Most but not all of these women have run out of eggs, sometimes naturally, or alternatively because the individuals have received anti-cancer drugs or radiotherapy. However, we should not underestimate the possible influence of nutrition from birth to the menopause. If cessation of smoking and a long-term improvement in diet could delay the menopause by three or four years, this could make a substantial difference to the duration that many of these women took HRT for, and in their exposure to some of the long-term delayed risks, especially that of breast cancer.

Jill's Story

Jill was only thirty-six when she began an early menopause. She was on HRT for several years, but eventually the side-effects became too great and she had to come off it. She is a health visitor and counsellor from Leicestershire, with three children. She first approached the WNAS for help seven years ago, at the age of forty-seven.

'In 1976 we were living in Zimbabwe. I was thirty-six years old and my children were aged eight, five and two. When I first missed a period my first thought was – was I pregnant again? I didn't feel pregnant, but I saw my doctor and had a pregnancy test which was negative. Nobody was unduly concerned, although I had always had a regular menstrual cycle, so I kept thinking it would come soon. But it didn't.

'My doctor referred me to a gynaecologist, who went through my case history and checked my thyroid levels, and then pronounced that he thought I was going through an early menopause. By this time I had missed five periods. He asked me to keep a temperature-chart and lo and behold I suddenly ran a high temperature and experienced abdominal pain, which was followed by a period. My response was to think: that proves him wrong – fancy suggesting an early menopause!

'At about this time we were making arrangements to return to England, and there was a lot of stress to deal with, the move,

19

sorting out our house which had been let out while we were away, and had gone to rack and ruin in five years, and the fact that my husband was starting his new job and working all hours, including weekends. To crown it all I injured my neck carrying my youngest child in a heavy rainstorm. I was subsequently in agony and unable to sleep.

'My doctor prescribed a course of iron tablets for my absent periods, which had not returned, but these did nothing. I remember seeing him one day and saying tearfully that something needed doing, otherwise I felt my marriage would be heading for divorce. I seemed to be constantly tired and irritable, I was getting headaches, felt anxious, my memory wasn't so good and sometimes I felt quite confused. I found it difficult to concentrate and was feeling very low.

'I was referred to a consultant who after doing various tests said that my ovaries were not functioning. He prescribed HRT, which I had never heard of until then, and I remember feeling very lucky to live near one of the only HRT clinics in the country at the time. Within days of commencing Cycloprogynova I began to feel a new person, like my old self again, with the sense of humour I hadn't realized I'd lost! Also I could sleep again, and the pain in my neck and the numbness in my arms I had been experiencing as a result, went too.

'As the weeks and months progressed I found a pattern emerged. I would have approximately sixteen days when I felt great, then I began to feel edgy and sailed into a week of PMS symptoms. At the HRT clinic I was prescribed vitamin B6, and also Premarin to take the week I was off the Cycloprogynova. I was also prescribed Moduretic, to deal with the fluid retention. As I also had insomnia again during my bad week, my GP also prescribed Halcion.

'In March 1985 I read a piece in *The Times* – "Diet could End Women's Bad Days". It was a report on the research conducted by the WNAS. I wrote for some information which I found very interesting and I passed it on to my health visitor colleagues and also to my clients. Looking back, I do not know why I didn't ask for some help for myself at that point.

'The next eighteen months became increasingly stressful. My husband had to take early retirement because of government cuts. We seemed to have endless marital crises, which he blamed on me and my problems. My GP prescribed Diazapam to help relax me during my bad week, which was when things got really out of hand.

'I finally phoned the WNAS for myself and spoke to a very reassuring person. She sent me some questionnaires which I duly completed and returned, and a programme was worked out for me to follow. I changed my diet, which I had previously thought was very healthy, took supplements and increased my exercise regime.

'Within three months most of my symptoms had gone and I was able to reduce or omit most of the medication I had been taking, but I did continue with the HRT. I progressed on and within six months all my symptoms had gone.

'The following summer I developed an odd rash on my legs, like lots of little blood blisters. Because we were not sure of the cause my GP suggested I come off the HRT for a month. My husband had just been posted abroad, and as the whole family was about to go abroad to be with my husband for nearly two months, and I would have plenty of time to relax, I thought it would be a good time to try coming off the HRT. I felt fine off the HRT this time, despite the fact that the trip was very stressful, and my relationship with my husband was at breaking point. He refused to communicate or spend any time with me alone, without the children. But, amid all the stress, I still felt more "myself", I had no desire to be back on the HRT and felt I could cope.

'So I came off the HRT finally in May 1988 and haven't taken it since. I mostly observe the WNAS dietary recommendations, still avoiding caffeine, whole wheat and chocolate. I usually manage very well by eating Ryvita and drinking small amounts of decaffeinated coffee. I find that whenever I lapse to any great extent, I start getting digestive problems, can feel very tired and sometimes feel anxious, irritable and moody.

'Sadly I came to recognize the total futility of trying to work at any sort of positive relationship within my marriage and in 1990 I obtained a divorce. Regardless of the stress of the breakdown in my marriage, the divorce, having to move house, my father developing senile dementia giving increasing concern for both my parents, three bereavements in the family, financial worries and other problems, I coped very well indeed. I have built a new life

21

PMS Symptom Questionnaire

✓ JILL

Symptoms	Week after period (Fill in 3 days after period)				Week before period (Fill in 2-3 days before period)			
	None	Mild	Moderate	Severe	None	Mild	Moderate	Severe
PMT-A								
Nervous tension	✓				variable depending on stress factors			
Mood swings	✓						✓→	✓
Irritability	✓						✓	
Anxiety	✓					✓		
PMT-B								
*Weight gain	✓						✓	
Swelling of extremities	✓						✓ legs	
Breast tenderness	✓					✓		
Abdominal bloating	✓					✓		
PMT-C								
Headache	✓				sometimes ✓			
Craving for sweets	✓					✓	✓	
Increased appetite	✓					✓		
Heart pounding	✓				✓			
Fatigue	✓						✓	→✓
Dizziness or fainting	✓				✓ (during teens)			

22

PMT-D					
Depression	✓			✓	✓
Forgetfulness	✓			↑✓	↑✓
Crying	✓			↑✓✓	
Confusion	✓			✓	✓
Insomnia	✓			✓	↑✓
OTHER SYMPTOMS					
Loss of sexual interest	✓				
Disorientation	✓			✓	
Clumsiness	✓				✓
Tremors/shakes	✓		✓	✓	
Thoughts of suicide	✓			✓	
Agoraphobia	✓				
Increased physical activity		✓			
Heavy/aching legs	✓			✓	✓
Generalised aches	✓				
Bad breath	✓			✓	
Sensitivity to ~~noise~~/light	✓			✓	✓
Excessive thirst	✓				*sometimes*

Do you have any other PRE-MENSTRUAL SYMPTOMS not listed above

1 _____   4 _____

2 _____   5 How much weight do you gain before your period

3 _____   *3-4 lbs*

23

Follow-up Menopause Questionnaire

Do you suffer from any of the following? Please ensure each symptom is only ticked *once*.

JILL	*How many times per month	None	Mild	Moderate	Severe
1 Hot/cold flushes*		✓			
2 Facial/body flushing*		✓			
3 Nightsweats*		✓			
4 Palpitations*		✓			
5 Panic attacks*		✓			
6 Generalised aches and pains		✓			
7 Depression		✓			
8 Perspiration		✓			
9 Numbness/skin tingling in arms and legs		✓			
10 Headaches			✓		
11 Backache			✓		
12 Fatigue		✓			
13 Irritability			✓		
14 Anxiety			✓		
15 Nervousness		✓			
16 Loss of confidence		✓			
17 Insomnia		✓			
18 Giddiness/dizziness		✓			
19 Difficulty/frequency in passing water		✓			
20 Water retention		✓			

21	Bloated abdomen			✓
22	Constipation			✓
23	Itchy vagina			✓
24	Dry vagina			✓
25	Painful intercourse			✓
26	Decreased sex drive			✓
27	Loss of concentration			✓
28	Confusion/Loss of vitality			✓

Are any of the above symptoms cyclic? (i.e. come in cycles, for example on a monthly basis) _No – they were due to_ _stress at work and in my personal life at the time._

25

for myself and feel happier, more confident and in fact am healthier now than I think I have ever been. Also I now look and feel ten years younger than I did ten years ago.'

When PMS meets the menopause

It's pretty bad luck if your premenstrual syndrome bumps into the start of your menopause symptoms, and you have the worst of both worlds. It is a common problem, but fortunately one that can be sorted out effectively within the space of a few months. Numerous studies reveal that the occurrence of cyclical physical and mental symptoms that are present just before the arrival of menstruation and diminish or disappear with or shortly after its arrival are at their most prevalent in the mid-thirty age group. So what are they doing here in a book on the menopause? Well, for some women PMS never quite goes away and can even be worse in the perimenopausal phase. This is presumably due to the hormonal instability at this time. This and other hormone-related factors has caused many researchers in the past to attribute PMS to a lack or an excess of any hormone you care to mention. The medical profession do not speak with one voice in this matter. More critical research, however, has found no consistent hormonal abnormality in the majority of PMS sufferers and a more modern understanding is to ascribe the cause of PMS to an undue sensitivity, on the part of the sufferer, to the normal hormonal changes that take place in the last half of the cycle. Now this makes it a lot easier to see how PMS might fit in with some women's perimenopausal experience.

Most women who suffer from PMS do not enjoy the hormonal roller-coaster. Furthermore, the most successful treatments include anything that effectively switches off the ovaries. No working ovaries means no PMS! Oestrogen implants work like magic, producing a near-religious experience for some women. But alas, the benefit may not last as the body adjusts to a new hormonal balance and the natural cycle re-imposes itself.

Our own substantial experience and that of others who have also published their results is that PMS can be helped by a change of diet, the use of certain nutritional supplements, and physical exercise. These factors can all influence female-hormone chemistry, nervous-system chemistry, general well-being and physical fitness. They can do so in a far more gentle and as effective a way as the 'best' hormonal treatment.

In our survey mentioned in Chapter 1 we also looked at the relationship between previous PMS suffering and current meno-pausal symptoms. The difficulty with this sort of question is that the person's perception of the past may be influenced by their current state of health.

There did seem to be a moderate connection between the severity of past premenstrual symptoms and some current menopausal symptoms. This held true for symptoms of depression, anxiety, confusion and insomnia in particular. Physical symptoms, such as hot flushes and nightsweats showed only a minor degree of association with past PMS.

It would therefore seem that symptoms that are mainly attributable to oestrogen withdrawal, such as hot flushes, are not greatly influenced by a history of PMS. 'Mental' symptoms, however, do seem to show some kind of continuity. It is not possible from the questions we asked to discern how much of this was due to psychological problems, or hormonal or other health problems.

As diet and lifestyle seem to make such a big difference to many women's PMS, there seems to be good hope for many menopausal women suffering with similar mood changes at the time of the menopause.

Annabelle's Story

Annabelle, a florist from Hertfordshire with three grown-up children, was forty-seven when she approached the WNAS for help. Her PMS symptoms had reached a crescendo, as her menopause symptoms were beginning.

'My periods had gradually become very heavy, leaving me feeling exhausted. During the run-up to each period I felt extremely anxious and irritable, with incredibly sore breasts, having gained about half a stone in weight, which felt like half a ton around my middle.

'I thought this was bad enough. Then one day I began having hot flushes and nightsweats as well. My head would throb continually and my heart would pound, and I honestly thought I was going insane. I was so relieved to hear about the WNAS and apart from anything else I discovered I was addicted to caffeine. I made dietary changes, which incidentally I had to follow closely otherwise I fell behind again, and I began an exercise programme, which I felt much better for, and took specific nutritional supplements.

'Within a couple of months I was like a different person. All my PMS symptoms disappeared, the flushes and sweats went, and I felt human again. I can honestly say life is normal again and I feel like the storm is over. I have even managed a three-month trip with my husband to visit our daughter in Australia. I feel like I have been reborn.'

Further information on the treatment of PMS and the experience we have had in treating the women attending the Women's Nutritional Advisory Service's clinics can be found in the book *Beat PMS Through Diet*. That said, there will be some women in the perimenopause with premenstrual symptoms who will benefit from some form of hormonal therapy. For them a small dose of HRT in the form of tablet or patch will help smooth out the hormonal swings. Those women with a uterus will need to take a cyclical dose of progesterone and this is associated with a return of PMS symptoms in 20–30 per cent.

If you have some premenstrual symptoms, are in the perimenopause and are undecided about HRT, then read on. PMS is only one factor to consider in deciding how best to control the symptoms of the change.

Hysterectomy

Hysterectomy is the surgical removal of the womb and is one of the commonest operations performed in the UK. Some 20,000 take place here each year and a staggering 590,000 are performed each year in the USA. It involves the removal of the womb, either through an incision in the abdomen or, in about 25 per cent of cases, by it being removed through the vagina. A total hysterectomy just removes the womb including the cervix or neck of the womb. Sometimes the ovaries, which are at either side of the uterus, are also removed together with neighbouring tissues; this is called a radical hysterectomy. The ovaries may need to be removed if they are diseased with large cysts, endometriosis or cancer.

Studies have revealed a great variation in the frequency with which hysterectomies are performed, especially in different regions of the USA. Though there is agreement about the need for hysterectomy in women with uterine cancer, there is not so much agreement about its need for non-cancerous reasons such as fibroids, heavy periods and pelvic pain. Recently, two detailed American publications have looked at the reasons why hysterectomies are performed and their outcome. Data collected by the National Center for Health Statistics in Atlanta revealed the rate of just under 600,000 hysterectomies per year for the years 1988–90. The overall rate per year was just below six hysterectomies for every 1,000 women rising to ten in the thirty to fifty-four years age group. The overall rate was slightly higher in black women compared to white. The commonest reason was uterine fibroids followed by endometriosis, prolapse and cancer among others. Fibroids were listed as the reason twice as commonly in blacks compared with whites and cancer twice as commonly in whites when compared with blacks. The ovaries were removed in 50 per cent of the operations and this became more likely with increasing age. However, oophorectomy, the medical term for the removal of the ovaries, was still performed in 29 per cent of the youngest age group listed, the twenty-five to thirty-four years category. For virtually all of these HRT will be necessary.

The outcomes of 418 hysterectomies were assessed in the second study from the Massachusetts General Hospital. For those women who had the operation because of fibroids, abnormal bleeding or pelvic pain, the outcome was frequently very favourable. New problems arose in some with hot flushes

(13 per cent), weight gain (12 per cent), depression (8 per cent) and lack of interest in sex (7 per cent) being recorded one year after the operation in those who were not troubled by these problems before it.

Hot flushes were, as you would expect, more likely in those who had had an oophorectomy (14 per cent) but still occurred in 3 per cent of those whose ovaries were not lost. On a more positive note, only 3 per cent of women still had negative feelings about themselves as a woman one year after the operation.

It seems that many women will continue to enter the menopause as a result of a hysterectomy with loss of their ovaries. HRT will be offered and taken by a majority of these women, especially in the USA. Those women who have had a hysterectomy because of uterine cancer will not be able to take HRT. This may change if future research shows that HRT is safe in those women in whom the cancer has not recurred.

Sarah's Story
Sarah, who lives in Essex, was in her early fifties when she contacted the WNAS for help. She had previously had a hysterectomy and was using Estraderm patches.

'I started my menopause when I was forty-five. My periods became irregular and extremely heavy. I experienced night shivers which were followed by hot flushes, and disturbed sleep, waking every two hours with tingling limbs. As a result I felt constantly tired and intolerant to others during the daytime. I also had a bloated tummy and evening flushes, which made me disinterested in travel or evening outings in particular.

'Although my doctor had prescribed Estraderm patches, I read about the WNAS programme in a magazine and decided to contact them for some additional advice. I found the programme written for me reassuring and experienced some instant benefit, gradually feeling less fatigued. I have continued to avoid red meat, spirits and fried foods.

'I am sixty years old now and I still feel great. I'm full of energy and I sleep well. I look forward to each day, meeting friends, going away and returning home. After a good night's sleep I am more tolerant generally and cope far better with my semi-invalid husband. As a result of following the WNAS programme I am now more able to enjoy living instead of it being an effort to get through each day.'

Contraception and the menopause

Women over forty *do* get pregnant, and though fertility certainly declines from the late thirties onward, contraception is still an important issue for the perimenopausal woman. A study of older women between the ages of forty and fifty-five who were menstruating regularly found that 93 per cent were still ovulating. At the age of forty-five the rate of pregnancy is still 10 to 20 per cent of women per year. Hence the need for contraception.

Barrier methods are often the choice. More mature couples may be prepared to use condoms, the diaphragm or contraceptive sponge and foam. The intra-uterine contraceptive device, the coil, may be suitable. Infection and rejection may not be the problems they are in younger women but heavy periods can easily be worsened and the coil will then need to be removed.

Perhaps no contraception is necessary? No period for a year in a woman aged over fifty, and for two years in a woman aged forty-five to fifty, makes pregnancy unlikely but not impossible. If ovulation can be influenced and sustained by an improvement in diet, then be warned! Oral contraception is still possible for the perimenopausal woman, who is not looking to increase the size of her family. HRT, it must be remembered, is not an effective contraceptive, as the dosage of oestrogen is not great enough to inhibit natural ovulation should it occur.

There are two different types of oral contraceptive: the combined (oestrogen and progestogen) oral contraceptive or COC, and the progestogen-only pill, POP. Progestogen is the name for synthetic progesterones of which there are several types; these are also used in some HRT preparations to produce a regular withdrawal bleed. COCs can now be given to women of any age provided they are healthy non-smokers with no

31

reason to avoid oestrogen. As the oestrogen in COCs is synthetic, and many times more potent than natural oestrogens, there has to be a greater degree of caution with its use than with that in HRT. COCs cannot be given if there is a history of or the presence of most types of heart disease, a history of blood clots, sickle cell anaemia, most types of liver disease, breast and gynaecological cancers and many rare but serious conditions that were worsened during pregnancy. Particular care needs to be taken with those who have other medical problems or are taking a variety of drugs.

The advantage of COCs in the perimenopause is that they will help to control irregular cycles, they will reduce the symptoms of oestrogen withdrawal and they can minimize bone loss. However, side-effects include breast enlargement, fluid retention, an increase in blood pressure, leg cramps and pains, depression, loss of libido, headaches, weight gain, nausea, patches of increased skin pigmentation, vaginal discharge, cervical erosion and breakthrough bleeding. So it is very much up to each individual to decide whether the possible disadvantages outweigh the benefits.

The large variability in tolerance of the oestrogen-containing oral contraceptives has encouraged interest in the progestogen-only pill, POP. Here, a small dose of a progestogen is taken every day throughout the cycle even when bleeding occurs. Progestogens may stop ovulation but they also thicken cervical mucus and inhibit implantation of a fertilized egg. They do not stop the hormonal changes of the menopause and do not diminish the symptoms of oestrogen withdrawal. In fact, they could aggravate such symptoms. Their advantage is that they are safer than COCs and are particularly suitable for those who cannot take COCs, especially smokers. Again, POPs cannot be taken by those with a history of severe heart disease, circulation problems and blood clots, those with a history of ectopic pregnancy and in a few other rare situations. They interact with several drugs and special care needs to be given when they are taken by those with high blood pressure, severe migraine and ovarian cysts. Side-effects are not too common except for irregular bleeding. Breast discomfort, acne, ovarian cysts and headaches can still occur and some women experience depression and haemorrhoids.

So there are the choices. The short- to mid-term risks of these oral contraceptives, provided you can take them, are not great but the full magnitude of the long-term risk will not be apparent until a large series of women in their forties have been using oral contraceptives for ten years or more. And what will be the risk for these women of then going on to HRT? Again, the answers will still be many years in coming.

For most women in the forty-plus age group who need contraceptive advice there is much benefit in seeking expert advice from a family-planning counsellor, practice nurse or general practitioner with special interests in these problems. Do bear in mind that if your menopause begins before the age of fifty you will need to use contraception for at least two years following your last period, and after fifty it's still contraception for a year, please!

Four

The Symptoms of
the Menopause

These fall roughly into three groups: physical symptoms, some of which are directly due to the withdrawal of oestrogen, some not so directly, and mental symptoms.

The significance of oestrogen
The main and predominant symptoms that can be attributed to the withdrawal of oestrogen are:

Hot flushes
Nightsweats
Vaginal dryness
Loss of libido
Difficulties with intercourse
Urinary symptoms
Skin changes

Oestrogen acts like all hormones by stimulating a change in certain tissues. It acts predominantly on the tissues of the female reproductive system, the uterus or womb, the vagina, the vulva and the end portion of the urethra – the outlet for the passage of urine from the bladder. Breast tissue is also influenced by oestrogen; it also affects skin tissue and blood vessels, although this does not result in the production of hot flushes.

HOT FLUSHES

DEGREE OF HOT FLUSHES IN A SURVEY OF 500 WOMEN

None	Mild	Moderate	Severe	Total suffering
12.5%	23.5%	36%	28%	87.5%

Hot flushes as they are known in the UK, and hot flashes in the USA, are the commonest symptom of the menopause and actually have several components to them.

In our *Woman's Realm* survey of 500 women they were reported by 87.5 per cent. Other surveys have found that they affect 70–80 per cent of menopausal women. In our survey we also found that they were more likely to be a problem in women who experienced their menopause at a younger age. For these women there is perhaps a more abrupt hormonal change being imposed on a system that has had less time to adapt.

The flush is usually felt over the upper trunk, neck, face and arms. The first event is an increase in blood flow to the affected area of skin. This is followed by redness or a flush, a rise in skin temperature of about 1° Celsius, and then sometimes by sweating which acts to cool the skin. There may be a rise in pulse rate at about the same time as the sensation of heat is experienced, and there can be a small rise in blood pressure. As you would expect with the increase in the flow of blood to the skin and the subsequent sweating there is loss of heat from the body and a tiny but perceptible drop in the temperature of the inside of the body. At the time of or just before the flush there are some changes in the levels of certain hormones – but not in the level of oestrogen!

The flush is preceded by a surge in hormone activity, not by the pituitary gland, but by an area of the brain called the hypothalamus, adjacent to the pituitary. Many hormones are released including the one that causes a rise in the level of LH from the pituitary. It also appears that there is a surge of activity in the part of the nervous system that controls the adrenal glands, blood pressure and blood flow. Not surprisingly this is connected to the hypothalamus. So the hot flush is not due to a sudden change in sex hormones but to a change in the activity of that part of the brain that has the main influence over the pituitary. It seems that the pituitary is not the conductor of the hormonal orchestra but the conductor's baton and it is the hypothalamus that is calling the tune. This part of the brain also controls the appetite, the timing of the menstrual cycle and temperature regulation. It appears therefore that the hot flush is as much a 'brain event' as it is a hormonal one.

But what part does oestrogen play?

It appears that these events of the flush only take place if oestrogen has been present in the system and is then withdrawn. Young girls before puberty do not flush, neither do those very few unfortunate girls whose ovaries are unable ever to make oestrogen. They will flush if they are given oestrogen and it is then stopped. Some women on HRT feel better if they can take oestrogen all the time without stopping and starting it, but oestrogen can only be taken continuously if you have had a hysterectomy (because of the risk of cancer of the uterus).

So a hot flush is due to a withdrawal of oestrogen rather than a lack of it. It can even happen when the oestrogen level is high and falling. There is more information about this aspect of the menopause in Chapter 8 which deals with the side-effects of HRT.

Not all women are flushers and women clearly show enormous variability in the degree to which they do flush. Experiments on women who do flush have shown that between hot flushes they experience small but definite irregularities in the flow of blood to the skin of the forearm and that these irregularities are diminished by giving oestrogen. So HRT acts both on the brain and the blood vessels of the skin to combat the hot flush.

Hot flushes, if frequent, greatly affect the quality of life. The flush is strongly associated with sweats in the day or at night. The flushes at night disturb sleep and this may be due to the changes in brain chemistry that precede the flush rather than just the flush itself. Flushers tend to have more menopausal symptoms than non-flushers and these include mental symptoms such as irritability and depression as well as physical symptoms such as aches and pains and tiredness.

Eventually (well, almost always), the system adjusts itself to the withdrawal of oestrogen. This can take months or years. The menopause is really a testing time for many women and the test is in part 'How well can your body chemistry cope with a falling level of oestrogen?' The solution is often just to give oestrogen in some form, but other approaches that help your chemical and nervous system can also be of benefit.

Alison's Story

Alison is a fashion designer from Cheltenham in Gloucestershire. She was forty-nine when she contacted the WNAS for help with her hot flushes. I remember speaking to her when she had just retired from teaching and was hoping to set up her own business. We decided that the day of her consultation was going to be the first day of the rest of her life in more ways than one.

'When my periods became irregular I assumed my menopause was underway. I didn't seem to have any problems, until the flushes began. The flushes became very severe both during the day and at night. I lived in dread of them, and as their timing was so unpredictable I never knew when one was going to strike. They made me feel very uncomfortable, especially the cold dampness that remained afterwards. I was unable to get enthusiastic about anything – and I live on my creativity. I just felt stressed, irritable and extremely tired. I used to get at least twelve hot flushes during the day and about eight each night. It was quite exhausting. If I exerted myself even slightly, just by walking up a hill, or experienced the simplest problem at work, I would instantly have a hot flush. And many other flushes came without any apparent reason.

'A friend at a yoga class happened to have had similar problems, and was helped by the WNAS. I didn't hesitate to contact them myself and was soon on a new diet, taking special vitamin and mineral supplements and doing more exercise. It took exactly one week for the symptoms to disappear. I was utterly amazed at the speed of recovery. I have not looked back since, except for one or two hiccups which I can pinpoint the cause of. That was a year ago. My friends comment all the time on how much better I look, and my close friends would admit that I'm not crabby any more. It's so nice to be back in control.'

NIGHTSWEATS

DEGREE OF NIGHTSWEATS IN A SURVEY OF 500 WOMEN

None	Mild	Moderate	Severe	Total suffering
25%	18%	32%	25%	75%

Nightsweats commonly accompany hot flushes as they are both due to the same mechanism. In our survey, nightsweats did not seem to tie up with any symptom other than hot flushes. This confirms the concept that they are both due to the withdrawal of oestrogen and that with the other symptoms some other factors apart from hormonal change are at play.

VAGINAL DRYNESS

DEGREE OF VAGINAL DRYNESS IN A SURVEY OF 500 WOMEN

None	Mild	Moderate	Severe	Total suffering
41%	20%	24%	15%	59%

This was very strongly associated with pain on intercourse especially in the slightly older hysterectomized women. It was also associated with loss of libido. It appears that vaginal dryness is a relatively late menopausal problem and this concurs with other research.

The decline in oestrogen results in a decrease in the blood flow to the area, with a loss of elasticity in the tissues and a shrinkage of the cells in the vagina, vulva, uterus, bladder, urethra and breast tissues. Similar but lesser changes also take place in the skin. As a result the vagina becomes drier and less elastic. These changes can be reversed by the use of oestrogen preparations by mouth or applied in the form of a cream to the vagina and vulva. As we shall see later, oestrogen as HRT is not the only way to promote a return to youthfulness in these tissues. They can also respond to natural oestrogens in our diet.

Oestrogen also influences the nerves that sense touch in the area of the vulva and vagina. Touch perception is obviously important when it comes to sexual arousal and response. The responsiveness of these nerves is reduced as oestrogen levels fall at the menopause but it can be restored to its previous level of sensitivity with the use of HRT. Again it appears that some of the effects of oestrogen are due to its effects on the nervous system and not just on the tissues of the vagina and vulva. Dietary changes, particularly those that include the plant forms of oestrogen, phytoestrols, have also been shown to return the vaginal tissue to normal (see page 129).

The changes in the health and sensitivity of these tissues can obviously influence sexual activity. Vaginal dryness makes intercourse more difficult and, together with a reduction in touch sensitivity, less satisfying. A lessening of interest leads to less intercourse and this increases the rate of change in the vaginal tissues. So it's a bit of a vicious circle!

LOSS OF LIBIDO

DEGREE OF LOSS OF LIBIDO IN A SURVEY OF 500 WOMEN

None	Mild	Moderate	Severe	Total suffering
38%	18%	21%	23%	62%

This, not surprisingly, was associated with vaginal dryness especially in those who had had a hysterectomy. Pain on intercourse was not a very strongly associated symptom. Anxiety, insomnia and even aches and pains were all mildly associated with loss of sexual interest. So what does this all mean? It looks as though there are a mixture of factors at work. Loss of libido in this group did not have the pattern we would expect if it were a straightforward 'hormone-deficiency' problem as some experts argue. Nor did it have the characteristics of being a predominantly psychological problem. It would seem to vary from person to person with some influence due to hormonal change causing vaginal dryness.

Diane's Story

Diane is a fifty-year-old wife, mother and carer from Aberdare in Wales. When she approached the WNAS for help she had been suffering with her symptoms for seven years.

'I was still working full-time in the education department of our local government office. The first menopausal symptom I experienced was that I found it harder and harder to concentrate. This in turn led to a lack of self-confidence which affected my performance at work and my life at home.

'I had to take time off and get others to stand in for me, as jobs that should have taken five minutes were taking hours. I even apologized to my boss for my incompetence and told him that I was thinking of resigning. I had always loved my career, but for

the first time in my life I was thinking of giving it up.

'I then started to feel constantly ill with migraine headaches and constant hot flushes. I felt that I had hit rock-bottom emotionally. I felt haggard and undesirable. I seemed to have aged almost overnight.

'My husband had always been very supportive but my irrational behaviour and my loss of libido were putting quite a strain on our relationship. I knew my behaviour wasn't fair to anyone, including myself, so I went to see my doctor and was given a prescription for antidepressants. They didn't work and made me feel that not only was I experiencing menopause symptoms, but also that I was mentally ill. Still feeling low I saw another doctor, who this time prescribed HRT.

'For six months I felt on top of the world. Most of my symptoms disappeared, although my libido didn't fully recover. Then the migraines returned with a vengeance and once again I couldn't sleep and was feeling sick and suffering with diarrhoea. My legs felt like lead, in fact I had no energy at all and found it an effort to walk. Plus I had terrible sugar cravings. I felt as if I was back to square one. I actually took myself off HRT and contacted the Women's Nutritional Advisory Service for help.

'I was instructed to make specific dietary changes, took nutritional supplements and exercised regularly. The hot flushes stopped within two weeks. My migraine headaches lifted completely and within a short time my whole attitude to life became more positive. From lying in bed feeling depressed, I noticed that come the morning I wanted to jump out of bed and get on with the day, just like I had when I was younger. Once again I had lots of energy, my moods were much more constant and I no longer felt irrational. Thankfully my libido returned and a normal loving relationship with my husband was resumed. I felt much more confident and even the laughter lines on my face noticeably faded.

'It's been four years now and I still feel absolutely brilliant. I am delighted with my progress and feel as if I have been released from a prison. My husband is very relieved too as he felt so helpless at the time. Within six months I was a totally different person and I have never looked back. I need far less sleep now. I'm planning to take an Open University degree course and I'm learning to play the piano. I feel tremendous, like a new woman, and best of all I look like one too.'

DIFFICULTIES WITH INTERCOURSE

DEGREE OF PAIN ON INTERCOURSE IN A SURVEY OF 500 WOMEN

None	Mild	Moderate	Severe	Total suffering
64%	15%	12%	9%	36%

As we have already seen this was mainly associated with vaginal dryness especially in older, non-hysterectomized women.

URINARY SYMPTOMS

Though we didn't ask about these in our survey they do deserve a mention as they can sometimes be a problem at this time of life.

Loss of control, especially when coughing, laughing or sneezing, an increase in the frequency with which the bladder needs to be emptied during the day or night and a feeling of urgency can all be problems associated with the menopause. It is not clear how much these are due to the fall in oestrogen and how much to the passage of time.

Although urinary symptoms can respond to treatment with HRT, improved control can also be obtained by the use of exercises to improve the muscles around the bladder.

It does appear that some women are also troubled by more frequent urine infections at this time and this is perhaps due to a change in the health of these tissues.

SKIN CHANGES

Oestrogens also influence the quality of our skin. The decline in quality at the time of the menopause is associated with thinning of the skin, a reduction in the blood-flow to the skin and a loss of elasticity. These to a large degree reverse with the use of HRT. Good nutrition and exercise also seem to have a significant influence on skin quality. Which will dominate will vary from person to person. Very thin skin is, it seems, a reasonably good pointer to those who may also have thin bones. Bones are not just made of minerals: one-third is made up of collagen, the main connective tissue of skin. Though some benefit to skin can accrue as a result of HRT it is not known for how long this will last. Perhaps diet and even exercise level will be of more importance with the passage of years as now appears to be the way with the bones.

Other physical symptoms of the menopause

Again in our survey of 500 women, we asked about some other physical symptoms that can also be a problem around the time of the menopause.

ACHES AND PAINS

SEVERITY OF ACHES AND PAINS IN A SURVEY OF 500 WOMEN

None	Mild	Moderate	Severe	Total suffering
29%	19%	32%	20%	71%

Aches and pains have not always been considered part of the menopause and postmenopause. However, recently some doctors have come to regard these as a fairly common associated problem that can respond to HRT. But is this really the case?

When we looked at this group of women we found no association between aches and pains and either hot flushes or nightsweats! Nor did it relate to vaginal dryness. What did come up was that aches and pains were most usually associated with panic attacks in the hysterectomy group and tended to be more of a problem in the younger women in this group. It would seem that many of the women who had had a hysterectomy were not as well as some of their contemporaries. It is not possible to say why, but there could be a dietary rather than a hormonal connection.

For the remaining women who still had their womb there was no connection with panic attacks but aches and pains were related to insomnia. So it would seem that this could be a reason for some of these women's disturbed sleep.

Again we see that not all women at the time of the menopause fall into the same category, and that the symptoms are not always hormonally related. Clearly, a lot more research and a flexible attitude to the possible causes of these problems is needed before we can say why women are troubled in the way they are at this time of their lives.

PALPITATIONS

SEVERITY OF PALPITATIONS IN A SURVEY OF 500 WOMEN

None	Mild	Moderate	Severe	Total suffering
47%	24%	23%	6%	53%

Palpitations were not often a severe problem. They were an interesting physical symptom to look at because the different schools of thought could relate them to the hot flushes and the surge of nervous-system activity that accompanies them, or to underlying feelings of anxiety or to the consumption of caffeine from tea and coffee: three quite different possibilities.

FATIGUE

This is another common symptom which unfortunately we were unable to ask about because of lack of space on the magazine page. A low energy level is a more common complaint in women than men, and some women report improvement when they take HRT. HRT the elixir of youth? Not quite. A more considered assessment of the cause and treatment of fatigue and other physical symptoms is that if these symptoms are strongly associated with symptoms of oestrogen withdrawal then they may improve with the use of HRT. This has been described as the domino-effect. Well worth having and probably more relevant for the younger woman with more severe hot flushes. As we will see later, and from Phillipa's story, HRT is not the only way to control hot flushes and the symptoms of oestrogen withdrawal.

Phillipa's Story

Phillipa is a forty-five-year-old wife and mother from Reading in Berkshire. She was given HRT by her doctor to help with her menopause symptoms, but was unable to continue taking them as they made her migraine headaches unbearable.

'I had been helped by the WNAS some twelve years ago when I was suffering with severe PMS. With those awful symptoms behind me for years it did not occur to me that I would have a rough menopause.

'When my periods became irregular and lighter I suspected that I was starting my menopause. Gradually I became tired, irritable and tearful, with no confidence at all. I visited my doctor to discuss the problem, but he only prescribed antidepressants, which did improve the tearfulness and nausea, but I was still getting the flushes and my vagina had become dry. I was feeling so low by this time I couldn't be bothered to talk to people or make the effort to visit them, which was so unlike me. I couldn't face having anyone to dinner either because of the effort it would take.

'I generally felt so tired, drained and tearful, and the worst thing for me was that I didn't have the energy to look after my grandson. I remember sitting on a stool at the kitchen sink after dinner, looking at the dishes that needed clearing away, and wanting to cry because I had not got the energy to just put them in the dishwasher.

'I went to visit my doctor again to discuss the possibility of taking HRT, which I had read so much about in the media. He wasn't sure if I could take it as I make breast lumps and have to have regular checks at the hospital. He wanted me to check with the consultant on my next visit. I was so desperate to feel normal again that I wrote to the consultant for the OK!

'I was put on Prempak-C at first, but I started to experience intense migraine headaches. I was changed to a lower dose to see whether that made any difference and finally I was put on Trisequens. As the migraines persisted I was unable to continue on HRT and that's when I contacted the WNAS for some natural help.

'Once again the WNAS formulated a programme for me to follow, this time for my menopause symptoms. I made some dietary changes, took different nutritional supplements and resumed an exercise programme. Within a few months I was feeling better. I have never looked back. My confidence returned.

I find myself running up the stairs now, whereas before I felt as if I were climbing a mountain, every stair was such an effort. The nausea has gone. I am much more able to socialize and go to work. I have even taken some courses on computers at an adult college, which I could never have done before. Once again I am delighted with the help of the WNAS.'

BOWEL PROBLEMS

In addition to typical menopausal symptoms we also asked in our survey about bowel problems and how many women suffered from constipation, diarrhoea or both. I knew that women with severe PMS seemed, in nearly 50 per cent of cases, to have bowel problems, too, and other surveys have shown that over 20 per cent of the normal adult female population admit to bowel problems.

The pattern of bowel problems in this group was as follows: constipation: 39.5 per cent; diarrhoea: 20 per cent; both: 15.5 per cent. This means that a total of 59.5 per cent of our sample were experiencing bowel problems. Although we cannot relate this to the hormonal changes, it again seems surprisingly high. As there is a known strong connection between diet and bowel problems, these figures would seem to strengthen the need for dietary advice to be given to menopausal women.

WEIGHT-GAIN FOLLOWING HRT

From our sample, 62 per cent of those who took HRT claimed that they had experienced weight-gain as a result. The average claimed weight-gain was sixteen and a half pounds. We have no way of accounting for other causes of weight-gain in this survey. Suffice it to say that many women perceive weight-gain as being a problem that goes hand-in-hand with taking HRT.

Menopause and your Mind

Having looked at physical menopausal symptoms, we now come to the 'mental' symptoms of the postmenopause.

Many researchers have already tried to determine if depression, anxiety and insomnia become more of a problem to women as they approach the menopause. The results have been rather mixed, probably because of difficulties in the methods of looking at psychological problems, in relying on subjective reports rather than using standardized tests. This is indeed a criticism of our survey but then we do not wish to rely on our findings alone.

Dr Myra Hunter, a psychologist and the author of *Your Menopause* has developed, together with colleagues, a more scientific method of assessing symptoms. They surveyed 850 women aged forty-five to sixty-five who were not attending a menopause clinic and were thought to be fairly representative of the normal female population of this age. Women around the time of and after the menopause had greater levels of depression and insomnia but not anxiety. The increase in these symptoms was nowhere near as great as the increase in hot flushes. There was no increase in many physical symptoms or in problems relating to thinking.

Overall it seemed that the experience of the menopause would make for a modest but definite increase in a change in mood.

So what pattern did we see in the group of women from *Woman's Realm*?

INSOMNIA

DEGREE OF INSOMNIA IN A SURVEY OF 500 WOMEN

None	Mild	Moderate	Severe	Total suffering
27%	18%	28%	27%	73%

Clearly a common problem, one as common as hot flushes and nightsweats.

Insomnia was more of a problem in those with anxiety and to a slightly lesser degree with nightsweats. Depression and aches and pains also seemed to be mildly associated. So again there could be hormonal, psychological or possibly other physical factors behind insomnia at this time of life. It all depends on the individual.

It is well-documented from other research that insomnia is a common accompaniment of nightsweats. In fact, the disturbance in sleep begins before the sweating does and is in time with subtle changes in the electrical brainwaves, again testimony to the involvement of the nervous system in the symptoms of the menopause.

ANXIETY

DEGREE OF ANXIETY IN A SURVEY OF 500 WOMEN

None	Mild	Moderate	Severe	Total suffering
30%	21%	27%	22%	70%

A strong association with panic attacks was observable in those who had had a hysterectomy and also to a lesser degree in those who had not. Depression was also associated with anxiety and so was insomnia. Here we see quite a strong grouping of different mental complaints. Some would argue that this is good evidence of the need for treatment with drugs to control either the anxiety or depression. Not so fast we say! With the problems of Valium, Ativan and other benzodiazepine drugs still fresh in our memories there must be another way for the majority of women. We know from our experience of women with premenstrual syndrome that many can do well through dietary change, the use of some nutritional supplements and physical exercise, and have been seeing similar results in menopausal women too for many years now. Don't jump to conclusions yet.

Eleanor's Story
Eleanor is a forty-three-year-old mother of three from Kent, who had to give up her job at the time her menopause began because she felt so ill.

> 'Although I was still menstruating at the time, I was feeling so "unwell", constantly exhausted, with loss of memory, with an imbalance of mind, headaches, anxiety, panic attacks and rapid mood changes. I felt desperate and quite dreadful, and afraid of being institutionalized.
> 'I was recommended to the WNAS by a friend. I followed a

postal and telephone course of treatment which gave me instant hope. It was practical and positive and I felt the benefit almost immediately. Now three years on I am much better. I still avoid caffeine, alcohol and wheat-based products. I am much more balanced and can have normal relationships. Thank God I heard of the wonderful work the WNAS are doing.'

DEPRESSION

SEVERITY OF DEPRESSION IN A SURVEY OF 500 WOMEN

None	Mild	Moderate	Severe	Total suffering
31%	23%	30%	16%	69%

As you may well expect, this clusters together with anxiety in the main, and slightly with panic attacks and insomnia, and is in complete agreement with what we would expect. But again, don't reach for the happy pills as something a little more natural is to hand.

Moira's Story

Moira is a teacher from Dyfed in Wales who had suffered with menopausal depression for seventeen years, at one point so severely she tried to commit suicide. After years of tranquillizers and psychiatric treatment, at the age of fifty-nine she followed the WNAS programme which changed her life.

'The menopause took me by surprise at the age of forty-three. I had hot flushes, dizziness and abdominal bloating, but my main symptom was depression, which led to a nervous breakdown. Everything was an effort, even getting up in the morning. I had the feeling I wasn't really there. It was a great disappointment after leading such a full life with a busy and satisfying career.

'My husband was very supportive, but at a loss to know how to help me. No-one really understood how I felt. My GP tried me on different treatments but nothing really helped. Eventually, a psychiatrist gave me mood stabilizers and taught me how to relax. I recovered and returned to my teaching career. However, once I retired the depression got worse and I was just existing. I completely lost confidence and nothing in life seemed to give me any pleasure.

'Luckily I read an article which mentioned the Women's Nutritional Advisory Service. After asking me lots of questions and taking a thorough medical history, they worked out a diet, supplement and exercise programme to suit me. Within three weeks I experienced dramatic improvement. During the following four months I had monthly consultations during which adjustments were made to my programme and I felt better than I could remember for many years.

'It has been four years since I followed the WNAS programme. I continue to enjoy life now. I'm still symptom-free and I no longer need to take psychiatric drugs. But I do wish I hadn't left it so late to find effective help. I would like to stress to other women how important it is to get help early on. You do need something other than tablets. So often when you are down you feel powerless to help yourself, and family and friends are at a loss to know how to help. I'm just glad I found the WNAS and can now look to the future with enthusiasm.'

CONFUSION

SEVERITY OF CONFUSION IN A SURVEY OF 500 WOMEN

None	Mild	Moderate	Severe	Total suffering
39%	24%	26%	11%	61%

Though not that common as a severe symptom, confusion was often marked as a moderate or mild problem. The pattern of its association marked it down as more of a mental symptom than a hormone-related one.

PANIC ATTACKS

SEVERITY OF PANIC ATTACKS IN A SURVEY OF 500 WOMEN

None	Mild	Moderate	Severe	Total suffering
47%	22%	21%	10%	53%

Not as common as some other symptoms and the clustering showed that it mainly tied up with anxiety and depression as well as with one physical symptom (see page 43).

By now a very strong pattern of symptoms is appearing. Those that were due primarily to hormonal change of oestrogen withdrawal were clustered together and those that related to anxiety and depression were also clustered together with very little apparent crossover and no influence of age at the meno-pause.

It would seem that the full range of menopausally related symptoms could not be easily explained by the simple and attractive notion of 'a lack of hormones'. This might also lie behind some women's dissatisfaction with HRT in not tackling all their symptoms and solving all their problems. It would seem that a more broadly based lifestyle approach would be needed to give the best chance of success in controlling the troubles of the postmenopause.

Five

The Bone Robber:
Osteoporosis

Although it is not strictly part of the menopause itself, osteoporosis has become closely associated with it, to the point where no book on the menopause would be complete without a chapter on the subject.

What is osteoporosis?

Osteoporosis is thinning of the bone. The bones are composed of a 'skeleton' or scaffold of connective tissue around which minerals in crystalline form are laid down, rather like bricks being built up on to a steel framework. The framework has a certain flexibility as well as great strength and the minerals give the structure resistance to compression or crushing. So the structure of bone is rather similar to that of reinforced concrete.

In osteoporosis there is a reduction in both the amount of the connective tissue and the mineral content of the bone. The loss of bone mass reduces its strength and increases the likelihood that the bone will break when pressure is brought to bear on it.

What determines bone strength?

Bones are living tissue. They are not dead or inert but grow, get stronger or weaker, are damaged and heal just like other tissues of the body, and their health and strength are influenced by a variety of factors.

Bones grow with us from birth and reach their peak in size and strength not in our late teens when we have stopped growing in height, but in our mid thirties! Also at this time muscle bulk and lung function are at their peak, so Mother Nature expects us to be at our most physically active at this point.

There are several important factors that determine the strength of our bones:

Diet, especially the intake of calcium;
Physical activity, especially weight-bearing exercise;
Genetic factors that determine the size of our body; and
Hormonal factors, especially the balance of oestrogen in women.

After the peak, the size of which is normally determined by the first three of these factors, there is a gradual decline. Now it should be a very slow decline and one that hardly has any impact on our health. Its impact is due to the increased risk of fracture that it brings, should we fall or be involved in an accident.

Osteoporosis becomes more of a problem if the peak bone mass in the mid thirties is not very high, if the rate of subsequent loss is rapid, or if the individual lives a long time and if there is a significant risk of falling. Currently in most developed countries all these four factors are present and hence we have an epidemic of osteoporotic fractures which looks set to continue for many decades. Linda Edwards of the National Osteoporosis Society estimates that at least two million out of the eleven million postmenopausal women in the UK have oesteoporosis and most of them require some form of treatment. In financial terms the care of older patients with osteoporotic fractures poses an enormous burden on health-care resources in developed countries. In the UK in 1990 it was estimated to be half a billion pounds per annum. Furthermore, the fracture event is often a turning point in the lives of elderly people. Some 20 per cent will die in the six months following their fracture. Many have lasting disability or find that they subsequently become dependent on others for their daily needs.

In short, osteoporosis has become a twentieth-century challenge which, until recently, has been an increasing and silent epidemic. If half as many men felt threatened by this bone-degenerating disease, substantially more money would be poured into research and larger National Health screening and awareness campaigns would be mounted.

Which bones break?

Osteoporosis becomes an important issue at the menopause because of the influence of the withdrawal of oestrogen on bone mass. This results in a marked increase in the rate of loss to 2 per cent of bone mass each year. Certain bones become particularly vulnerable to fracture as a result.

HIPS
Fracture of the neck of the femur, to give it its proper title, fills nearly 25 per cent of all orthopaedic beds in the UK. It is more commonly a problem in those aged sixty-five and over and usually occurs after a fall. There are over 40,000 such fractures a year: at least one for every 1,500 of the population each year. Each fracture means a stay in hospital, an operation to repair the fracture site with a steel pin, and a period of disability. Some will need a hip replacement.

SPINE
The vertebrae are the bones of the spinal column and are like strong building blocks between which there is a rubbery disc. The mass of the vertebrae reduces rapidly after the menopause, and fracture is common from the age of fifty. The fracture happens without any fall, usually in the course of normal daily activity. An episode of back pain, which is worse on movement or on taking a breath, is common. Eventually, if there are several such fractures, loss of height, increased curvature of the spine or a marked stoop develop. It is estimated that well over half of vertebral fractures go undetected. Sadly there is no treatment other than the use of pain killers.

WRIST AND ARM
Fracture of the wrist, Colles' fracture, and fracture of the humerus, the upper arm, usually follow a fall. Again they are more common from the age of sixty-five. These fractures are

influenced not only by bone strength but also by poor balance and coordination which increase the chance of a fall.

Who will get osteoporosis?

Much of the research into osteporosis has centred on determining who will get it and what are its risk factors. It is hoped that strategies to prevent it from occurring will reduce the rate of fractures in later life.

The risk factors for osteoporosis include:

HORMONAL FACTORS

- An early menopause, especially before the age of forty-five
- Age and in particular the number of years since the menopause is extremely important
- Cessation of periods for anything more than a few months due to:
  Being underweight e.g. in anorexia
  Excessive exercise e.g. in athletes or ballet dancers
  Some drugs e.g. in the treatment of gynaecological problems
  A late start to the periods can also be a factor.
- There is some protection in women if they have been pregnant and have breast-fed
- Previous use of the oral contraceptive pill might also offer a little protection from osteoporosis in later years.

GENETIC FACTORS

- A strong family history of osteoporosis is sometimes relevant
- Race is important as osteoporosis is much more of a problem in those of Caucasian and Asian origin and less for those of African origin
- Height is a factor as osteoporosis is more common in those of short stature.

DIETARY FACTORS

- The intake of calcium during childhood and young adult life is very important. The intake of calcium at the time of the menopause is not a good predictor of bone mass. It may predict the rate of loss and future risk
- The inability to tolerate cow's milk or milk sugar – lactose. Cow's-milk allergy in children is quite a common cause of eczema and digestive problems and some children and adults find that milk and cream give them diarrhoea, a common problem in those of Eastern including Eastern European origins. Some people unwittingly consume little milk because they can only digest small amounts of it
- Coffee does slightly increase the risk of osteoporosis but thankfully the risk vanishes if you drink it with milk
- Bran interferes with the absorption of calcium and this is another possible risk factor in some cases
- Alcohol consumption, if heavy, is a factor. Moderate consumption may predispose the elderly to a fall
- A generally poor-quality diet may increase the risk. There is evidence that in postmenopausal women calcium is not the only important nutrient and that the rate of loss is least in those with higher intakes of protein, phosphorus, zinc and folate, a type of vitamin B. Magnesium may also have a small effect
- Other food-risk factors include sugar, salt and excessive consumption of phosphates which all help to reduce the bones' uptake of calcium. The intake of other minerals including magnesium might also be important.

EXERCISE

In all age groups this is a major factor. Plenty of exercise in childhood, including sport at school, helps to build up a high peak bone mass in the mid thirties. Subsequently, exercise reduces the rate of loss and increasing the amount of physical activity in the elderly can actually increase the strength of the bones especially when combined with calcium or HRT. Different types of exercise influence different parts of the skeleton.

Walking will help the hips and spine, but hand and wrist exercises are necessary to strengthen the wrist bones. The disabled, the bedbound – even for a few weeks – and housebound are very much at risk and so are astronauts because of their weightlessness.

Body weight is also a factor. It helps to be heavy and being too light increases the risk. The woman with a petite build is more likely to experience problems.

SMOKING

Smoking deserves its own category as this is now being appreciated as a major preventable risk factor. Smoking seems to accelerate the rate of postmenopausal bone loss. Women who stop smoking at the time of the menopause may reduce the risk of hip fracture by as much as 40 per cent. Smoking is an even bigger risk factor for fracture of the spinal vertebrae.

DISEASE

A number of health problems are known to reduce the uptake of minerals by the bones. This includes:

• Conditions where there is reduced absorption of calcium because of malabsorption. This is common in diseases of the pancreas, after part or all of the stomach has been removed, and problems of persistent diarrhoea with weight loss
• Other hormone-related problems including an overactive thyroid or excessive production of steroids
• Liver disease of any type especially chronic biliary cirrhosis, a problem mainly of middle-aged women
• Rheumatoid arthritis which can be associated with an increased risk of osteoporosis especially in the bones adjacent to the affected joints.

DRUGS

Steroids are associated with an increase in the loss of calcium from the bones. It is minimized if calcium supplements are taken.

Some drugs may protect the elderly from bone-thinning. To date, there is some evidence that diuretic drugs used in the treatment of heart failure and high blood pressure may do this as a beneficial side-effect.

In summary, there are many risk factors for osteoporosis and for a few individuals one or two of the rarer reasons can be very important. For the majority of older women the most important risk factors are:

- Age at the menopause
- Years since the menopause
- Low body weight
- A previous fracture due to fragile bones.

Even detailed studies have found that assessment of many risk factors can only account for less than half the variation in bone mass. So there are clearly more important pieces of the osteoporosis jigsaw missing.

Tests for osteoporosis
Interest in osteoporosis has increased enormously in the last decade because of the more widespread use of detection methods, in particular the ability to measure the density of bone. This is normally assessed in the hip and in the vertebrae of the spinal column.

There is indeed a relationship between the bone-mineral density of the neck of the femur and the force required for its fracture, but for a given bone density the force needed to produce a fracture can vary by as much as twofold. The bone-density guide may be imperfect but it is the one most relied on at present. What it is good at is observing change: either deterioration with age or improvement with treatment. There are different types of scans available but a discussion of the merits of these are outside the scope of this book.

Other tests look for the changes in body biochemistry that

take place in those who are rapidly losing bone mass. A series of blood and urine tests can look at how much calcium, other minerals and breakdown products of the connective tissue of bone are being lost from the body. As yet they have not replaced bone-density measurement.

Treating osteoporosis

The real test for any treatment for osteoporosis is not 'Does it increase bone density?' but 'Does it reduce the rate of fracture?' The larger and more recent studies have tried to answer this important question.

The tried and tested treatments that actually reduce the rate of osteoporosis-related fractures are:

- Oestrogen;
- Calcium;
- Calcitonin, a calcium-modifying hormone.

Other treatments of uncertain value are vitamin D, a mineral called fluoride, anabolic steroids, hormones similar to the male sex hormone testosterone, and multivitamins with magnesium and calcium.

Improved diet, increase in exercise, and giving up smoking are all very important too.

OESTROGEN
This is at its most effective in preventing or slowing the rate of the rapid loss of bone that results from the withdrawal of oestrogen at the time of the menopause. It is also effective in older women but the beneficial effect does wane with the passing years. After the age of seventy-five, women who have been on HRT for about ten years following their menopause have a bone density that is only 3 per cent greater than those who had not been on HRT. So though HRT is currently the most tried and tested form of prevention, its benefit is probably greatest for those women who rapidly lose calcium after the menopause. The advisability of staying on HRT for more than ten years to prevent osteoporosis will depend on the

risks of HRT, particularly the delayed risk of breast cancer (which you can read about on page 92).

HRT in the form of patches, implants and some of the newer preparations also seems likely to help osteoporosis, though this remains to be fully proven. Large studies assessing the effect of HRT on the rate of fractures show that tablets of oestrogen in one form or another lowers the rate by 45–60 per cent: certainly an effect worth having. The rate may be greater if oestrogen is combined with exercise.

CALCIUM

Supplements of calcium have long been popular. An effective dose is at least 1 gram (1,000 milligrams or mg) of the element calcium each day. This is on top of the average dietary intake of calcium of about 700 mg each day. Unfortunately, 10 per cent of the adult female population in the UK consume less than the minimum recommended intake of calcium of 400 mg each day. So though the average intake for the UK may be acceptable, it is not for the bottom 10 per cent and even the lowest half might benefit from extra calcium depending on their activity level. Nearly half our dietary calcium comes from dairy products, hence the need for those who consume little or no dairy products to eat other calcium-rich foods or take supplements.

The effectiveness of supplemental calcium is in the region of 25 per cent reduction in hip-fracture risk. This is less effective than oestrogen but it has the attraction of being an approach virtually without any substantial risk. Only those with a history of kidney stones may need special advice. It does seem that calcium supplements, especially if combined with other dietary measures, regular exercise and the cessation of smoking, are an attractive long-term option appropriate for many women.

Many of these calcium supplements are available on UK prescription and these are known to dissolve in the stomach and be well absorbed. Many others are not! An analysis of some of the preparations available in health food shops found that the calcium preparation produced by Healthcrafts was one of the few likely to be assimilated by the body.

The more easily absorbed forms are calcium citrate and gluco-
nate but calcium carbonate is cheap and suitable for most people if
it is taken with food. The very elderly and those with absorption
problems may be better off with the citrate preparations. The very
elderly and those who are housebound should also have a small
supplement of vitamin D to ensure a good absorption.

Calcium and Etidronate

One problem with just giving calcium is that it is easily lost from
the bones. Improving the diet generally and enough exercise are
ways of helping to keep the calcium where you want it. The
same has also been achieved by giving an altered form of the
mineral phosphate called biphosphonate, which helps to 'lock'
the calcium in the bone. It does this by reducing the activity of
the cells that help to remodel bone, the osteoclasts. Combining
calcium with intermittent use of the biphosphonate drug, etidronate, achieves an improvement in the density of the vertebral
bones and a reduction in the rate of their fracture. It seems to
have little or no effect on hip-fracture rate. The etidronate
portion needs to be taken on an empty stomach in the middle of
a four-hour time period without food.

Tips about dietary calcium

These other dietary measures below are of little importance in
the short term but in the long term will help increase the
absorption of calcium and its deposition in the bones.

1 Avoid bran and bran-containing foods. These may interfere
   with the absorption of calcium
2 Avoid carbonated drinks high in phosphate, e.g. some brands
   of cola. Again this reduces the ease with which calcium is
   absorbed
3 Do not eat very large amounts of protein-rich foods. It too
   can increase the loss of calcium in the urine
4 High intakes of sugar can displace calcium from the body and
   it will spill out into the urine
5 Salt can have the same effect as sugar. Their effect is admittedly

small but may be significant over ten to twenty years

6 Vitamin D helps in the absorption of calcium from the diet. Supplements are only needed by those over seventy-five years and those who have either liver or kidney disease or who do not obtain adequate sunlight. Do not take more than the recommended dosage

7 Magnesium and the trace element boron, both of which are found in vegetables and fruit, may also play a part in maintaining bone-mineral content and strength. Zinc and fish oils may also play a part in the prevention of osteoporosis

8 Take supplements of calcium with food as this may help their absorption. Taking them with the main meal or a few hours before retiring may be the best times

9 Exercise. Nothing but nothing helps increase bone uptake of calcium as much as exercise. Regular daily exercise, especially walking, helps. So walk for at least thirty, preferably sixty, minutes each day in shoes with a leather heel or a non-cushioned heel so that the impact of putting your foot to the ground is transmitted to the hip and spine. Walking to the greengrocer and carrying the shopping home is ideal! It may sound totally impractical but don't forget that is what used to happen routinely fifty or so years ago. See also Chapter 12.

CALCITONIN
Calcitonin is a hormone from the thyroid gland that helps to inhibit the release of calcium from the bones into the bloodstream. It sounds ideal and the results of trials are quite good. Unfortunately it has to be given by injection. It has proved popular in Italy and other parts of Continental Europe. Its use appears to be associated with a 30 per cent reduction in the risk of hip fracture. It should be considered more frequently for women who cannot take HRT and for men.

Bone health in the long term

A great drawback of many of the studies on the different treatments for the prevention and treatment of osteoporosis is their effectiveness and suitability in the long term. We just do not know the answer to many relevant questions, and it will be some ten to twenty years before we have a good idea of the best treatments for the different categories of those who are at risk of osteoporosis. This lack of certainty and the importance that diet and lifestyle factors play on a long-term basis has encouraged some authorities to consider what the message to the general public should be, bearing in mind that it seems unlikely that the majority will be swallowing pills or having 'treatment' of whatever sort.

So some simple, safe advice for all women from the time of the menopause onwards who wish to prevent osteoporosis or help in their treatment of it is:

- Eat a good diet rich in calcium from dairy and non-dairy sources. You will find the list of foods rich in calcium and magnesium on pages 205–6
- Do not smoke
- Do not drink heavily
- Keep physically active. A daily walk is best
- Get out on a regular basis and do not become housebound
- Avoid falls. This requires a good senses of balance, sight, safety in the home and ensuring a good level of mental and physical health
- See your doctor if you have one or more of the risk factors detailed in the early part of this chapter.

Part Two

HRT: THE ADVANTAGES AND DISADVANTAGES

Six

HRT – The Choices

Apparently the first attempts to give replacement hormones to women involved the use of animals' ovaries! In the 1920s the hormone oestrogen was identified and by the late 1930s synthetic oestrogen was being made. Experimental work in the 1940s led to the use of oestrogens in the USA in the 1950s and elsewhere in the 1960s. Historically the US has had a significant lead on the rest of the world in the use of HRT.

Oestrogens were mainly used for the first twenty years in the form of natural oestrogen derived from the urine of pregnant mares. This provided the inspiration for the name of one such preparation, Premarin (*pre*gnant *ma*res' u*rine*). This type of oestrogen is also called conjugated, as it is joined to another natural chemical, and this is broken down when it is taken by mouth. These natural or conjugated oestrogens are less powerful in their actions than the synthetic oestrogens that are found in the oral contraceptive pill. As a rule they have fewer side-effects and may have certain beneficial characteristics, particularly with regard to their possible benefit in reducing the risk of heart disease.

Oestrogen in whatever form, if given by itself, as was the case for many women in the US in the 1970s, results in a proliferation of the lining of the womb and a real increase in the chance of developing cancer of the endometrium (the lining of the womb). For this reason virtually all women who have not had a hysterectomy will need to be given the second female sex hormone, progesterone. Giving this for ten to fourteen days and then stopping it abruptly will cause the lining of the womb to be shed – a vaginal bleed. Many women call this 'a period'. More correctly it is 'a withdrawal bleed'. This form of therapy is called 'opposed HRT' and has been in use mainly in the last ten years. A lot of research has been going on to look at the difference between the benefits and risks of these two types of HRT.

As well as different types of oestrogen there are now different types of progesterone. Most of the progesterones, in contrast to oestrogen, are synthetic and not natural. Natural progesterone is not very effective when given by mouth. So a natural progesterone preparation, Cyclogest, is given in the form of a pessary and a specialized form of natural progesterone, micronized progesterone, is available in some countries but not the UK at present. As for the different types of progesterone, the older ones have some properties similar to the male sex hormone testosterone, while the newer ones tend not to have this effect. The older ones may reduce the beneficial effect that oestrogens have on blood fats such as cholesterol. So for those women who need to take HRT and are at high risk of heart disease, some of the newer progesterones may be preferable.

In addition to all this there are some natural oestrogen and progesterone-like substances that are present in some foodstuffs. More of that later. Let us stick with the prescribable forms of these hormones for the time being.

In 1994 we conducted a survey of 1,000 general practitioners to determine which HRT preparations they favoured and also to find out what treatment they offer to women who cannot take HRT.

The survey showed that half of the GPs questioned experienced problems when using HRT, with 43 per cent claiming that they experienced problems when treating menopausal women.

The six most popular choices of treatment were forms of HRT. Oestrogen implants were not a treatment option. The commonest choice was tablets of oestrogen and progesterone which were prescribed by 95 per cent of the sample. Eighty-five per cent used patches, 79 per cent used oestrogen only pills, 69 per cent oestrogen and progesterone patches, 52 per cent tibolone, and 40 per cent oestrogen, oestradiol and progesterone pills.

The survey also examined to whom doctors refer patients with continuing difficulties. Twenty-two per cent felt that they had no need to refer patients and 68 per cent of the total referred to a consultant gynaecologist or specialist hormone clinic. Some doctors gave more than one choice usually in addition to a gynaecologist and these included endocrinologist, psychiatrist, nutritionist or complementary practitioner. As such a large percentage of doctors refer patients to gynaecologists, at the time of going to print, we are in the process of surveying the gynaecologists in the UK to examine how they deal with menopausal patients who can and cannot take HRT.

The administration of HRT

The great problem with oestrogens is that the human system is very efficient at getting rid of them! The liver removes them from our blood-stream, chemically alters them and packages them off in the bile to be passed out into our own intestines. That isn't quite the last of them as some of these oestrogens are absorbed back into the system to go round once again. Thus our blood-stream contains some second-and third-hand oestrogens. There does seem to be a fair degree of variation in the levels of oestrogen found in women before the menopause at different times of the menstrual cycle and as a result of taking HRT preparations.

OESTROGENS BY MOUTH – PRESCRIBED BY 79.5 PER CENT OF GPS IN OUR SURVEY

This has been the commonest way of giving oestrogen in the USA and the UK. As all the oestrogen given in this way will first go to the liver before it then reaches the skin, breasts, vagina and so on, a proportion is 'lost' by being converted, by the liver, into forms that are less powerful. They also tend to cause some very slight change to the function of the liver and are more likely to cause feelings of nausea than are other forms.

The disadvantage of this method is that a pill has to be taken daily. However, it is easy to stop or change the dosage as necessary.

OESTROGEN VAGINAL CREAMS

These deliver oestrogen to the vagina and vulva and help greatly with vaginal lubrication. They are useful for those women for whom this is the main complaint. They can also help with hot flushes but absorption of oestrogen can be erratic, especially at the start of treatment. It is not suitable for most women as long-term treatment.

OESTROGEN BY SKIN PATCH – PRESCRIBED BY 69.2 PER CENT OF GPS IN OUR SURVEY

This has been a clever innovation in HRT delivery. A natural oestrogen 17B-oestradiol, which is similar to human oestrogen, is contained in a reservoir held next to the skin by a sticky rim. The patch comes in different strengths and is applied twice a week to the skin of the lower abdomen or hips. The patch releases a steady supply of oestrogen which by-passes the liver and avoids the slight adverse effects of some oral preparations.

The advantage of the patch is that it is similar to the woman's own ovary. Progesterone will need to be given to those who have a uterus and this can be in the form of tablets, pessaries or a separate patch containing progesterone, which is elegant but rather expensive. The disadvantages are that the patch can become dislodged and the level of oestrogen can rise dramatically in very hot weather or climates, or if the woman exercises vigorously. Skin irritation is reported as occurring in 5 per cent of users, which reminds me of an amusing story. I had a patient recently who was the daughter of a well-respected gynaecologist. He was emphatic that she should wear an oestrogen patch and have her uterus removed. She couldn't quite face the surgery, but went ahead with the patch, which caused her a great deal of skin irritation. One night in bed, she tossed and turned so much and felt so irritable that she ripped the patch off. When she woke up in the morning she noticed that her husband was now wearing her patch. I didn't have the heart to ask her where it was positioned!

OESTROGEN BY IMPLANT

Another method of giving oestrogen is the use of an implant that can provide a supply of oestrogen for up to six months. Again this form of delivery means that the oestrogen does not have to

Are you sure we don't have our patches mixed ??

go through the liver before reaching the tissues. The implant is placed under the skin of the lower abdomen by means of a small operation under local anaesthetic. Occasionally the pellet is rejected or becomes infected. This method has been popularized by some specialists in the UK in particular. The advantage is that once given you can forget about it, though women with a uterus will need to take progesterone every month to induce a withdrawal bleed. An attraction to many women has been that response to this form of HRT can be dramatic. But though implants undoubtedly have their fans, both professional and public, there can be problems.

The implant can result in very high levels of oestrogen and some women may feel unwell on it. Additionally, some women's bodies adapt to these high levels and, as they fall, even though they are still high, menopausal symptoms of hot flushes can return! This rapid fall results in a further round of oestrogen-withdrawal symptoms, despite there being no deficiency. It is not possible to give another

71

implant and very often the woman may have to wait several months for this effect to wear off before another type of HRT can be given. This effect has been reported in up to 15 per cent of women with implants. Perhaps it is best reserved for those women who have been on HRT for a while, and want to try something more convenient.

HRT WITHOUT A BLEED – PRESCRIBED BY 51.8 PER CENT OF GPS IN OUR SURVEY

The real trick, if doctors and scientists can achieve it, is HRT without a bleed for those women who have a uterus. The monthly bleed or irregular bleeding is a major reason why many women give up on HRT or do not even start it. Some new treatments have tried to conquer this problem.

Livial (also known as Tibolone) is a synthetic substance with mild oestrogen and progesterone effects combined (with a little bit of testosterone too). If taken continuously it controls oestrogen-withdrawal symptoms without stimulating the lining of the uterus so there is no withdrawal bleed. The best results are after three months of therapy but bleeding can still be a problem in younger women whose last natural period was within one year of starting their treatment with this compound. So this is really one for women a little later on through the menopause. It does seem to have some beneficial effects in reducing the rate of loss of calcium from the bone, but its effect on the risk of heart disease is still unknown.

A further development in the use of opposed therapy is to give oestrogen and progesterone together throughout the month. This has the effect of preventing proliferation of the lining of the uterus. No bleeding results and symptoms can be well controlled. This type of HRT is currently being evaluated and is not routinely available.

Other methods of controlling the unwanted bleed are to give continuous progesterone by the use of an intra-uterine device, like a coil, that contains progesterone, together with the removal of the lining of the womb by an operation called uterine ablation. No doubt these methods will see the light of day with their protagonists in full voice. (For a listing of HRT formulations, see Appendix 5.)

The future

It seems that the number of methods of giving HRT is rapidly increasing. In many ways this is a good thing, giving more choice to the consumer and more options for doctors when dealing with other health problems that alter HRT requirements. Short-term side-effects and risks may be fairly easy to assess. However, the big question is 'What are the long-term side-effects?' This is a much harder question and as we already have an effective and relatively safe form of HRT, natural or conjugated oestrogen, the onus is on the newcomers to prove their safety. In the time it will take to do this, the longer-term and delayed risks of all forms of HRT, particularly with regard to breast cancer, may become apparent. In the end, women may well be presented with greater choice and more uncertainty. The conservative recommendation may then well be for most women only to take HRT for a few years. It could well be several generations before a fully informed choice is possible.

Seven

HRT – Who Can't Take It?

The benefits of any therapy must be balanced by its risks. This is true for drugs that treat high blood pressure, operations for heart disease – in fact all treatments that doctors now wish to use have to be looked at from the risk as well as from the benefit point of view. An enormous advance over the last twenty years has been the near-universal adoption of this approach to health care. This has been made possible because large studies of treatments involve tens of thousands of patients to be followed. If there is an increase in the risk of certain diseases developing, then this may be rapidly apparent. Furthermore, the use of large numbers and the careful reporting of adverse events after a drug is in use allow even rare events – such as those occurring in one in 10,000 or more patients – to be detected. Modern science has brought some sophisticated and useful methods of assessing both benefit and risk.

Many of the conditions that prohibit the use of HRT are well-documented and are detailed in the information given to both doctor and patient alike. Most are uncommon or even rare but because of their importance to the individual concerned we see no alternative but to mention each of them with a brief explanation of the condition and how those affected might know they are at risk.

The following information has been extracted from the May 1994 edition of the *Monthly Index of Medical Specialities* (MIMS), the standard guide to commonly prescribed drugs in the UK. It accords with the advice given by individual pharmaceutical manufacturers.

Contra-indications
The following are the situations where HRT cannot be given

PREGNANCY AND LACTATION
The reasons are pretty obvious!

CANCER OF THE BREAST, GENITAL TRACT AND OTHER
OESTROGEN-DEPENDENT CANCERS
Oestrogen can stimulate the growth of these tumours. The treatment of breast cancer often involves giving a drug that blocks the action of residual amounts of oestrogen on the tumour.

A pelvic examination and breast examination should be undertaken before treatment of HRT is begun and it should be performed regularly during its administration.

Some experts feel that those women who have had these types of cancer and have been treated successfully with no evidence of its return for five or ten years can sometimes be given HRT. This is a contentious issue and one very much for individual appraisal by the patient's specialist.

VAGINAL BLEEDING
As this could be due to cancer of the womb or the cervix, then the cause of the bleeding must be determined before HRT is begun.

ENDOMETRIOSIS
This condition is characterized by painful periods and infertility. The lining of the womb, the endometrium, may sometimes extend outside the womb and occur in small pockets around the uterus and bladder. This displaced endometrial tissue will increase in size under the influence of oestrogen and then cause painful internal bleeding. So if you have painful periods, especially if the pain starts before the period begins, then you may have endometriosis. This should be detected by internal examination.

ACTIVE THROMBOPHLEBITIS OR THROMBOEMBOLIC DISORDER
These are conditions where blood clots form in the legs or elsewhere. This can happen after an accident, operation or after several days of inactivity. Sometimes blood clots form in the

veins for no obvious reason. The first sign of this may be painless or painful swelling of the leg and, rarely, the arm. The clot can silently dislodge from the vein and travel to the lung (a pulmonary embolism) which can cause breathing difficulties or sudden death.

In addition to the above situations blood clots can also occur in women with certain blood conditions that may pass undiagnosed. Though rare they should be suspected if there is a history of unexplained blood clots in the patient, blood clots in a near relative, recurrent unexplained miscarriages or other blood or heart disease.

A case was reported in the British press not so long ago of a woman who had a history of thrombosis that had not been taken into consideration. Her doctor prescribed HRT, which did not seem to help her symptoms. During a follow-up consultation the doctor increased the dose of HRT hoping it would be more effective; instead a short while later the patient died.

SEVERE CARDIAC, LIVER OR KIDNEY DISEASE
Oestrogens can worsen these conditions or cause blood clots to develop.

OTHER LIVER DISEASES
Do tell your doctor if there has been a problem with any illness affecting your liver in the past. HRT can worsen some types of liver disease. Mild hepatitis in the past is not reason enough not to have HRT. Some people may have a chronic low-grade form of hepatitis, hepatitis C, which would prevent them from receiving HRT. This type of hepatitis is most usually found in those who have been users of intravenous drugs or have come from developing countries. It can be detected by a simple blood test.

Special precautions
As well as the absolute reasons for not giving HRT the following are conditions where special attention is required or tests should be performed.

HISTORY OF THROMBOPHLEBITIS
The details in the previous section apply here too. Some women may be able to take HRT under careful supervision. The risk of blood clots forming with the oral contraceptive pill is well-known. This risk is not so apparent with HRT, but nevertheless should not be ignored.

MILD CHRONIC LIVER DISEASE
Liver function should be monitored by taking blood tests every eight to twelve weeks.

GALL STONES
Again, HRT can be given but care should be taken. Oestrogen administration approximately doubles the risk of developing gall-bladder disease.

OTOSCLEROSIS
This is a type of deafness that usually develops in pregnancy and is due to stiffness in the three small bones in the ear. These may be unduly sensitive to oestrogen.

PRURITUS DURING PREGNANCY
A very few women experience hormone-induced skin-itching or pruritus during pregnancy. In theory this might return if the same woman received HRT. It is a symptom that we have often dealt with in women on their voyage through the perimenopause and beyond.

SEVERE HERPES IN PREGNANCY
Severe widespread herpes in pregnancy may again be hormone-related and is listed as a contra-indication to HRT. As the oestrogen levels achieved by HRT are a fraction of those in pregnancy, the risk again seems more theoretical than actual.

MIGRAINE
This often improves at the time of the menopause. It can worsen with HRT and the oral contraceptive pill. If it is severe or is associated with numbness or tingling down one side of the body or

severe disturbance of vision, then HRT should usually be stopped.

MULTIPLE SCLEROSIS
This can worsen with HRT. Although rare, take care if neurological symptoms become worse during pregnancy, or when on the oral contraceptive pill.

EPILEPSY
Again it can worsen with HRT. The dosage of some anti-epileptic drugs may need adjustment.

DIABETES
Increased monitoring of blood-sugar levels may be needed. Some oral-opposed regimes can increase insulin requirements slightly, though oestrogen patches may avoid this effect.

HIGH BLOOD PRESSURE
Usually there is little or no change in blood pressure with HRT and some recent trials have reported a small fall in blood pressure. Those with mildly elevated blood pressure can take HRT, especially if they are also given advice to limit salt intake and, if relevant, to lose weight. However, a few women experience a large rise in blood pressure and this should be suspected if there was a history of high blood pressure when they were on the oral contraceptive pill. Blood pressure should be regularly checked in all women on HRT.

PORPHYRIA
This is a rare condition affecting the liver which may go unnoticed. Does anyone in the family have it?

UTERINE FIBROIDS
This is a common problem especially in women in the perimenopause. It will probably cause heavy periods and should be easily picked up on internal examination. The fibroids may or may not increase in size with HRT. You may need expert advice if there are problems.

TETANY

A low blood-calcium level can cause muscle spasms and this might come to light in someone beginning HRT. It is rare and as the fall in blood calcium from HRT is minute, the risk is more theoretical than actual.

Despite all the above contra-indications, many general practitioners have seen few such patients. Perhaps the commonest problem is when a woman experiences persistent bleeding on HRT at times other than those intended. Because of the possibility of endometrial cancer, some kind of sample from the lining of the womb will need to be taken and this often means a dilation and curettage (D&C).

DRUGS

Finally, there are many drugs that can interact with different HRT preparations. They all have the common feature of being processed by the liver which is also busy processing all the forms of HRT. These drugs include certain antibiotics – Erythromycin and Rifampicin – some antifungal agents, drugs for epilepsy, barbiturate sleeping tablets and some antidepressants. Adjustment to the dose of HRT or a change in the other drugs used may be necessary.

Well, there you have it. Those are all the main reasons why some women cannot be given HRT or may have medical problems with it once they try it. A much more common situation is when there is no reason why a woman cannot try it but experiences unacceptable side-effects as a result and then has to stop. This will be covered in the next chapter.

So what's on offer instead?

Although there are a number of treatment approaches for women who cannot take HRT, none of them are surrounded by the publicity and the hype that HRT currently enjoys. The pharmaceutical industry has gone to great lengths to get its promotional message across to general practitioners and has spent vast sums of money on postgraduate education, which is mostly product-oriented. The result is that GPs often have a one-sided view and although they are sometimes reluctant to prescribe HRT for certain patients, they are not so familiar with the alternatives as they obviously should be.

From our recent survey of 1,000 GPs we discovered that by their own admission 82 per cent had no training on the nutritional approach to the menopause and osteoporosis.

The survey showed a great inconsistency in prescribing habits for alternative treatments to HRT, with 36 different treatment approaches nominated. This was hardly surprising as there is such a shortage of information for doctors on how to treat a woman who cannot take HRT.

Fourteen per cent of the doctors in the sample failed to reply or felt that there were no alternatives. Fifteen per cent listed one alternative, 23 per cent listed two alternatives and a further 23 per cent listed three alternatives. Fourteen per cent listed four alternative treatments, and 11 per cent listed five approaches.

The most popular non-hormonal treatment was Evening Primrose Oil used by 37 per cent of the doctors. Calcium supplements were used by 33 per cent. Other treatments including antidepressants, vitamins, minerals and tranquillizers are listed on the following table in order of popularity.

This demonstrates that there is a great deal of confusion amongst the medical profession, which obviously needs addressing urgently, to prevent women who cannot tolerate HRT being left on a 'medical scrap heap'.

GENERAL PRACTITIONERS' PREFERENCES FOR ALTERNATIVES TO HORMONAL TREATMENTS FOR MENOPAUSAL WOMEN

Treatment	1st choice n = 169	All choices n = 473
Clonidine/Dixarit	43	82
Evening Primrose Oil	29	70
Didronel PMO	15	45

Calcium supplements alone	11	46
Beta-Blockers	11	21
Dietary advice and self help	10	20
Antidepressants	6	32
Anxiolytics	6	13
Oestrogen creams	5	10
Depends upon symptoms	5	6
Vitamin B6	4	16
Progesterone	4	7
Homeopathy	4	6
Diuretics	3	23
Exercise	3	11
Tibolone	3	7
Calcium and Vitamin D	2	9
Multivitamins	1	11
Exercise and Diet	1	3
Psychotherapy	1	3
Hormone implant	1	3
Replens – vaginal lubricant	1	2
Vitamin E	0	6
Stop smoking	0	6
Calcium and magnesium supplements	0	4
Refer for bone density assessment	0	2

OTHERS: The following were all listed once as a non-first choice: Ossopan, Vitamin D alone, Stanazolol, Sanomigran. Aromatherapy, Royal Jelly, Herbal Preparations, Acupuncture and Hypnosis.

When I heard that a common attitude among gynaecologists in Beverly Hills is to advise 'prophylactic hysterectomies', I assumed it was to prevent the 'prophylactic removal' of their new Mercedes Benz!

On a more appropriate note for the UK, the vast majority of GPs, while they are sympathetic, lack knowledge and are therefore unable to provide effective care for the majority of middle-aged women with health complaints. There is no doubt that pressure has to be brought to bear on the medical authorities to reverse this situation in the future.

Eight

The Not-so-serious Side-effects

Like all medicines there can be side-effects to HRT. These may be relatively minor, occur at the start of treatment and settle down after a few weeks. Many are not. In our experience we see a significant number of women who have tried HRT and didn't get on with it. They have had to stop even though they would have liked to continue because they found that it was effective in controlling some of their menopausal symptoms. We think that some of the side-effects of HRT have been underplayed and some have been overplayed. The published work reveals that there is much scientific concern about the short-and long-term effects of HRT.

The side-effects can be broadly divided into two categories. First there are adverse reactions which usually begin within a few weeks or months of starting the preparation. These types of reactions, such as irregular bleeding, are not life-threatening and may be diminished by changing the dosage or type of HRT – but not always. The second type are the more serious effects on life-threatening ills such as cancer. These will be dealt with in the next chapter.

Adverse reactions to HRT
The first list has been compiled from the data supplied by the manufacturers of different HRT preparations and from the UK doctors' guide to drug prescribing, the *Monthly Index of Medical Specialities* (MIMS):

Gastrointestinal upset

Nausea and vomiting
Weight-gain
Breast tenderness and enlargement
Breakthrough bleeding
Headaches or migraine
Dizziness
Leg cramps

There are also a variety of other relatively minor problems that can be triggered or aggravated by HRT. They include:

Increase in the size of uterine fibroids
Intolerance of contact lenses
Certain skin reactions
Loss of scalp hair
Increase in body or facial hair

Gastrointestinal upset may well seem familiar to those readers who have been pregnant. Its effects are due in the main to the action of oestrogen and the body may take a few weeks to adjust to it. It is estimated to occur in 5–10 per cent of women taking oestrogen-based HRT. Some women may tolerate natural oestrogens better than the synthetic ones, others may not. A change from tablets to patches may help some women: the patch has the advantage of delivering oestrogen into the circulation without going through the liver first and some women may tolerate this better.

Despite all this, a number of women do not feel at all well on HRT. Mood changes, an alteration in libido and a feeling of being different may persist and become troublesome enough for some of them to change their minds about continuing with HRT.

A disadvantage of the oestrogen implant (which gives a very high dose of oestrogen for six months) is that if there are any adverse effects then these may be severe and persist for several months.

PREMENSTRUAL SYNDROME CAUSED BY HRT!
Yes, it really can happen. A price sometimes to be paid for

turning the clock back on our hormones is to turn the clock back on some of our most undesirable symptoms.

Premenstrual syndrome (PMS) is a collection of physical and mental symptoms – particularly mood swings, irritability and depression – that come about because of fluctuating levels of female sex hormones through the monthly cycle. It is not usually due to a lack or excess of any one hormone but to an undue sensitivity to the changes in hormone levels.

Those women who have to take cyclical progesterone with their oestrogen-opposed therapy also have fluctuating levels of hormones virtually identical to that of the natural menstrual cycle. It should therefore come as no surprise that some women on this type of HRT will experience a pattern of symptoms similar to PMS.

Adam Magos together with John Studd and other researchers from Dulwich Hospital, London, discovered that some 20–30 per cent of women receiving progesterone experienced symptoms of breast discomfort, nausea, irritability and water retention during and particularly towards the end of their treatment with progesterone and especially with the higher doses of progesterone. Progesterone has to be given to women with a uterus, who wish to receive HRT, to prevent the overgrowth of the lining of the womb. These specialists commented that this was quite often a reason for some women to discontinue HRT and this agrees with our own experience. Reducing the dosage of progesterone may be helpful to some women.

Geraldine's Story

Geraldine is a retired schoolteacher from Cardiff, married with one grown-up child. She was fifty-eight when she approached the WNAS for help. She had been suffering with menopause symptoms since her late forties and had tried HRT. Although it improved her general health, it did not help her migraine headaches and made her feel light-headed; she also gained weight.

'When my menopause began I was in my late forties. My periods became scanty and I started to get regular migraine attacks. I also suffered from bilious attacks, had a bloated abdomen and felt "out of sorts". I would alternate between feeling dispirited to feeling "high" and yearning for sweet, sugary food, especially before my period was due. I always felt exhausted.

'My doctor prescribed Prempak-C, and although I felt better generally, I gained weight, felt light-headed and had awful migraine headaches every three weeks. The migraines were devastating: they left me feeling depressed, unsociable and unable to enjoy life. After the pain had passed I was thoroughly exhausted for three or four days. I felt utterly frustrated as I couldn't keep up with my daily routine. My vision was affected, so too were my speech and my concentration. I couldn't go out anywhere as I was continually vomiting.

'As I was unable to attend work because of my symptoms, I eventually took early retirement, regrettably, from my infant teaching job which I loved. At home I had my aged mother and aunt to care for which I found tremendously difficult because of the migraines and the exhaustion.

'I read an article in my local paper about the work of the WNAS. The case-history reported sounded just like me. I didn't hesitate to contact the WNAS for help and enrolled on their postal and telephone service. It was a wonderful experience. After completing the detailed questionnaire and diet diary, I was asked during my first consultation to make specific dietary changes, to take moderate weight-bearing exercise and to have some daily nutritional supplements. The whole programme made so much sense. The presentation and the information was excellent and I derived much pleasure from following the directions and had great hope for a cure.

'During the monthly consultations we continued to make adjustments to my diet and to the programme in general. I still avoid tea, coffee, chocolate and confectionery, salty foods, smoked foods, citrus products and wheat products. The programme has helped me enormously. I am more able to cope with my aged relatives, despite the emotional strain, and my bloating and constipation have completely disappeared.'

BREAKTHROUGH BLEEDING

A further common problem for some women who take HRT and have a uterus is breakthrough bleeding, or bleeding that happens other than at the time of progesterone withdrawal. Irregular bleeding is reported to be more likely in younger women who have only recently stopped menstruating or are still having occasional periods – the perimenopause. This can be a problem for up to one-third of women, though it usually settles down within a few months of treatment. If irregular bleeding persists or is heavy, then assessment by taking a sample of tissue from the lining of the womb and usually having a dilation and curettage (D&C) will be necessary. This is because of the possibility of cancer of the endometrium – the lining of the womb. This is a rare event and many of these D&Cs will in fact turn out to have been unnecessary.

Adjustment of the dosage and type of HRT is often needed. Certain types of HRT, Tibolone (Livial), are prone to cause breakthrough bleeding and this sort should not be used within a year of the last natural period.

WEIGHT-GAIN

From our *Woman's Realm* sample, 62 per cent of those who took HRT claimed they had experienced weight-gain as a result of taking it. The average claimed weight-gain was sixteen and a half pounds. We have no way of accounting for other causes of weight-gain in this survey. Suffice it to say that many women perceive weight-gain as being a problem that goes hand-in-hand with taking HRT.

The 'addictive' nature of HRT

This has caused genuine concern in the minds of many women taking HRT and in those who are wondering whether to or not. There is no question of HRT being addictive in the way that heroin is, but the pattern of response to its use and the effects of sudden withdrawal give it addictive-like properties.

The commonest reason that most women currently take HRT is for the control of hot flushes and there is no doubt that oestrogen administration is highly effective in this respect. In fact, it is almost too effective! When natural oestrogen was compared in a trial with placebo (dummy tablets) for three months, both reduced the number of hot flushes. Not surprisingly, HRT was more effective than placebo, virtually abolishing the hot flushes whereas placebo produced a creditable 60 per cent reduction. In the second part of the trial those who first took placebo were then transferred to natural oestrogen and they too noticed a virtual disappearance of their hot flushes. Those who had first been given HRT were then transferred to placebo. Not surprisingly their flushes returned. After a month they were back to 50 per cent of their original level but by two and three months they experienced a 25 per cent increase in their original level of symptoms at the start of the trial.

So natural oestrogen is without doubt highly effective but beware if you should stop it suddenly. This pattern of deterioration following the abrupt withdrawal of a potent drug is also known to happen with drugs used to lower blood pressure, those used in the treatment of epilepsy and with Valium, the now discredited anti-anxiety cure-all. A trial of Valium published in the 1980s also showed that its use reduced anxiety levels more effectively than placebo but when those who were taking it were transferred to placebo their anxiety scores rapidly rose to levels higher than at the start of the trial. Those who had remained on placebo throughout the trial had not experienced this sudden relapse and were clearly better off.

A slightly different but similar phenomenon occurs in women who receive oestrogen implants. Initially, these give a very high level of oestrogen which falls rapidly, though levels are significantly raised for six months or so. However, some women experience a return of their hot flushes and other symptoms despite having levels of oestrogen in the blood-stream many times higher than is normally required to control these symptoms.

A possible interpretation of this is that the oestrogen-sensitive tissues have become accustomed to high doses of this hormone and no longer respond satisfactorily. Furthermore, the rapid decline in these artificially high levels again produces an oestrogen-withdrawal effect, even though the absolute levels are normal. This unhappy sequence of events is reported to affect 3–15 per cent of women receiving treatment by oestrogen implant. There is little alternative but to let oestrogen levels decline completely over one to two years before re-trying a different form of HRT. Not surprisingly, this suggestion often does not go down too well.

Smoking and HRT
Unlike the oral contraceptive pill, it appears that there is no adverse interaction between smoking and the use of most forms of HRT. Smokers, it seems, can take HRT, though they should always be advised to stop smoking or cut down as a matter of routine.

Surgery and HRT
Again the risk seen with surgery in women on the oral contraceptive pill is not seen with natural oestrogens in truly postmenopausal women. A report by the Royal College of Surgeons in Edinburgh is reassuring. Professor Wallace, writing about the report, states: 'Women on HRT should not have their medication discontinued

for elective (planned) surgery and do not appear to have an increased risk of deep vein thrombosis.' However, if a woman is receiving HRT, and is actually premenopausal, then she should discontinue her HRT for four weeks before any major operation. The difference here is that she may still have significant levels of her own oestrogen and HRT and this situation might increase the risk of blood-clot formation.

Coming off HRT

After a while, perhaps a few months or ten years or more, many if not most women will stop taking HRT. The rights and wrongs of this have yet to be decided. There seems to be a relative shortage of information about what happens to the majority of women who stop taking HRT. In general we would expect there to be quite a few who would again experience oestrogen-withdrawal symptoms. These seem to be less likely the older the woman is, the lower the given dosage of oestrogen and the more slowly it is withdrawn. The alternative is to stay on HRT for ever and, in the words of one popular American book, remain *Feminine Forever*. This seems unproven and possibly unwise. This is because of the long-term risk of life-threatening diseases, the subject of the next chapter.

In conclusion, we do not think there is any substitute for a woman who wishes to take HRT being treated by an understanding and informed gynaecologist or physician. The evidence points strongly to there being a substantial individual response to all forms of hormonal treatment. Your wishes, your concerns and the individual way in which your body responds all need to be taken into account if you want to get the best rather than the worst out of HRT.

Woman's Realm survey and HRT

Out of the 500 women in our survey, 240 women had never taken HRT and their average age at the time of the menopause was forty-seven.

The reasons for non-use were as follows:

- 23 per cent had a medical condition that prevented them from taking it or had been advised against it by their doctor
- 28 per cent were afraid of possible side-effects
- 49 per cent had no wish to take an HRT preparation.

Out of our sample it had been suggested that 60.5 per cent take HRT. Of these, a total of 51.5 per cent took it, which was 254 women. In the HRT users it had been suggested to them by their doctor in over 95 per cent of cases. In the non-HRT users, 246 women, HRT had still been suggested by their doctor in nearly 24 per cent of cases.

Of the 254 women who had used HRT, they had tried the following:

Tablets 84%   Patches 35.5%   Implants 5%

As you can see, some women had tried more than one form of HRT. In particular, of the 214 women who had tried tablets, 58 had also tried patches – probably after trying tablets.

Of the 156 women who had only tried tablets, 71 per cent reported benefit and a surprisingly high 57 per cent had experienced some side-effects.

Of the thirty-one women who had tried patches only, 84 per cent experienced some benefit, but 64.5 per cent had also experienced side- effects. This might have included symptoms of skin irritation. These side-effects seem surprisingly high. Even if 50 per cent of them relate to minor problems, this is still a disturbingly high percentage and not an expected one, according to HRT enthusiasts.

Nine

The Serious Side-effects

This chapter is about the serious side-effects of HRT, especially cancer. As you can imagine, this is a highly contentious issue and one that, fortunately for everyone, has been the subject of concerted appraisals in many countries, especially the UK, the EC and the USA. In brief, the risks are small particularly for any one individual. The dose of oestrogen is significantly less than that used in the oral contraceptive pill and the risks, such as they are, only show up after several years of taking HRT. It has also taken some massive studies to demonstrate what the risk is. The importance of quantifying these risks, even if they are small, is because many millions of women may in the end take HRT and may do so for years, even decades. As a rule, the risk of the conditions below rise with the dose and the timespan in which it is taken.

Cancer

There does not seem to be any increase in a wide variety of other cancers, apart from those mentioned below. Other cancers are more likely to be influenced by smoking and dietary habits.

CANCER OF THE WOMB

There is good general agreement that the use of oestrogen alone in women who have a uterus is associated with a substantial increase in the risk of endometrial cancer, or cancer of the lining of the womb. Early studies show a five-fold risk after five years rising to a ten-fold risk after ten years. For this reason alone, unopposed oestrogens are rarely if ever given to women who still have their uterus.

The introduction of cyclical progesterone virtually eliminates this risk by inducing a withdrawal bleed. Thus any cells in the lining of the womb that may be starting to undergo cancerous change are shed on a regular basis. However, it seems to be the progesterone that causes many of the side-effects.

In the large survey of 4,544 women drawn from specialist menopause clinics in the UK, not one woman was found to develop cancer of the womb after receiving HRT for at least one year. However, 36 per cent of these women had had a hysterectomy and the women tended to be of a relatively higher social class than the general population. This group had used HRT for an average of six years and seven months.

The first sign of cancer of the womb is irregular or heavy bleeding and this type of cancer is most common in women aged sixty. It is also linked to being overweight.

CANCER OF THE OVARY

The risk of cancer of the ovary seems to be less in those who take birth-control pills but the picture in HRT users is not clear. Recently Dr Jacobs and Dr Loeffler from London concluded that 'at the present time one cannot exclude an adverse effect of long-term treatment on the risk of ovarian cancer'.

Abdominal pain, swelling and vaginal bleeding may be the first signs.

CANCER OF THE BREAST

Cancer of the breast is the commonest female cancer and there is much evidence to link oestrogen exposure to the risk of developing this cancer. Recent detailed expert assessments of currently published data suggest that the risk of developing breast cancer is increased in HRT users by between 10 and 25 per cent after about ten years. Some authorities suspect that the real risk may be higher than this and there will probably be more precise assessments with longer studies. Results from the Medical Research Council's surveillance of postmenopausal women on HRT in the UK has seen an unwelcome change in the risk of breast cancer. This mixed group of women who had used a variety of HRT preparations for a year or more initially had a lower-than-average risk of developing breast cancer which began to approach the population average ten years after their first exposure to HRT. The latest information from this group of women suggests that the risk has continued to increase, turning this initially low-risk group into at least an average-risk group. Concern is mounting about the effect of giving HRT to a more mixed group of women in the UK which would include those with an average-to-high risk of breast cancer at the start of their therapy.

There is also some suggestion that the risk might be less in those receiving natural or conjugated oestrogens and that it might be higher in those taking opposed oestrogens; the picture is not clear enough. The risk is likely to be greater in those who have a history of benign breast problems, or in those who have a first-degree relative (mother, sister and possibly daughter) with breast cancer. For this reason regular breast examinations and mammograms are part of the routine for all women receiving HRT of whatever type. It is also possible that giving HRT may make mammography less sensitive at detecting early breast cancers. Again we do not know for certain.

The most worrying data is that breast cancer has become much more common in women as a whole at a time when oestrogens in the form of oral contraceptives and HRT have become popular. In England and Wales, breast-cancer registrations rose by 50.7 per cent between 1962 and 1987. Fortunately with early and thorough treatment the outlook appears to be improving.

The high and increasing prevalence of this type of cancer in the majority of developed countries may also be due, in part, to the effect of dietary factors on hormone metabolism.

The strong suspicion remains that the total exposure to oestrogens from a variety of sources from childhood to old age will be a large factor in determining the risk of breast cancer. The main sources of oestrogens during a woman's lifetime are those from her own ovaries, those in the oral contraceptive pill and those in HRT. The metabolism of all these is influenced by the individual's diet and probably by her inherited metabolism.

To better quantify the risk of HRT on breast cancer we shall also have to quantify the risk or benefit of these other factors and that is going to take a very long time. There is no room for complacency, however, in the meantime and if you are going to take HRT for more than five years make sure that you have a good reason for doing so.

Sarah's Story

Sarah, from Enfield in Middlesex, is married with two grown-up children and has a full-time job as an art teacher. She was fifty when she contacted the WNAS.

'The symptoms first began three years ago when I had hot flushes every half an hour. The flushes were so draining it took me about half an hour to recover from each one and consequently I felt tired and wiped out. I felt very depressed as I couldn't predict when the flushes were coming and they were totally out of my control. My hands used to swell up and I had insomnia too. I would go off to sleep and then be woken by the flushes and sweats and then not be able to get back to sleep. I also suffered with palpitations, panic attacks and anxiety. I was foul and morose towards my family. They coped with me by keeping me at arms' length. I felt intolerant towards them, very irritable and couldn't be bothered to respond. I am usually so active and cheerful, it was such a change for me and I felt utterly exhausted by my symptoms.

'I went to see my GP, but unfortunately he said it was inadvisable for me to take HRT as I have a history of breast cancer, and I was a migraine sufferer. He did prescribe some pills for migraine, but they made me very constipated.

'I don't know how I managed to keep going at work. I was so tired, it was difficult to act as if nothing was happening. I managed somehow, it was a sort of pride thing, but deep down I was desperate.

'I heard about the work of the WNAS through a friend, but I must admit I was sceptical as I always considered that I ate a healthy diet. The initial programme that was suggested for me by the WNAS included cutting down on coffee and to stop eating foods that contained added sugar. I took multivitamins and minerals and did some regular exercise.

'The programme has helped to reduce the flushes and I am able to sleep now, so I am not feeling exhausted any more. I feel much more in control of my own body and I'm probably a much easier person to live with! My relationship with my family has greatly improved. However, I do lapse on the diet sometimes and notice that the symptoms start to return when I return to my old ways of eating and drinking. Knowing that my well-being is under my control and that I have the knowledge to put things right if I have lapsed is very welcome.'

Other causes of death

One of the main UK studies, that of 4,544 long-term HRT users who have been monitored by Kate Hunt from the Medical Research Council, found that HRT users were slightly more likely to die from 'injury, poisoning and violence as well as suicide and suspected suicide'. This seems more likely due to the social characteristics of the group than just the taking of HRT itself. But does a society or a group within society that is prepared to take HRT mean that we are less tolerant of stressful situations and more prepared to take a pill to solve an ill even if it is too much of a pill?

Cardiovascular disease

Now for some good news. The other major area of concern about the use of HRT has been its possible effect on heart disease. With the oral contraceptive pill there had been a definite increase in some types of cardiovascular disease especially among those who smoked (and were overweight and had high blood pressure). This pattern has not been observed with HRT. The oral contraceptive pill uses a relatively high dose of a synthetic oestrogen combined with a synthetic progesterone, whereas the HRT studies that have shown a fall in heart-disease risk have used unopposed natural oestrogen at a dose less than that in the pill.

The thirty or more published studies that looked at the risk of using HRT in the form of unopposed natural oestrogen and developing coronary heart disease have also been recently reviewed. Most of these studies have found a small reduction in the risk of either having a heart attack or of dying from one. The degree of reduction in risk is of the order of 30–40 per cent and seems most noticeable in those who have taken it for long durations, five years or more, and in those who had a relatively high risk to start with. This would include smokers, those with a high cholesterol level, those with a family history of heart disease and those who had not been eating a diet rich in fresh fruit and vegetables.

In the large Medical Research Council study in England and Wales the relative risk of cardiovascular death seemed to reduce with time as that for breast cancer slightly increased. By and large the administration of natural oestrogen results in a fall in the total level of cholesterol in the blood. There can also be a rise in the level of HDL cholesterol – cholesterol thought to be being removed from the circulation to be excreted by the liver. These effects are comparable to those obtained by following a fat-reduced, high-fibre diet. Physical exercise can also lower the level of cholesterol in menopausal women but that of oestrogen appears to be greater – though of course taking HRT does not make you fit or automatically bring with it the many proven benefits of regular exercise.

Progesterone, on the other hand, may lessen the potential blood-cholesterol-lowering effects of oestrogen. This has been true in the past and depends on the type of progesterone used. Currently the jury awaits the evidence of on-going trials of opposed therapy (oestrogen and progesterone) on cardiovascular risk.

The effect of HRT in the form of patches and implants on cardiovascular disease has not yet been evaluated. Patches that combine oestrogen and progesterone can have a potential beneficial effect on blood-cholesterol levels.

So it would seem that a reasonably clear advantage of HRT is the use of natural unopposed oestrogens (in women who have had a hysterectomy) as a means of lowering her risk of heart disease. Indeed, some improvement in the survival of women with established coronary heart disease has been shown by the giving of HRT.

Does the story end there? Well, not quite. The initial interest in the menopause and heart disease was triggered by the observations that heart attacks, and death from coronary heart disease, are rare before the menopause and that the risk rises from the time of the menopause be it naturally late, naturally early or as a result of the loss of the ovaries. In other words, oestrogens looked protective from the start.

It was subsequently shown that the rate of heart disease is already rising well before the time of the menopause and the rate of rise does not actually increase further at this time of hormonal change. So we need to understand better what is going on and the part that hormones, diet, smoking, exercise and genetic factors all have to play. This is vitally important because a heart attack is the commonest cause of death in postmenopausal women and one that is potentially preventable. The bad side of HRT might be forgivable to many if there was a large reduction in cardiovascular deaths, particularly in those that occur at an early age and if the women who take it feel particularly well on it. Individual risk assessment and the personal choice of how a woman might like to meet her maker may well come into it.

Stroke – more good news
This too has been the subject of careful review and there appears to be no increase in risk. The only proviso is that a few women will experience a rise in blood pressure on HRT. This should be detected and either their HRT stopped or their blood pressure controlled by drug or non-drug therapy. Otherwise they will carry an increased risk of having a stroke. The main risk factors for stroke are high blood pressure, obesity, high alcohol intake, lack of physical exercise, smoking and a diet lacking in fresh fruit.

It seems that a picture of sorts is appearing. It is not entirely clear, and with the rapid, perhaps all too rapid, introduction of different types of HRT, assessment of the risks remains difficult. To its credit HRT is, in the short term at least, a relatively safe form of treatment for many menopausal complaints. But many big questions relating to its long-term safety remain unanswered. Safe for some and unsafe for others seems the likely outcome. At this point we can do no better than to quote the final conclusion given by a large group of American authorities who published their appraisal of HRT trials in the *Annals of Internal Medicine* in December 1992:

'Hormone therapy should probably be recommended for women who have a hysterectomy and for those with coronary heart disease or at high risk of coronary heart disease. For other women the best course of action is unclear.'

Part Three

THE NATURAL APPROACH TO THE MENOPAUSE

Ten

Why You Should Change Your Diet and Lifestyle

So far, we have been looking at the mechanics of the menopause and how some of the symptoms in some women could be helped by oestrogen replacement. But in doing so, we discovered that some of the symptoms are not particularly related to a fall in oestrogen levels and thus there must be some other underlying cause.

What we haven't inspected closely is our diet and lifestyle and the relationship they have to our health and well-being, or lack of it. Our twentieth-century diet is very different to the practices of our relatives in times past.

When we examine our early ancestors' diet, we begin to realize that it is not 'natural' to eat meat protein, for instance, in the quantity that many of us do today. Evidence shows that diet approximately three million years ago consisted largely of hard seeds, plant fibre, some roots and stems – a diet high in vegetable matter.

Animals today are bred to be fat. Modern meat contains considerably more fat than the wild meat our ancestors ate. Our ancestors' meat also contained more of the good polyunsaturated fats than today's meat, which is high in the potentially harmful saturated fats. The ancient diet was also richer in vitamins and minerals, largely composed of fresh, raw foods.

Lifestyle is different too, for as recently as the 1930s approximately four proper meals were consumed each day, with only one or two in-between-meal snacks. Whereas in the 1990s we now consume on average one or two proper meals, with approximately four or five in-between-meal snacks. Convenience food and pre-prepared meals are often served instead of wholesome home cooking, largely because time is at a premium. We no longer have the extended family to fall back on and very often women have to be the wage-earner now, as well as '*Haus frau*' and mother.

We exercise far less as well. In the age of the motor car, many of us have forgotten what our legs were designed for. We drive from one place to another, do more sitting down than is good for us and allow our metabolic rate to rest!

The net result is that we are suffering far more from conditions that were not so common in the past. Heart disease, cancer, diabetes and osteoporosis are just a few of the disorders that are on the increase. So too are symptoms like irritable bowel syndrome, including constipation, diarrhoea with a painful and windy, bloated abdomen, migraine headaches, nervous tension, irritability, insomnia, feelings of aggression and fatigue. Let's just take a quick look at the magnitude of some of the major problems and how they are influenced by our diet and lifestyle.

The price of illness

It is estimated that in 1993 the NHS bill for the taxpayer was £37 billion. In the USA in the last twenty years or so, the medical bill has increased from $27 billion to over $200 billion! The awful fact is that despite these amounts of money being spent, some of us have been getting sicker.

HEART DISEASE

Cardiovascular disease is still the biggest killer in developed countries and undoubtedly the commonest preventable cause of early death in young to middle-aged men and women. Approximately 170,000 people die each year in the UK from heart attacks and strokes. There has been little improvement, as yet, in these figures, though the USA and Finland have begun to achieve a substantial fall in their incidence of heart disease. Smoking, lack of exercise, obesity, high blood pressure and high blood cholesterol are all well-documented risk factors and these last three are all influenced by diet.

CANCER

Cancer, too, it appears, is on the increase. There seem to be three main factors for this. The first is age. With a few exceptions the incidence of most cancers rises steeply with age from about forty years onward. In the past, many people did not live long enough to be at risk of developing cancer. Second, it is highly likely that there has been a true increase in the rate of cancer this century, regardless of age, and that this reflects the increased use of chemicals in the environment. Many industrial chemicals, pesticides and even drugs linger in the environment for years.

Finally, the type of food we eat also influences cancer risk. Consumption of smoked and pickled foods is associated with an increase in some cancers, especially of the stomach and oesophagus, while a high intake of fresh fruit and vegetables may well protect against many types of cancer. These protective foods are rich in vitamins C, E and carotene – vegetable vitamin A – which help limit the damage to tissues by cancer-inducing chemicals.

PSYCHIATRIC ILLNESSES

'Mental' illnesses are also on the increase and this too may be influenced by our diet, consumption of alcohol, medical and illicit drugs. Obviously, social factors, education and life-skills are also all important in helping us cope with times of stress or ill-health. The stresses and strains of twentieth-century living have not made it easy for some of us to cope and for many women, working and raising a family and coping with aged relatives proves to be particularly stressful.

ALLERGIES

Allergic problems have also become much more common in the last forty years. The reasons for this are not clear but they include family or genetic factors, chemicals in the environment, dietary habits and the pattern of feeding in childhood.

Menopausal symptoms, diet and lifestyle

What, I hear you ask, has this pessimistic view of the state of our health got to do with the menopause? Quite simply, it appears that the development of symptoms at the time of the menopause may very well be influenced by the same factors: diet, exercise or the lack of it and possibly environmental chemicals. It is possible that these diverse conditions have common causative and aggravating factors.

In 1990 the Women's Nutritional Advisory Service completed a national survey of 274 women in the UK in conjunction with a national newspaper. We found that 86.8 per cent of them suffered in varying degrees with symptoms at the time of the menopause. This figure concurs with other reported surveys. Over two-thirds of the women in our sample suffered with hot flushes or nightsweats. Fatigue was the next most commonly complained about problem, followed by sexual problems and weight-gain. These are not all oestrogen-withdrawal symptoms, but can all be influenced by diet, as you will see.

Our bodies were not built to cope with refined and processed foods, very often empty of nutrients. We have had to live with pesticides and insecticides being sprayed on our crops, with growth hormones and antibiotics pumped into animals, and with environmental pollution and acid rain as the finishing touches. Many of us overeat and under-exercise and women nowadays tend to lead far more stressful existences. So it is logical, really, that we can't honestly expect our 'machines' to go on indefinitely without breaking down when we don't treat them with respect. We generally treat our cars better than we do our bodies – you wouldn't dream of putting the wrong fuel in your petrol tank, would you?

In order to look at diet more closely we need to examine how our habits have changed. As little as 100 years ago, meat, animal fat and sugar were a much smaller part of our diets than today. The consumption of cereal fibres has also dropped considerably. These are important factors in relation to the menopause, as we shall see.

These days, in order to eat a 'normal, healthy diet' we have to pay far more attention to the foods and drinks we choose. If you concentrate on avoiding the nutrient-deficient and contaminated foods we have listed below, you will be making changes for the better in your diet – changes which will not only help your menopause symptoms, but will help you feel healthier all round. There is less you can do to combat the unhealthy effects of our polluted environment, but there are some suggestions in the pages to follow.

- We have increased our consumption of sugar. The UK has become one of the world's largest chocolate and sweet-eaters, with the average person consuming some 188 lb or 85 kilos each per year. We currently spend over £4 billion per year on chocolate alone.
- Our diet is particularly high in saturated fats (animal fats). It is thought that this has much to do with our also having a high incidence of heart disease and breast cancer.
- We eat far too much salt – ten to twenty times more than our bodies really require each day. Salt can contribute to high blood pressure.
- We often drink far too much coffee and tea which can impede the absorption of essential nutrients and aggravate hot flushes, symptoms of irritability, nervous tension, insomnia and headaches. On average we consume four mugs of tea and two mugs of coffee each day, which delivers approximately 800 mg of caffeine into our system each day. Anything over 250 each day can give symptoms of caffeine excess, and that's in a healthy individual who has no existing symptoms. Count the number of teas and coffees you have had so far today; you may be consuming even more than average.
- We consume volumes of foods with a high level of phosphorus, which again impedes the absorption of good nutrients and interferes with calcium absorption by bone tissue. Examples of these foods are soft drinks of low or normal calorie types, processed foods, canned, packaged, prepacked convenience foods and ready-made sauces.
- Alcohol consumption has almost doubled in the UK since the end of the Second World War. Alcohol not only knocks most nutrients sideways, it also can bring on the hot flushes.
- Unbelievable as it may seem, we actually eat less food than we

did thirty years ago and more. It seems that today's women actually expend less energy than those of a generation or two ago and this has resulted in a 10–15 per cent reduction in food intake. This means that our intake of essential nutrients has also fallen, particularly if we eat refined or convenience foods.

- Many of the foods available contain chemical additives in the form of flavour enhancers, colouring and preservatives. While some of these are not harmful, some of them are and our bodies are certainly not designed to cope with them.
- Our water contains certain pollutants which are thought to be a risk to public health.
- Our meat has become contaminated with antibiotics and growth hormones, so much so that vegetarians now have an easier menopause than meat-eaters.
- Nitrate fertilizers have been used to obtain fast-growing and abundant crops. It is now recognized that nitrates are harmful and can produce cancer, at least in animals.
- Almost all our fresh fruit, cereals and vegetables are sprayed with pesticides at least once. In addition, milk and meat may retain the pesticides from feed given to livestock.

ANTIBIOTICS

Because antibiotics are being so widely used on animals, the conditions that would normally be treated by antibiotics are becoming resistant to them. Apart from being used as a medicine for individual sick animals, they are given to whole herds as a preventive measure and they are again used for growth promotion.

My advice is to try to use organic or additive-free meat where possible, meat which has not been subjected to drugs, growth promoters or contaminated foods. Organic and additive-free meat is becoming more widely available. Certainly local farms and even supermarkets often keep stocks. If you can find 'clean' meat, it can be included in your diet approximately three times a week. An alternative is to limit your meat intake to moderate quantities of good quality lean meat or to become a vegetarian. It's the fat in the meat that will carry much of the pollutants, so avoid it – and also eat more fish. When eating chicken, don't eat the skin and don't make the gravy from the fatty part of the juices: pour it off first.

FAT CONSUMPTION

Britain has the honour of having the highest incidence of heart disease in the world. This was not so in the past, when other countries such as Finland and Australia were way ahead.

It seems that the saturated fats increase the level of cholesterol which leaves the bloodstream and settles down in the arteries, resulting in a gradual blockage of those supplying the heart, brain and other organs. This leads to heart attacks, strokes and poor circulation. It is worth noting that smoking accelerates the process.

By 1966 the Australian and US rate of heart disease began to decline, but that was not so for the UK, whose casualties were on the increase. In other countries, such as Finland, for example, who were previously 'top of the coronary pops', a national nutritional education campaign was undertaken. The result is that today they are a much healthier nation with a far lower incidence of heart disease than many other countries.

THE SWEET FACTS

Over the past 100 years there has been a twenty-five-fold increase in world sugar production. This is a real change from the days when sugar was an expensive luxury that we locked away for high days and holidays and was only consumed by the wealthy. Refined sugars simply didn't exist for our ancestors. Their diet consisted mainly of vegetables, fruit, cereals and some wild meat. It wasn't until this century that we developed an addiction to the sweet and sticky sugar family.

We clearly don't need refined sugar. What seems to have been overlooked is that our bodies can change complex carbohydrates and proteins into the sugar they require. Sugar contains no vitamins, no minerals, no protein, no fibre and no starches. It may contain tiny traces of calcium and magnesium if you're lucky, but primarily it provides us with loads of 'empty calories'.

It is actually a fair skill these days not to consume large amounts of sugar because it is added to so many foods. What do you think the following have in common? Cheese, biscuits, fruit yogurt, tomato sauce, baked beans, pickled cucumbers, muesli, beefburgers, Worcestershire sauce, pork sausages, peas, cornflakes and Coca-Cola – well, they can all contain sugar. Cola-Cola contains some eight teaspoonfuls per can.

THE NITTY GRITTY ABOUT COFFEE

Over the last ten years reports have begun to filter through about the health hazards attached to coffee, probably because increasing amounts of coffee are being consumed. Since 1950 the consumption of coffee in the UK has increased fourfold. Many people become quite addicted to it unknowingly, and couldn't give up the habit easily.

We now know that coffee worsens nervous tension, anxiety and insomnia. So obviously, no matter how much we may enjoy it, drinking coffee to excess is not a healthy habit. In fact, coffee contains caffeine which is a mental and physical stimulant. This can be of benefit, of course, but even with two to four cups each day, adverse effects can be experienced. These include anxiety, restlessness, nervousness, insomnia, rapid pulse, palpitations, shakes and passing increased quantities of water. Regular coffee drinkers not only enjoy the flavour but in many cases come to rely on the stimulation to get them through the day. If you cannot get going without your first fix of the day, you will know what I mean!

Weaning yourself off coffee can sometimes be a fairly traumatic experience. It can sometimes produce symptoms not unlike a drug withdrawal, in particular a severe headache, which may take several days to disappear. However, rest assured, the headaches do eventually go completely, as long as you manage to abstain and use alternatives with which you are relatively happy.

How to Kick the Habit

- Cut down gradually over the space of a week or two.
- Use decaffeinated coffee instead, but limit yourself to two to three cups each day.

- Try alternative drinks like Barleycup, dandelion coffee or Bambu which you can obtain from healthfood shops.
- If you like filter coffee, you can still use your filter, but with decaffeinated versions or with roasted dandelion root instead of coffee (get this from good healthfood shops; it has a very pleasant malted flavour).

THE TRUTH ABOUT TEA

The British are famous for their tea consumption. Tea, like coffee, contains caffeine, about 70 mg per cup, compared to coffee's 120 mg per strong cup. Tea also contains tannin, which inhibits the absorption of zinc and iron in particular. Excess tea produces the same effects as coffee and you can also experience withdrawal headaches. Plus, tea can cause constipation.

By drinking a cup of tea with a meal you can cut down the absorption of iron from vegetarian foods to one-third. Whereas a glass of fresh orange juice with the same meal would increase iron absorption by twice as much because of its high vitamin C content. Vegetarian and vegan women need their intake of iron to be readily absorbed, so drinking anything other than small amounts of weak tea may mean they risk becoming iron deficient.

'Herbal teas' don't count as tea as such. It's really a confusing name. Most herbal teas are free of caffeine and tannin and just consist of a collection of herbs. Unlike regular tea, they can be cleansing and relaxing. My favourite herbal tea 'look-alike' is Rooibosch Eleven O'Clock tea, which looks just like tea with milk but tastes even better. Many patients prefer it to ordinary tea, although it does take a week or two to get used to. It is available from most healthfood shops.

MORE ABOUT ALCOHOL

On average, women consume one unit of alcohol each day, and men three units (one unit = one glass of wine, one pub measure of spirits, one small sherry or vermouth, or half a pint of normal strength beer or lager). These average levels are now the maximum recommended daily intakes for women and men respectively. Although many of us may be teetotallers or drink substantially less than this, there will be those who regularly consume more. It is recognized that some women hit the bottle at the time of the menopause in an attempt to blot out reality.

Alcohol in excess destroys body tissue over the years and can cause or contribute to many diseases – for example, cardiovascular diseases, digestive disorders, inflammation and ulceration of the lining of the digestive tract, liver disease, brain degeneration, miscarriages, damage to unborn children and malnutrition. Last but not least, sustained heavy drinking can be a risk factor for osteoporosis.

As most of these conditions come on gradually, we often don't see the real dangers of alcohol. There is no impact like that of an accident or the drama of an ambulance arriving to carry you off. Instead, there is a slow process of destruction which conveniently escapes our awareness.

If you like your drink and notice that your consumption is becoming heavier because you feel low, you will be aware of the social problems that go with it, such as mood swings and personality changes. When this occurs others around become affected and relationships may be strained at home and at work. It is a fact that one-third of the divorce petitions cite alcohol as a contributory factor. Local courtrooms are always having to deal with people who committed offences while under the influence of alcohol – so take stock.

SMOKING

Smoking tobacco has become a widespread habit among Western societies. In 1922 in the UK, for example, twenty-to thirty-year-old women smoked an average of fifty cigarettes each year, but by 1975 this had risen to an average of just over 3,000 cigarettes per woman, per year. Despite the more educated classes reducing their cigarette consumption, smoking has become relatively common in those women who are less well educated.

It is generally acknowledged that women who regularly smoke in excess of fifteen cigarettes each day are likely to have their menopause two years earlier than their non-smoking counterparts. Smoking also affects bone density; it should either be drastically cut down, or, better still, stopped before the menopause.

DRUGS
Western societies have become drug-oriented. In the USA in 1991 nearly £35 billion was spent on medicines by a population of 250 million, and in the UK it was £3.5 billion or £69 per man, woman and child. Doctors issue some 15 per cent more prescriptions than they did a decade ago. In England alone, over 425 million prescriptions were written in 1992, nearly ten million for antidepressants, amounting to £81 million. None of this is surprising, in view of the power and influence that drug companies have been allowed to assume in the education of doctors.

In the last few years there has been tremendous concern by medical practitioners worldwide about the excessive use of benzodiazepine tranquillizers and sleeping tablets. It is now recommended that these drugs, which include Valium, Mogadon and Ativan, are used as a temporary measure for only a few weeks. Those who have been taking them long-term should, if at all possible, have their dosage and frequency gradually reduced under medical supervision.

THE QUALITY OF DIET
Our diet this century has gone through, and continues to go through, several substantial changes. By the end of the 1970s there was evidence, from certain surveys, of a deterioration in the quality of the UK diet, particularly since the Second World War. A high intake of sugar, refined foods, animal fats and alcohol had meant a relatively poor intake of essential vitamins and minerals.

Some fifteen vitamins, twenty-four minerals and eight amino acids have been isolated as being essential for normal body function. They are synergistic, which means that they rely on each other in order to keep the body functioning at an optimum level. When one or more is in short supply, alterations in body metabolism occur. Minor deficiencies can often be tolerated, but major or multiple deficiencies result in the body becoming inefficient, with the development of symptoms and possibly disease.

There is, however, some heartening recent evidence. All the food advice from numerous individual experts and expert committees, government ones included, has finally got through to some of the British public. Many of us have increased our intake of fruit and vegetables and this greatly offsets the potential fall in intake from eating refined foods or eating smaller amounts of food in general. However, this has not happened with the unemployed or those who come from families where the main wage-earner is unskilled. From the recent dietary survey of British adults in the UK, the single biggest factor that determined nutrient intake was not age, sex, illness, or whether on a diet or not, but whether the person was unemployed. Like it or not, it seems that we already have a nutritional underclass who don't have the money and the knowledge to improve their diets. Fats and sugar are cheap calories and when you are hungry calories are more important than fibre, vitamins and minerals.

WATER

Our most important nutrient is water, and sadly it is becoming one of our major sources of pollution. Not only is the water contaminated with lead, aluminium and copper, we now have nitrates to contend with as well. Nitrates are chemicals used in fertilizers to promote crop growth. These are harmful because they go through a chemical change and at the end of the day turn into nitrosamines which are believed to be strong cancer-producing chemicals.

LEAD AND OTHER TOXIC MINERALS

Toxic minerals in the form of lead and mercury are in the soil, the air and the water, as well as being present in our food. During this century their levels have been rising rapidly, at times to a point where our bodies have not been able to cope.

Lead pollution has been much discussed in the media over the past few years. High lead levels are acknowledged to be linked to low birth weight and low intelligence in children. As a result of extensive research on lead, many countries have removed lead from petrol and are trying to keep lead levels down in cities. However, it is far more difficult to remove it from the water supply as the filtering systems at water-purification plants can't always cope with the load.

How to avoid toxins

- Concentrate on eating a nutritious diet, particularly high in zinc, magnesium, calcium and vitamins C, B and E (see also page 200).
- Take a well-balanced multivitamin supplement and some extra vitamin C if you are at particular risk.
- Scrub all fruit and vegetables with a brush to clean off as many toxins as possible, and remove the outer layers of lettuce and cabbage, etc. But don't *peel* fruit and vegetables unless you don't like the peel – very often the bulk of the nutrients is just under the skin. Use organic vegetables and salad stuff or grow your own where possible, without using chemicals.
- Water filters tend to filter out a great deal of the toxic metals. Every so often the filter needs replacing and it's amazing what collects in it. Rather the toxic deposits collect in the filter than in your body! Water purifiers can be bought in healthfood shops but they aren't so efficient.
- Do not spend too much time near busy roads if the local exhaust fumes contain lead (which may be easier said than done)
- Avoid copper and aluminium cookware unless with a non-stick lining
- Cut down on alcohol, as it increases lead absorption
- Do not eat refined foods: these give the body little protection against toxins
- Avoid antacids which contain aluminium salts

FOOD ADDITIVES

While there are some perfectly harmless substances added to food, the number of potentially harmful additives is significant. Many additives have been shown to cause hyperactivity in children, as well as asthma, eczema, skin rashes and swelling. It's obviously important to be able to differentiate between the safe and the not-so-safe additives.

After being bombarded by warnings about additives, is it any wonder that some of us have at one time or another avoided all foods containing them? Understandably, 'additive' has become a dirty word in some circles. But it's important to understand that some additives are, in fact, beneficial! For example, beneficial additives include riboflavin – vitamin B2 – and calcium L-ascorbate which is vitamin C, and the many preservatives which help keep our food from spoiling. Look in Appendix 3 on page 294 for details of booklets and books on additives which will help you to pick out the dangerous additives from the safe ones.

Take one positive step at a time

I am sorry to bombard you with so many depressing facts all at once. We the consumers definitely need more information about the food we eat and the environmental factors to which we are subjected.

Probably the first step towards reversing the effects of the twentieth century on your body is for you to acknowledge the value of that body if you haven't already done so. After all, you only have one body to last you the rest of your life, so it's important to treat it with respect.

It's up to you how often you expose your body to alcohol, cigarettes, drugs and additives, and how physically fit you keep through exercise. Making one change at a time is better than not changing at all.

As for environmental pollution, there are now many worthwhile national and local groups running campaigns to help overcome these problems. You will find a list of these on page 301. If you are concerned about your local situation, you can always contact your area government representative for help and advice.

If you have been neglecting your body to some extent, now may be the time to make some changes. Don't expect your doctor to piece you back together again when you have fallen apart through 'environmental wear and nutritional tear'! It's up to each one of us to look after our bodies to the best of our abilities and to treat them as well as any other of our treasured possessions.

Eleven

Nutrition and Hormone Function

There is now no doubt that our diet influences our hormone function. Medical researchers are beginning to work it out for women and eventually they will also work it out for men. So far it would seem that there are three main ways that our diet and nutritional state can determine our hormonal balance:

- The balance of fat and fibre in the diet
- The effects of individual essential nutrients
- The presence of natural oestrogen and progesterone compounds in foodstuffs.

Before we launch into these three areas we must first acknowledge that we do not actually know how important these components are. It is safe to say that they have been overlooked and that their importance will rise perhaps to a point where dietary change will be acknowledged for some women, by Uncle Tom Cobley and all, as a real alternative to HRT for the control of oestrogen-withdrawal symptoms. That is our impression from many of the women we have seen and advised in a clinic setting.

We are not talking about diet and oesteoporosis. That is a quite different topic and it is covered in an earlier chapter.

Fat and fibre
This duo, who took leading roles in the story of heart disease, have also been busy at work on the rise and fall of oestrogen. Scientific interest primarily came about because of the strong

relationship between the dietary intake of fat and not just heart disease but breast cancer. Those countries with a high intake of fat, especially saturated fat found predominantly in animal products, have a high rate of breast cancer. As yet we do not know whether reducing our intake of fat will reduce the rate of breast cancer. Such studies would be costly and complicated and have not yet been undertaken. What has been studied is the influence of our diet and its fat and fibre content on hormone function and thereby the possible risks of breast disease. Some of this information is of relevance when trying to understand the relationship between diet and hormone changes at the menopause.

In brief, the majority of studies have shown that:

- A high-fat, low-fibre diet is associated with relatively high levels of circulating oestrogen
- Dietary fibre enhances the rate of clearance of oestrogen from the body
- In premenopausal women, changing to a low-fat, high-fibre diet can, but does not always, lower the circulating oestrogen levels
- Vegetarians and those who are not overweight tend to have higher levels of a hormone-modifying protein, sex hormone binding globulin (SHBG), in their blood. This helps smooth out the highs and lows of hormone fluctuation
- Severe constipation is associated with a low level of oestrogen and menstrual irregularities
- Antibiotics, by killing off friendly bacteria in the intestine, may reduce the natural recycling of oestrogen by the body

What this jumble of information means is not fully clear. In essence, the extremes of diet and bowel function are associated with the more extreme levels of hormones, especially oestrogen. Being a lifelong high-fat, low-fibre eater, as is seen in many Western women, is more likely to be associated with menopausal symptoms of oestrogen withdrawal. This may be because their systems are used to a relatively high level of circulating hormones and that they tolerate the drop less well. In theory, making a dramatic change to a low-fat, high-fibre diet might aggravate the symptoms of oestrogen withdrawal in women in the perimenopause or early postmenopause. This effect is likely to be offset by the impact of improved nutrition on hormone function.

In summary there seems to be an excess hormonal vulnerability in those consuming a Western diet. Make the change but do not be too drastic about it at the time of the menopause: for example, don't suddenly go from being a meat-eater to following a weight-loss vegan diet! Changing your diet may help not only with the risks of heart disease but also with the risks of the hormonally related cancers in the breast and womb.

Individual essential nutrients

It appears that many nutrients are essential either for the production of hormones or to help the way in which the hormones do their job in the body. Nutritional deficiencies have to be severe before they have a profound influence, but several combined nutritional inadequacies will probably have a subtle adverse effect on hormone function. You may think that nutritional deficiencies are rare in the UK. True, if we confine ourselves to severe deficiencies. But from authoritative government surveys, poor intake of a number of nutrients are acknowledged in some 20 per cent of women of child-bearing age. So there is absolutely no room for nutritional complacency.

Let's take an individual look at some of the important nutrients.

IRON
The main function of iron is the production of the oxygen-carrying blood pigment haemoglobin. Iron is also needed by muscles and the brain, and a lack causes not only anaemia but also fatigue, loss of hair and brittle, split nails. Anaemia occurs in 4 per cent of women of child-bearing age but has to be severe to result in cessation of periods. Mild lack of iron is more likely and can be present in a further 10 per cent of the menstruating

population. It can cause fatigue and should be considered in any perimenopausal woman in whom this is a problem.

VITAMIN B

There are several members of the vitamin B family. Broadly speaking, they are involved in energy release from food and the health of the nervous system. Severe deficiency of two of these vitamins is on record as causing cessation of menstruation or menstrual irregularities. These are vitamin B12 and vitamin B3. Deficiencies of either of these is rare.

Lack of vitamin B12 can occur in long-standing strict vegans and in older people who lose the ability to absorb this vitamin. Weight loss, fatigue, tingling in the feet and loss of balance are other features of this deficiency.

Lack of vitamin B3 – nicotinic acid or niacinamide – should only develop in the heavy alcohol consumer, those on very poor low-protein diets and those with serious digestive problems. Depression, a red, scaly rash on the face, backs of the hands or other light-exposed areas and diarrhoea are other features. In malnourished women deficient in this vitamin, menstrual irregularities were apparently common. It might occasionally be a problem in the perimenopausal woman if she is drinking rather heavily.

Vitamin B6 is often linked with premenstrual syndrome. Mild deficiency diagnosed by a low blood level is surprisingly common and together with lack of vitamin B1, thiamin, is known to be a common finding in both men and women with anxiety and depression. Deficiency of this, however, is not known to be associated with any menstrual disturbance. Vitamin B6, however, is involved in the way in which tissues respond to oestrogen and is apparently needed for that part on the surface of the cell that interacts with oestrogen to refresh itself. Hence increased amounts of vitamin B6 may be needed by some women who are taking relatively large amounts of oestrogen, as in the oral contraceptive pill. HRT seems to have a much less disturbing effect in this respect. It is theoretically possible that the response of tissues to oestrogen would be improved by correction of a vitamin B6 deficiency or by taking an extra amount of it.

Though severe lack of these and the other B vitamins are fairly infrequent, mild deficiency is not that uncommon even in relatively well-fed populations. Such has been the concern about the poor intake of folic acid in women of child-bearing age that, since December 1992, all women in the UK who wish to become pregnant are now advised to take a daily supplement of 400 micrograms, nearly twice the average dietary intake, before conceiving. Doing so greatly reduces the chance of the mother giving birth to an infant with spina bifida. There may well be other adverse effects of mild vitamin B deficiency in women of child-bearing age that are not yet documented. Menstrual disturbance is one possibility.

VITAMIN E
The use of Vitamin E in women of reproductive age was stimulated by the early discovery that in rats, deficiency caused pregnant females to abort and lose their offspring. Indeed, the proper chemical name for vitamin E is tocopherol, which in Greek means child-bearing. In premenstrual women, in fact women with premenstrual syndrome, supplements of vitamin E have been found to raise oestrogen levels but the response varied considerably with the dose. Its effect on hormone chemistry in perimenopausal and postmenopausal women has unfortunately not been studied. However, its effect on hot flushes has been recorded since 1949. In the earliest study a response rate of over 50 per cent was recorded when high doses, in the region of 1,000 IUs per day were given. Although the trial was not scientific enough to convince today's doctors, this early report included the case of one woman who resumed menstruation ten months after she had received radiation treatment to destroy her ovaries. So we cannot rule it out completely. Again, we would like to know if some menopausal women have a relative lack of this vitamin. Lower-than-average levels have been associated with a higher-than-average risk of breast cancer. So it might help some women: perhaps those in the perimenopause rather than those who are truly postmenstrual.

We often use vitamin E as part of our programme for menopausal women: try 200 IUs initially each day.

MAGNESIUM
This mineral has come from obscurity to the verge of fame in the last ten years. The cousin of calcium, it is necessary for normal bone, muscle and nerve function. It is also the sister of potassium and like her is found mainly inside cells controlling energy functions. Good sources of potassium are fresh fruit and vegetables, especially green ones. From dietary assessments it appears that between 10 and 20 per cent of women of child-bearing age consume less than the minimum recommended amounts of these nutrients.

Magnesium and some other minerals are also involved in hormone function. Experiments have shown that this mineral is needed by the ovaries in order for them to respond satisfactorily to the stimulatory effect of the pituitary hormones, LH and FSH. The failure to respond to them on the part of the ovaries is exactly what happens at the menopause. Now, we don't think that lack of magnesium is the cause of the menopause! However, it does often seem to be moderately lacking in women of all ages with premenstrual syndrome; and we know that supplements of it can help PMS. So it wouldn't be too surprising if it was having some influence over some menopausal problems. Good candidates would include an early menopause, erratic cycles, fatigue, depression and aches and pains.

A high-magnesium diet is very nutritious and supplements are harmless enough; the only likely side-effect is diarrhoea which, for those who are constipated, might be a help. No studies, as yet, have looked at the relationship between magnesium and either the timing or the symptoms of the menopause. From our own experience we have seen a rather variable picture when we have looked at the results of red-cell magnesium levels, which are known to be low in 50 per cent of women with PMS and do seem to be low in some women with menopausal difficulties. Again, it is asking too much to blame everything on to one nutrient; what is needed are large studies that look at nutritional factors in detail. We have found a magnesium and calcium supplement called Gynovite useful in treating hot flushes, and it may also encourage bone regeneration.

Madelaine's Story

Madelaine was thirty-five when she had one of her ovaries removed because of a large cyst. Eleven years later, her periods were becoming irregular and even though she was not experiencing hot flushes she wondered if she might be approaching the menopause. Along with her periods, of which she had had six in the preceding twelve months, she was experiencing migraine headaches, breast tenderness and lumps, and fluid retention. The breast tenderness had been partly helped by Efamol Evening Primrose Oil.

Investigations showed significantly increased levels of the hormones FSH and LH into the 'menopausal range'. Nutritional tests showed low levels of vitamin B, magnesium and essential fatty acids of both the vegetable and fish-oil types, so it was therefore possible that Madelaine's hormone function was being compromised by her nutritional state.

A change in her diet was suggested to reduce the intake of saturated animal fats and to increase her intake of the polyunsaturated essential fats. Foods known to be common triggers of migraine were also to be avoided, as were salt and salty foods. Supplements of multivitamins, magnesium and evening primrose oil with fish oils were recommended to be taken for several months. These measures resulted in a reduction of her migraine headaches and a substantial lessening of her breast problems.

Initially there was no influence on her periods and it seemed likely that HRT might well be necessary. After four months she had three periods at three-to four-week intervals and after a further eight-week gap there then followed a further four periods, all at regular intervals. The period-associated symptoms had all diminished greatly and the need for HRT had seemed to fade. In fact, a repeat of the hormone tests showed a substantial fall in the levels of FSH and LH to premenopausal levels, supporting the notion that Madelaine's ovaries were responding more easily to the cyclical stimulation from the pituitary. The previously deficient nutrients had also improved.

This is an example of how attention to nutritional problems in the perimenopause might influence the regularity of the menstrual cycle and the symptoms associated with it.

ZINC
This mineral is certainly important for men, as even a mild lack of it, if prolonged, can have a profound effect on sperm and testosterone production. By rights it should be important to women but we do not know of any evidence to this effect. Intakes in the UK are pretty close to the minimum recommended amounts and absorption is easily reduced by alcohol, bran and many other foods. The best dietary source is Atlantic oysters followed by beef and most other meats (so you know what to give him for dinner tonight). It would probably take a severe lack to upset hormone function and this is only likely in the heavy alcohol consumer and those eating a low-protein diet.

ESSENTIAL FATTY ACIDS
Some fats, like vitamins and minerals, are essential. These essential fats are the polyunsaturates found in most vegetable oils and oily fish. We've heard a lot about them in heart disease and the story doesn't end there. They are not easy things to study. First, your body only needs a tiny amount of them, which is just as well as that's all it usually gets with our modern-day diet. A deficiency builds up over years, possibly decades, before it takes its toll. We know so far that severe deficiency is rare and is confined to premature infants, alcholics (again) and the malnourished. A mild or relative deficiency can develop in the 'normal' population and this could be a factor in heart disease. Intakes and blood levels generally fall with increasing age.

On the hormone front, essential fatty acids are doing something very interesting. These fats are used in the building of cell walls and in particular seem to influence the function of those pieces of cell machinery that are actually embedded in the cell wall, such as the receptors for hormones. Complicated but interesting. So it is possible that a relative lack of these essential fatty acids over many years might modify the way in which our bodies respond to certain hormones. So what's the evidence?

Well, in the cheetah a lack of the essential fishy fatty acids, more properly known as the omega-3 series, results in infertility because of an inability of the female to ovulate. Sounds familiar? And in the human? Sorry, right now we don't know but again it's a possible factor. Certain specialized preparations of these essential fatty acids have already been of demonstrable benefit in a variety of diverse areas. So far we have seen Efamol evening primrose oil benefit women with premenstrual breast tenderness and also help some adults and children with dry eczema.

The fish oils have also made their mark in reducing the pain and inflammation of rheumatoid arthritis and they help to lower elevated levels of some blood fats – not cholesterol. A pilot study in patients with osteoporosis who took Evening Primrose Oil, with fish oil, showed an increased calcium balance with increased bone formation. Efamol have recently added calcium to their new formulation, now called Efacal, and studies are on-going.

The essential fatty acids are all going to have other uses too but it would seem that their full benefit will only be realized if they are taken long-term for months, possibly years, and are accompanied by a very healthy diet rich in these same oils. And any associated deficiencies of vitamins and minerals need to be corrected, as they too influence the chemistry of these fats; and any underlying disease, like diabetes, for example, also needs to be treated. So it is not a quick fix.

CHOOSING YOUR NUTRITIONAL SUPPLEMENTS
If you plan to take nutritional supplements you will need to choose them with care. We don't advise women to take random supplements without first seeking proper advice. Our bodies are fairly sensitive mechanisms with specific needs and too much of any one particular nutrient can cause imbalances which may lead to other problems in the long-term.

Before choosing your supplements, take a look at the chart opposite on the physical signs of nutritional deficiency. You may recognize some deficiency which you have had for years, but have accepted as being 'normal'. There are some further hints on page 202.

PHYSICAL SIGNS OF VITAMIN AND MINERAL DEFICIENCY

Sign or symptom	Can be caused by deficiences of
Cracking at the corners of the mouth	Iron, vitamins B12, B6, Folic acid
Recurrent mouth ulcers	Iron, vitamins B12, B6, Folic acid
Dry, cracked lips	Vitamin B2
Smooth (sore) tongue	Iron, vitamins B2, B12, Folic acid
Enlargement/prominence of taste buds at tip of the tongue (red, sore)	Vitamins B2, or B6
Red, greasy skin on face, especially sides of nose	Vitamins B2, B6, zinc or essential fatty acids
Rough, sometimes red, pimply skin on upper arms and thighs	Vitamin B complex, vitamin E or essential fatty acids
Skin conditions such as eczema, dry, rough, cracked, peeling skin	Zinc, essential fatty acids
Poor hair growth	Iron or zinc
Dandruff	Vitamin C, vitamin B6, zinc, essential fatty acids
Acne	Zinc
Bloodshot, gritty, sensitive eyes	Vitamins A or B2
Night blindness	Vitamin A or zinc
Dry eyes	Vitamin A, essential fatty acids
Brittle or split nails	Iron, zinc or essential fatty acids
Pale appearance due to anaemia	Iron, vitamin B12, Folic acid, essential to consult your doctor

Depending on the symptoms you are currently suffering, there are several useful supplements that can be tried in conjunction with each other. Assuming your symptoms are severe and that you are looking for the most effective treatment, I shall first suggest the optimum regime to begin with, regardless of cost. I shall then go on to discuss cheaper alternatives.

Vitamin and Mineral Supplements
The best all-round option is to take a multivitamin and mineral supplement which contains good amounts of the essential nutrients mentioned. The supplement we favour, which has been through a clinical trial, is called Gynovite. It was formulated by Dr Guy Abraham in the USA and is the sister preparation to Optivite, the clinically tried and tested supplement for PMS. In the UK it is available from healthfood shops and by mail order from Nutritional Health (address below). For severe symptoms you will need to take between four and six tablets each day, ideally splitting the dose between breakfast and lunch. Work up to the full dose gradually over a week or two. If your symptoms are moderate, you could probably manage with between two and three tablets each day.

Once you have selected your basic supplement, you will need to add other appropriate products. Read through the chart below and decide which extra supplements you need. Where two or more options are listed for one set of symptoms, try one of the supplements under that heading first. If after a few months you are not convinced that it is helping, switch to the alternative. As we are all so individual, we may respond to different supplements, so it is sometimes a matter of trial and error. Keep a note of what you try on your personal programme chart on page 195.

MATCHING SUPPLEMENT TO SYMPTOM

Problem	Type of supplement	Daily dosage	Available from
Hot flushes and nightsweats	*Natural vitamin E	200–400 IUs	Boots, chemist, healthfood shops and Nutritional Health (by mail)
	Siberian ginseng	1–2 600 mg capsules	Boots, chemist, healthfood shops

126

	4:40 Plus (vitamin E + ginseng)	1–2 600 mg capsules	Chemist, healthfood shops
Anxiety, irritability, mood swings, depression	*Gynovite	2–4 tablets	Healthfood shops or Nutritional Health (by mail)
Eczema, dry skin	*Efamol/Epogam	2–8 500 IU capsules	Boots, chemists or Nutritional Health (by mail)
Heavy periods	*Gynovite	Dose as above	As above
	Iron-ferrous sulphate	1 200mg tablet with fruit juice	chemists
Painful periods	*Magnesium amino acid chelate	2–4 150mg tablets	Healthfood shops or Nutritional Health (by mail)
Breast tenderness	*Efamol/Efamast	As above	Boots, chemists, healthfood shops or Nutritional Health (by mail)
Constipation	*Magnesium amino acid chelate	2–5 150mg tablets at night	Healthfood shops or Nutritional Health (by mail)
	Linusit Gold	2 tablespoons	Healthfood shops
Osteoporosis	Calcium carbonate, gluconate or citrate	1000mg of elemental calcium	Chemists and healthfood shops
	*Magnesium amino acid chelate	150–600mg elemental magnesium	Healthfood shops and Nutritional Health (by mail)
	Efamol with fish oil and calcium	6–8 500 IU capsules	Boots, chemists, and healthfood shops

* Available by mail order through Nutritional Health, PO Box 926, Lewes, East Sussex, BN7 2QL

Herbal Supplements
Siberian ginseng has been through clinical trials and has been proved to be helpful in controlling hot flushes. It comes in supplement form from healthfood shops, and can also be used in

the form of ginseng tea. Ginseng is on the list of phytoestrols, the oestrogen-like substances (see page 129).

Other herbal supplements have been suggested to help re-balance hormones, but I am not aware of any medical papers published to endorse their effect. The two best-known herbs are *dong quai*, the Chinese herbal remedy which, as it also contains plant-like oestrogen substances, may be worth a try, and *agnus castus*, which has been shown to help headaches. Both these remedies are available from healthfood shops.

Important points

- Never take supplements without the consent of your GP if you have a current medical problem.
- Always begin taking your supplements gradually. For example, if you are due to take two or four of a particular supplement each day, begin taking one tablet each day and gradually build up to the optimum dosage over a week or two. Take them after meals unless otherwise specified.

Should you keep taking the supplements for ever?
If you have decided not to take HRT, or can't take it for any reason, apart from wanting to control your symptoms associated with the menopause, you will need to prevent osteoporosis in the long-term. For this reason, more than any other, continue to take supplements that include calcium and magnesium for as long as you can. You are most at risk of bone-loss for the five years following the menopause, and although the loss slows down in the following ten years, it is still pretty significant. We recommend eating well, doing weight-bearing exercise and taking a moderate dose of supplements in the long term.

What about drugs?
If you are currently taking prescribed drugs from your doctor, you are not advised to stop taking them or to reduce them without his or her consent. Having said that, we do find that, once established on their holistic programme, many women no

longer feel the need for their tranquillizers, antidepressants or sleeping pills.

Vitamins and minerals can be taken quite happily alongside most drugs, as can HRT. There are a few exceptions, however. Any antibiotic in the tetracycline family should not be taken with a supplement of minerals. Evening primrose oil should not be taken by anyone with epilepsy.

When you feel the time has come to reduce your drugs, do go to see your doctor for a discussion before taking any action, especially if you have been taking them for a long time. Coming off drugs suddenly may bring on nasty withdrawal symptoms so make it a gradual process.

Phytoestrols

Natural oestrogens

Mother Nature has given us a number of plant foods which are rich in natural oestrogens. These phytoestrols, or phyto-estrogens as they are known, can provide us with a constant source of oestrogen if we know where to look for them. Although in small quantities, these plant-based oestrogens may well help to maintain falling oestrogen levels at the time of the menopause, and protect us against oesteoporosis in later life.

A validation of how effective phyto-oestrogens may be was published in *The Lancet* in 1992. The study concluded that Japanese women do not seem to experience hot flushes and other menopausal symptoms because the Japanese diet contains foods rich in plant oestrogens, like soya products and ginseng. These, it seems, have a constant top-up effect on oestrogen levels, and thus help avoid many common menopausal symptoms.

The diet section on page 213 has been designed to include phyto-oestrogens on a regular basis with a view to providing on-going protection. Plant-based oestrogens can be found in the following foods:-

• Soya beans and soya-bean products like soya flour, soy sauce,

tofu (soya bean curd), miso, tamari, soya bean oil etc.
- Sprouted soya beans and alfalfa
- Ginseng (dried to eat or as tea, or capsules/tablets)
- Celery, fennel and other green and yellow vegetables
- Anise and liquorice
- Rhubarb
- Linseeds
- Red clover (tablets, or sprouted seeds if you can)
- The herbs *dong quai* and *black cohosh*.

These should be available at your local healthfood shop, greengrocer or supermarket.

Twelve

The Benefits of Exercise

There is no doubt that regular exercise is beneficial to us at all stages in our lives. It is, however, even more important to establish an exercise routine at the time of the menopause. Not only does exercise help to improve energy levels, it may also help to overcome symptoms of depression, anxiety and insomnia, and increase confidence, self-esteem and well-being.

Weight-bearing exercise – in other words, anything that involves putting weight through your bones, so being on your feet, jogging, brisk walking, playing raquet sports, weight-lifting, doing a workout, skipping or even squeezing tennis balls! – is particularly important at the time of the menopause. We think that it stimulates the regeneration of bone tissue, reduces calcium loss and thus helps to strengthen bones and prevent osteoporosis.

Several studies have been conducted on groups of women entering the menopause and beyond. The general consensus is that you need to exercise moderately three or four times each week, for between twenty to forty minutes each time, so long as you do not suffer with cardiovascular disease. The pay-off is that within twelve weeks you should be more energetic, coping with stress more effectively, sleeping better, fighting off infections more successfully and feeling a lot better in general.

One study showed that when premenopausal women, with an average age of forty-one, trained for nine weeks, their volume of oxygen-intake improved by over 12 per cent and the postmenopausal group had an even greater improvement of 19 per cent.

Another study, conducted by Morgan in 1979, demonstrated that as a result of vigorous physical activity, muscle spasm was reduced and there was a significant decrease in the state of anxiety. He also demonstrated that exercising two hours before bedtime could lessen the symptoms of insomnia.

Similarly, a study of a twelve-week walking and jogging programme found the women felt better, enjoyed social functions more, participated in more activities and were not so tired at the end of the day. A more recent study conducted in the community of Linkoping in Norway showed that one year after the menopause, very few of the physically active women suffered with severe hot flushes – in fact only 6 per cent regarded their symptoms as severe, compared to 25 per cent in the less active group.

Exercise has also been shown to be better at improving the symptoms of depression and anxiety than psychotherapy. After a twelve-week aerobic programme, the exercise group had fewer symptoms than the psychotherapy group and at the follow-up, one year later, this was still the case. The added bonus for the exercisers, apart from the fact that they felt much better, was that they did not have to pay the psychotherapist's bill or for prescriptions for antidepressants!

The good news is that exercise may even offset ageing of the central nervous system, as well as being cardio-protective. People who exercise are consistently more alert and have a faster reaction time. It has also been shown that the greater the degree of fitness, the more functionally competent the individual. Recent studies have once again confirmed that as the physical fitness of women improves, their risk of death from cardiovascular disease and cancer decreases.

One researcher, Spiriduso, in 1984, concluded that 'Exercise seems to be one way for people to achieve maximal plasticity in ageing, approximating full vigor and consistency of performance until life's end. So there is absolutely no excuse why you shouldn't start today, unless you are currently seeing your doctor for some other serious complaint.

If you really dislike exercise you are probably groaning by now. But I assure you that you will reap the benefits of your labour. We have seen so many patients who have never previously exercised begin their exercise programme reluctantly and eventually come to love it. Apart from anything else, exercise improves your circulation. Your skin will look better after exercising and you will feel more alive.

The aim is to start a gentle exercise programme to get you fitter for life – you are not expected to run a marathon. It is not a competition: you are merely competing with yourself and aiming to improve your fitness level gradually over a period of months. So put the music on and start dancing!

Let me now introduce you to Helen Keighley who has been working with the YMCA for many years. She will outline some exercise options for you to choose from, depending on your social situation and your fitness level. Don't forget to check with your doctor first if you have any concerns about exercising.

Why exercise?

Perhaps the most important consideration is that it is never too late to start an exercise programme. However, unlike money in the bank which accrues interest over the years, exercise behaviour needs to be maintained if the benefits are to continue. Imagine a new drug coming on to the market offering increased mental alertness, greater energy and vitality, the ability to perform daily tasks without getting breathless or tired, greater ease of movement, faster reaction times, greater resistance to minor ailments and stronger bones. There is no doubt that the shops would be inundated and demand would far outstrip supply. The good news is that this 'drug' is a reality and available to all members of society, without a prescription, and at limited or no cost. Perhaps the only drawback is that, unlike a magic pill, we have to devote a little time in order to achieve these benefits, but this is surely a relatively small price to pay for even just a few of the possible improvements.

What is fitness?

The word fitness is frequently used in everyday vocabulary, but what does it actually mean? Physical fitness is not the exclusive domain of the young and active: it is something that can be achieved by most people, irrespective of age. It consists of a number of factors which can be categorized under three headings: stamina, strength and suppleness.

STAMINA

Stamina refers to the efficiency of the heart and lungs in delivering oxygen to the muscles, usually for sustained periods of time. If your stamina is poor you may feel breathless if you walk fast or feel tired after even a modest level of activity. It may be that you can only swim a few widths of the pool on holiday or have to keep taking frequent rests when walking uphill. If a situation arises which suddenly demands more activity than you are used to, you may find it difficult to cope or end up feeling exhausted and take a long time to recover. You may feel tempted to attribute these symptoms to the fact that you are no longer a teenager, but this is simply not the case. Improvements in cardiovascular efficiency can occur at any time, as has been

shown by patients recovering from heart attacks and surgery who have subsequently run marathons.

Improvements in stamina are cheap and easy to achieve and we refer to exercise that helps to stimulate such positive effects as 'aerobic'. Aerobic exercise is rhythmical, continuous and tends to use large muscle groups such as those in the legs. These big muscle groups demand more oxygen to keep working and so the heart has to work harder to supply what is needed. This in turn increases the strength of the heart muscle and allows it to cope better with the demands of increased activity. Reports have shown that walking is an excellent form of exercise.

The main consideration is to start any exercise programme gently. For those sedentary individuals who are just starting to become active, a fifteen-minute walk, three times a week, would be a good starting point. As this becomes increasingly comfortable and undemanding, the time could be extended in five-minute blocks. Depending on how much time you have, this could be increased up to an hour. If time is limited, you could attempt to reduce the length of the exercise period by walking more briskly and vigorously.

Unfortunately, the British climate often proves to be a deterrent to such activity, particularly in the winter months, and swimming could perhaps provide a better alternative. Increasingly, leisure-centres and health-clubs have fitness suites where you can sit in relative warmth and comfort and row or cycle your way to improved stamina. You could also continue your walking, but inside, on a treadmill, which is an excellent means of monitoring how far and how fast you are walking. Do not feel intimidated by what others are doing around you and don't fall into the trap of feeling that such centres are only for the young and superfit. The gymnasium is just as ideally suited to your needs and theirs.

STRENGTH
Even today, many women still believe that strength is somehow synonymous with having large muscles. Yet it has been shown that women can increase their strength by up to 50 per cent

without any increase in muscle size – and that even if they wanted to, the vast majority of women are incapable of producing the sort of muscle growth shown by many men. This is primarily because women simply do not possess anything like the levels of the male sex hormone testosterone. However, they can get stronger and this has many advantages. Stronger muscles can lift more weight, making it easier to carry shopping, lift, push or pull heavy objects and consequently you will be less vulnerable to injury. It is also possible to train the endurance of the muscles in order to keep them going for longer without getting fatigued, which can make domestic tasks such as decorating, gardening and cleaning much easier.

In order to achieve improvements in strength, we need to work a muscle harder than it is used to working. Probably the easiest way of achieving this is to lift weights, specifically to strengthen the muscles groups required. If you want to build up the endurance of a muscle, in other words to allow it to keep going without getting tired, then the activity has to be repeated. In the case of walking, not only do you improve the efficiency of your heart and lungs but you also develop the endurance strength of your legs. Initially, your legs may get tired but gradually they will be able to walk further and faster without becoming tired.

SUPPLENESS
This is probably the most underrated component of physical fitness, but it becomes increasingly important in later years as joints tend to stiffen up. The most important factor contributing to loss of joint mobility is lack of use. The old maxim 'use it or lose it' rather aptly describes what happens to flexibility levels. If you make a positive effort to maintain your range of movement, then you are less likely to tear muscles or injure yourself when called on to make sudden or awkward movements. Also, daily tasks become easier and less demanding because you are not working to your maximum movement range all the time.

Improvements in joint movement are achieved by stretching

exercises and these are probably the easiest to do at home. First, make sure that you are really warm: exercising after a hot bath is an ideal time. Slowly stretch your muscles, hold the stretch for a few seconds and then gradually release the tension by relaxing. Stretching should always be done slowly and can be easily performed while watching television or listening to music.

The benefit of exercise for postmenopausal women

So far, we have looked at physical fitness and briefly surveyed the general benefits which increased activity levels can bring for everyone but you may still be thinking it's a little late to start now. Nothing could be further from the truth – it's even more important to think positively after the menopause.

BONE DENSITY

Bones gain their strength and resilience from their mineral content and particularly from calcium. Our skeletons reach their peak bone density by our mid thirties. Bone-density levels in women then start to decrease as the cells removing and reabsorbing bone tend to work more efficiently than those cells which deposit new bone. After the menopause, the reduction in oestrogen levels causes an acceleration in this bone-removal process. This can result in as much as 30 per cent of your bone density being lost by the end of the first decade after the menopause. See also the chapter on osteoporosis.

Apart from good nutrition the stimulus for bone growth is exercise. Considerable work has been undertaken in this area and research shows that it is the pull of muscles on the bones in a weight-bearing situation that stimulates the bone-building cells to become more active and thereby increase bone density.

BONE-BUILDING EXERCISES

To prevent bone-thinning, a combination of strength and aerobic activities should be included in an exercise programme. The aerobic activities should include weight-bearing activities (see above) as these have been shown to produce better results than non-weight-bearing activities such as swimming. Ideally, these should be undertaken for thirty minutes or more every other day. However, when starting an activity programme, both the duration and the intensity of the activity should be reduced. For example, ten to fifteen minutes of moderate exercise two to three times a week would be an appropriate starting-point. Strengthening exercises will place a greater loading on the bones and it is possible to target key sites, such as the upper spine, wrists, hip and ankles, which are so vulnerable to fractures. This sort of programme can take place in a gym with weight-training equipment but it can easily be developed round home-based exercises.

Upper Spine

1 When lying in bed or on the floor, flat on your back, press your head back into the pillow or the floor and push for a count of five. Release and repeat. Make sure that you do not hold your breath (counting out loud might help) as this might make your blood pressure rise.
2 Lie on your front (preferably on a hard surface) and squeeze your shoulder-blades together. Then try to lift your head and shoulders a few inches off the floor. Lower and repeat a few times, gradually increasing the number of repetitions. Make sure that you don't tip your head back. Keep looking at the floor all the time so that your spine remains in a straight line.
3 In a sitting position, pull your shoulder-blades together and hold briefly before repeating a number of times.

Wrist

Stand about two feet or more from a wall, hands at shoulder height flat on the wall, arms straight. Slowly allow your elbows to bend, thereby bringing your face and chest closer to the wall. To complete the movement, simply extend your elbows smoothly and repeat. As you become more proficient, you can perform this exercise on the floor on your hands and knees. In this position, you should gradually lower your body towards the floor, ensuring that your back is kept in a straight line.

Ankles
Standing upright using a chair or worktop for balance, slowly lift your heels off the floor so that you rise up on to your toes. Check that your ankles do not roll outwards and keep your weight over your big toes.

Hips
Standing on one leg, take your other leg out to the side in a smooth, controlled manner. Slowly bring your legs back together again without putting any weight on the lifting leg. Repeat until your hips start feeling tired. Ensure that you stand upright throughout the movement and don't allow the supporting hip to push out to the side to compensate. This exercise can also be performed while lying on your side, this time with your upper leg travelling in a vertical plane.

Lie on your back with your knees bent and your legs positioned on the inside of two chair legs. Attempt to push your knees and legs apart (the chair legs will prevent this); hold for a count of five and then release. As with the neck exercise, be careful not to hold your breath.

Cardiovascular protection
Exercise has been shown to increase the amount of high density lipoproteins (HDL, or good cholesterol) and reduce the levels of low density lipoproteins (LDL or bad cholesterol). It is interesting to note that lack of exercise did not originally feature as one of the three major causes of heart disease. These were thought to be smoking, high fat levels and high blood pressure but more recent research now considers that being sedentary carries a similar risk – hence the modern slogan that 'inactivity can seriously damage your health!' So what type of activity should we consider as helping to counter the risks of heart disease? Look no further than aerobic exercise, which we discussed in the stamina section. This involves rhythmic activity using large muscle groups and needs to be sustained and moderately vigorous to be effective. We can see, therefore, that the brisk walk mentioned earlier can not only build stronger bones but can also help to protect against heart disease.

Posture

Looking at the population as a whole, it is probably true to say that our posture does not tend to improve as we age. We have seen that one of the major contributory factors to poor posture is the crumbling of the vertebrae in osteoporosis, but many people exhibit poor posture long before any bone changes have occurred. This is a result of weakness in certain muscles and undue tightness in others. Various factors may be involved. Too many of us spend a lifetime sitting at a desk, wearing high-heeled shoes, lying on soft beds or carrying bags on only one side of our body. Exercise can again help to redress the balance by strengthening weak muscles (such as the abdominals) and stretching those muscles which have become less pliant or shortened through the bad habits of our modern-day living. Muscles which can benefit from such a programme include those that give shape to the chest and that are so often associated with round shoulders.

Weight control

'Middle-aged spread' can be a frustrating and depressing experience and tends to provide the visual confirmation (we do not need) of the sort of changes happening around the menopause. This tends to stem from the fact that as we get older, our metabolic rate slows down. This is the rate at which we burn off our food and the calories it contains. Consequently, if we do absolutely nothing different through our advancing years, we will tend to put on weight. Unfortunately, we do tend to do something different but in the wrong direction – we generally tend to become more sedentary! Lack of time and inclination are usually given as the reasons for this but no matter how justifiable the reason, the effect is predictable and almost inevitable. If we want to maintain our youthful figures, we need to consider our dietary intake and increase our level of activity. Aerobic exercise can help to increase the metabolic rate and not just when you are exercising: the effects appear to last for several hours afterwards and, therefore, regular exercise with its elevated metabolic rate can lead to possible weight loss.

Precautions

If you have not exercised for some time, it is wise to adopt a cautious approach when starting to increase your activity levels and a brief discussion with your doctor will indicate whether any form of activity would be inadvisable.

Do remember that the old adage of 'no pain no gain' is most definitely outdated and it certainly does not 'have to be hell to be healthy'. You do not have to feel exhausted at the end of your activity: rather you should experience more of a feeling of invigoration. Listen to your body. Sometimes you will feel you have plenty of energy, that you can tackle almost anything, whereas on other occasions you will not be able to match your previous performances. If you have a cold or a viral infection, it is advisable to give your exercise session a miss until you feel better and, when you resume, remember to begin gradually and not to try simply to pick up from where you left off.

If you are not used to exercise, don't be worried if you start to sweat. This is not just another one of those hot flushes but an indication that your body is using more energy and needs to get rid of the excess heat you are producing. Sweating is not a sign of lack of fitness, just the reverse. The fitter you become, the more efficient your body becomes in removing excess heat. You may also start to huff and puff a little if you are working hard, but providing that you can still hold a conversation and are not in any distress this is nothing to worry about. It simply means that you need more air and that your system is adapting to provide your body with a steady supply. Gradually, if you persevere, you will find that these symptoms disappear for the same activity level and will only reappear as you begin to work harder.

Getting started

We can all think of incidents where we, or people we know, have embraced some form of activity with zealous enthusiasm, only to discover a week or two later that the novelty has worn off and a state of sedentary normality has returned. So the first rule of exercise is to choose something that you like doing. If you already like walking, whether on a treadmill or along a country lane or in the park, then do it! This is an excellent way to start. Or you may prefer to exercise with someone else or with a group of people. If so, try to make a realistic, regular commitment. This could entail attending an exercise class or going swimming or visiting the local leisure centre or selecting a good home-exercise video. Whatever it takes and whatever your pleasure, you have already jumped the most difficult hurdle – you've started!

How long and how often?

The second rule is undoubtedly to start slowly. Many people embrace exercise with such enthusiastic vigour that they experience major discomfort and possibly even injure themselves. Deconditioned muscles being put through their paces too dramatically often suffer the consequences. This leads to a cessation of activity and the return to a sedentary lifestyle – a vicious cycle of inactivity. To avoid this common problem, 'a little and often' should be the rule. It is worth remembering that, following by-pass surgery, cardiac patients are encouraged to walk, building up to three miles a day over a period of about three months after their operation. This sort of model would be just as appropriate for many unfit people starting on an exercise programme.

What type of activity?

Much has been said about walking but it really is a very underrated form of activity. It's free, it requires no equipment and can be undertaken anywhere and at almost any time. It does not demand a high level of skill but it can still be extremely effective.

If you prefer the privacy of exercise in your own home, there are a number of options. Probably the most economical method is to buy an exercise video but a word of caution is necessary here. There is no control over the standard of exercise videos and some should undoubtedly carry a health warning 'This video could seriously damage your health.' Sifting your way through this minefield is not easy but look for a graduated programme that starts off at an easy level and allows for

142

progress as your level of fitness improves. Many videos last between forty-five minutes to an hour and this may well be too long in the early stages. If you do buy one of these, just do the warm-up and cool down exercises initially, and then gradually include more of the main section over the coming weeks. Don't be afraid to use the fast-forward button if the exercises start to feel too strenuous. The YMCA Fitness Club videos are a good investment. They range from beginners' exercises to funky aerobics and are broken down into workable blocks of time.

For a bigger capital outlay, you could buy an exercise cycle or a rowing machine. These will undoubtedly improve the endurance strength of your legs and provide a good aerobic work-out for your heart and lungs. However, it would be a good idea to supplement such a programme with some specific strengthening exercises, which will help to load the bones at points vulnerable to osteoporosis and fracture.

Formal classes, such as those based on exercise to music, circuit-training, or step-training can be a social way of taking your exercise and may involve making a commitment either to go with someone or to pay for a number of lessons in advance. First check that your teacher is properly qualified and that the class will be suitable. If you have not exercised for some time, a 'Take it Easy' class will be more appropriate than an advanced aerobics session.

Warming-up

Whatever type of activity you decide to try, warming-up should form an essential part of your session no matter how long it's going to last. It can help you to gradually get into the mood for the more demanding exercise which will follow and prepare your body systems, thus making it easier for you to perform and reducing the chances of sustaining an injury. A warm-up is designed to make you feel warm and to get the blood flowing to the muscles, so that oxygen can be provided to meet your energy requirements. This can be achieved by walking, jogging gently, marching on the spot, cycling or by any simple graduated activity which uses large muscle groups in a rhythmic way. It should not be exhausting! In addition to these warming movements, you should try to move the joints through their full range of movement, loosening them up and enabling them to move more freely. Joints can easily become stiff through lack of use and, by warming the fluid which 'oils' the joints, they become more pliable and this results in easier movement. Once you are warm and your joints are loose, gently stretch the muscles you are going to use. Try not to bounce when performing these stretches and hold them for about six to eight seconds. Adequate preparation leads to a body ready for action.

Cooling down

If you have been working hard, even on a brisk walk, your heart rate will have increased and you will often be breathing more deeply and more rapidly. This means that your heart has been stimulated to make it work harder, which is exactly what is required if you are going to improve your cardiovascular efficiency. However, just as it is better to decrease your driving speed in a car by going down through the gears, it is better to reduce your activity level gradually, rather than suddenly stopping. If the muscles don't need so much oxygen, the heart doesn't need to beat as fast, so it can gradually be allowed to return to normal. Undertaking regular activity, particularly repetitive actions such as walking or jogging, will undoubtedly lead to stronger muscles which can keep going longer. It will also lead to shorter muscles which may be more susceptible to injury, so it is beneficial at the end of any exercise session to gently stretch out the muscles that have been working hard. Not only does this feel good but it also ensures that the range of movement around all your joints is maintained. Try also to build in some relaxation time for yourself. If you've been active, this is the reward period for all your efforts and an opportunity to release tension.

By now we hope you are convinced that some form of exercise can be beneficial, not just in helping to counteract some of the more unpleasant symptoms and effects of the menopause but in promoting a healthy lifestyle, which can be maintained well into old age.

Thirteen

The Benefits of Relaxation

Our lifestyle in the 1990s and the demands that life places on us are quite different from the experience of past generations. The average woman has so much more on her plate, without necessarily having the support network of bygone days. The net result of the excessive demands on our time and our attention may leave us feeling stressed.

While a certain amount of stress may be good for us, since it tends to keep us mentally on our toes, there comes a point when stress can be overwhelming. Feeling stressed-out for any length of time can take its toll, both physically and mentally. It has long been medically acknowledged that stress can affect the hormone cycle and in some studies of menstruating women it has been shown to suppress ovulation. When the menopause descends on us, bringing additional changes and strains, we need to learn to improve our ability to cope with life's stresses – which are unlikely to go away.

Debra's Story

Debra is a fifty-two-year-old wife and mother from Cardiff. She heard about the WNAS programme at a time when she was on HRT but still feeling very low.

'I first came to hear of the WNAS through an article in the local press. It interested me because the person about whom it was written had suffered severe menopausal symptoms and had been greatly helped by the WNAS programme. My own symptoms were really a continuation of premenstrual symptoms, which I had

Menopause Symptom Questionnaire

Do you suffer from any of the following? Please ensure each symptom is only ticked *once*.

DEBRA	*How many times per month	None	Mild	Moderate	Severe
1 Hot/cold flushes*		✓			
2 Facial/body flushing*		✓			
3 Nightsweats*		✓			
4 Palpitations*		✓			
5 Panic attacks*		✓			
6 Generalised aches and pains		✓			
7 Depression				✓	
8 Perspiration		✓			
9 Numbness/skin tingling in arms and legs		✓			
10 Headaches					✓
11 Backache		✓			
12 Fatigue				✓	
13 Irritability			✓		
14 Anxiety			✓		
15 Nervousness				✓	
16 Loss of confidence				✓	
17 Insomnia			✓	✓	
18 Giddiness/dizziness		✓			
19 Difficulty/frequency in passing water		✓			
20 Water retention					

21 Bloated abdomen	✓			
22 Constipation	✓			
23 Itchy vagina	✓			
24 Dry vagina	✓			
25 Painful intercourse	✓			
26 Decreased sex drive				✓
27 Loss of concentration				✓
28 Confusion/Loss of vitality				✓

Have you noticed since the onset of the menopause:

1 Loss of height   Yes/No

2 Difficulty in bending   Yes/No

3 Increased curvature of back   Yes/No

Are any of the above symptoms cyclic? (i.e. come in cycles, for example on a monthly basis) _____

_____

Have you gained weight since you started the menopause?   Yes/No   If yes, how much _____

Do you have any other menopausal symptoms not mentioned above?   **No** _____

_____

How long have you had menopausal symptoms?   _A continuation of pre-menstrual tension_

Did you suffer from pre-menstrual tension prior to the menopause?   Yes/No   If yes, for how long?   **30 yrs.**

147

Follow-up Menopause Questionnaire

Do you suffer from any of the following? Please ensure each symptom is only ticked *once*.

DEBRA	*How many times per month	None	Mild	Moderate	Severe
1 Hot/cold flushes*		✓			
2 Facial/body flushing*		✓			
3 Nightsweats*			✓		
4 Palpitations*		✓			
5 Panic attacks*		✓			
6 Generalised aches and pains			✓		
7 Depression		✓			
8 Perspiration		✓			
9 Numbness/skin tingling in arms and legs			✓		
10 Headaches		✓			
11 Backache			✓		
12 Fatigue		✓			
13 Irritability		✓			
14 Anxiety		✓			
15 Nervousness			✓		
16 Loss of confidence			✓		
17 Insomnia			✓		
18 Giddiness/dizziness		✓			
19 Difficulty/frequency in passing water		✓			
20 Water retention		✓			

21	Bloated abdomen		
22	Constipation	✓	
23	Itchy vagina	✓	
24	Dry vagina	✓	
25	Painful intercourse	✓	
26	Decreased sex drive	✓	
27	Loss of concentration	✓	
28	Confusion/Loss of vitality	✓	

endured for many years. It had not occurred to me that a nutritional approach would be beneficial. I had never sought help, believing that I would eventually get better!

'About two years ago or more, my periods became irregular and as well as the usual headaches, depression and nervousness, I began having nightsweats. That year was also the start of a very stressful period in my life when three members of our family died and some minor incidents added to the stress. My headaches became constant and very oppressive for some months and I knew I had to get help as I felt that I was rapidly going downhill. I saw my doctor and asked if I could start on HRT, hoping that this would ease my headaches and depression. After about four months on HRT I felt no better, but no worse either, so I decided to contact the WNAS.

'After a few weeks of starting the programme, I noticed a slight difference and very gradually I began to feel better. It certainly helped me through a very difficult time. Now, a year later, with regular exercise, a controlled diet and the supplements, my symptoms have eased considerably and I find I have much more energy. The quality of my sleep is better and I wake feeling refreshed most mornings, whereas I used to be so fatigued. I don't feel irritable any more and I have far fewer headaches. There have been two other benefits from the programme. I suffered a lot with swollen ankles for a couple of years but this has now stopped. I also had a problem with burning eyes, which often felt so tired and prickly, and this has also stopped.

'I came off HRT six months ago for a trial period and as things are going so well I have not restarted it.

'I hope that my experience will encourage other women to take the natural approach to the menopause and also to premenstrual syndrome. I certainly wish I had known about the WNAS a long time ago.'

Stress is also able to affect our digestive process, bringing abdominal and bowel symptoms that we may not have experienced before. When we are under considerable emotional and psychological stress, it's possible that we are more likely to develop food intolerances. Often the stress persists, the symptoms become chronic, or the individual may be passed off as neurotic or a hypochondriac – and things go from bad to worse.

Ineffective treatment, or inadequate belief in the physical nature of our symptoms, often contributes further to our stress.

Learning the art of relaxation

Stress and relaxation are at two opposite ends of the spectrum. When they are in balance you are coping, but when the scales tip and stress outweighs relaxation, symptoms often develop. As our lifestyle these days is far from relaxed, we should consciously protect ourselves from excess stress by learning relaxation techniques which, unlike stress, do not come naturally.

Relaxation has also been shown to influence hot flushes in a medical study conducted in 1984. They showed a 60 per cent reduction in the frequency of flushes in a group of women who were given relaxation training.

But relaxing may not be as easy as it sounds. When you are feeling wound up and tense, learning to release tension from tensed muscles is an acquired skill. Once you have mastered the art, however, it can be practised at any time, requires only space and time and is free of charge!

Instead of focusing on the outside world and the problems that it brings, you will need to learn to tune-in to your body and become sensitive to its tensions. Even if you have never been taught any basic relaxation techniques, what is involved is quite simple.

You will need to wear some loose, comfortable clothes and find a warm space where you will be uninterrupted. Either lie down on a mat, on a soft carpet or on a bed. Make sure you are comfortable with the room temperature and lighting. If you like music, you can practise this relaxation technique while calming music is playing in the background. Once you feel comfortable, do the following, step-by-step:

1 Place a pillow under your head and relax your arms and your lower jaw.
2 Take a few slow deep breaths before you begin.
3 Then concentrate on relaxing your muscles, starting with the toes on one foot and then the other. Gradually work your way slowly up your body.

4 As you do so, first tense each group of muscles and then relax them, taking care to breathe deeply as you relax.

5 When you reach your head, and your face feels relaxed, remain in the relaxed position for about fifteen minutes.

6 Gradually allow yourself to 'come to'.

YOGA

Yoga has been practised throughout the world for thousands of years. It works on the principle of bringing about a harmonious balance between your mind, body and soul. It is particularly effective at helping to relieve stress and stress-related conditions. To get started, it's best to attend a yoga class and then to practise the postures at home on a regular basis. There are many good books on yoga (see the suggested reading list on page 295) and there are now a few yoga videos which you might find helpful.

MASSAGE

Massage is a term used to describe a fairly ancient art of healing by touch, and if you think about it, we often subconsciously touch or rub a painful area in an attempt to bring relief. There are several different massage techniques to choose from, but essentially massage is designed to heal, relieve tension, improve circulation and help the body to rid itself of toxins.

Massage can also relieve pain by stimulating the production of brain chemicals called endorphins, the body's own painkillers, and by blocking out the transmission of pain messages by increasing the sensory input to the brain.

There are different ways of getting a regular massage, depending on your pocket and your situation. You can book an appointment with a registered masseuse, which can be quite expensive. You can enlist the help of your partner or a friend, or alternatively you can learn to self-massage, but this does have its limitations unless you have arms like Twizzle. If you enjoy being massaged but have a limited budget, you might enjoy learning how to massage by following a short course. Teaming up with another can be the cheapest way of getting a regular massage. Most local authorities have classes and there are several good books on the subject.

In the meantime, if you would like to experiment, take a few drops of an aromatherapy oil of your choice – lavender, orange and melissa are particularly relaxing – mix it with some almond oil and rub yourself in a clockwise direction on your abdomen, with stroking motions on your arms and legs, and gentle smoothing motions on your face and neck. Give your scalp and your temples a massage. Lastly, rub your ears between your thumb and forefinger, starting at the top and working your way down to the ear lobe, pulling gently at the same time. It feels wonderful and increases the circulation to your face and head.

INFLUENCING THE SUBCONSCIOUS
There are many ways of stimulating the subconscious mind to heal the body and medical studies have been done to show that it works! It's thought that the subconscious can be influenced by suggestion and imagination: hence the placebo response that we sometimes hear about in clinical trials, where the dummy pill apparently produced an effect. There are many different methods of stimulating the subconscious mind and it's important to choose a system that you feel comfortable with, in order to achieve your objective. To find the self-help measure that you feel happy with, you may have to experiment.

At the Centre for Climacteric Studies in Gainsville, Florida, Dr Morris Notelovitz has been testing non-hormonal methods of helping menopausal symptoms. One particular study, using biofeedback training, which had previously been shown to manipulate heart rate, skin responses, vascular diameter and muscle tension and had been used to help patients with migraine, was used to help overcome hot flushes.

Biofeedback is another relaxation technique. With this method a machine is often used and a deep state of relaxation achieved. The eight women on the study had never encountered biofeedback before, but were trained in the method before they started. The women were taught to consciously cool their hands for forty-five seconds during a hot flush and to consciously warm their hands in between flushes. Their progress was measured on the biofeedback machine. The training period lasted for four weeks and the trial was continued for a further four weeks, with the women recording hourly records throughout the day. While the duration of each flush remained the same, the associated discomfort dropped significantly. This looks encouraging although larger, controlled studies need to be conducted.

CREATIVE VISUALIZATION

This is probably one of the easiest and most pleasant ways of distancing yourself from the problems and stresses that affect you. It really just involves day-dreaming in a structured way. Choose a scene that you would like to be part of and spirit yourself there in your imagination. The skill you will gradually acquire involves blocking out everything else and being able to be in your desired scene, feeling warm, calm and relaxed.

SELF-HYPNOSIS

This method helps to bring about the feeling of calmness and mental agility. It is a system of implanting positive messages which have a therapeutic value. Half an hour each day can leave you feeling refreshed and in a more positive mood.

AUTOGENIC TRAINING

This is designed to tap into the body's own in-built powers of self-healing. It consists of repeating six different commands slowly in sequence until you reach a semi-hypnotic state. The end result is a much more relaxed and positive you – and initially requires only half an hour or so three times each week.

All these and many more relaxation techniques can be learned at specialist centres throughout the UK. It will really be worth investing a little of your time in order to learn how to relax and rise above the stresses and strains of everyday life.

Fourteen

Holistic Therapies and the Menopause

Holistic medicine looks at the whole person, the mind, the body and the spirit and how they interact. So as well as dealing with symptoms on a nutritional level it's important to make sure that you are functioning on an optimum level across the board. The years during which you may have suffered as a result of not eating the right diet, being pregnant and breast-feeding, coping with stressful situations and perhaps premenstrual symptoms before your menopause may well have taken their toll. The body is a complicated but delicate network of bones, muscles, ligaments, nerves, organs and blood vessels. Physical symptoms and nervous tension can affect the smooth running of the body processes. If your symptoms are intense, before and when you start your nutritional programme in Part Four, you might consider the value of acupuncture or acupressure, herbal medicine or cranial osteopathy as a means of speeding up the recovery process. They are powerful tools and can help to bring about the speedy relief of symptoms.

Acupuncture

Traditional Chinese medicine can be useful in the treatment of female health problems. According to the severity of the problem, there are two levels at which treatment can be taken. The first level is appropriate for severe symptoms and involves consulting an acupuncturist. Many of the problems mentioned, including hot flushes, insomnia, depression, aches and pains, mood swings and headaches may well respond to treatment by acupuncture. The second level involves acupressure (see page 157).

Chinese medicine is quite different to Western medicine in that it considers symptoms rather than named conditions and the diagnosis and subsequent treatment address the whole person, the mind, body and lifestyle.

THE PRINCIPLES

In order for good health to exist, Chinese medicine works on the premise that a universal energy known as *chi*, which has two complementary qualities known as *yin* and *yang*, must be in perfect balance. The term Yin encompasses the feminine principle – cold and the state of rest – whereas *yang* includes the male principle – heat and activity. These principles are active in appropriate degree in both men and women. When the balance is upset, illness is the result.

Chi flows through the twelve meridians or channels of the body, which are each associated with a particular organ, like the lungs, liver or spleen. Herbal remedies and acupuncture are used to restore the balance of *yin* and *yang* and thus promote healing.

TREATMENT

As well as taking an in-depth medical history the Chinese doctor will take your pulse at six different points on each wrist to get the measure of each of the twelve vital organs of the body. Your tongue will also be inspected closely as its texture reflects the condition of the vital organs.

Acupuncture uses stainless-steel needles, which are inserted into specific points, or meridians, in order to affect the energy flowing to an organ. The needles, which remain in place for approximately twenty minutes, don't actually hurt: they may tingle and cause a mild ache or heat sensation. Treatment often reaches the parts that Western medicine finds difficult.

You should always get help from a properly trained and registered practitioner. You can usually obtain information from your public library or Citizens Advice Bureau. A register is published by the Council for Acupuncture, listing all members of the five recognized and affiliated professional bodies.

Acupressure

A second level of treatment, more appropriate to the minor or occasional problems that you can sometimes alleviate by self-assessment and home treatment, is *shiatsu*, the Japanese finger-pressure method, sometimes called acupressure. In this system the body is influenced in various ways by the stimulation of key points, found along the course of energy channels circulating near the surface of the skin. These are the same as acupuncture meridians, but the points are stimulated by pressure rather than needles.

For *shiatsu* to be effective it's important to give the right kind of pressure for an appropriate length of time. It's no good pushing pressure points like 'magic buttons' and it's important to recognize by feel whether what you are doing is correct. Providing you adopt the right approach, *shiatsu* may be very helpful, whether you enlist the help of a friend or perform it on yourself.

Here is a summary of the method and a description of how to find just a few of the most useful points for some of the troubles mentioned.

DEPRESSION AND ANXIETY

First, try working with repeated steady thumb pressure along your inner leg between the edge of the bone and the calf muscle. Also, two inches above your wrist, in between the tendons at the centre of your inner arm, there is a good point to press firmly.

Breathing is very important to get your energy flowing smoothly, so try this simple exercise. Kneel on a cushion or carpet and join your hands together with your fingers back-to-back while pointing your fingertips towards your own upper abdomen. Let your relaxed fingers press into the centre, below the ribs but above the navel. As you do this, lean gently forward and exhale. The pressure should lend a little force to the exhalation. Wait for the inhalation to come naturally and raise yourself back again to the upright kneeling position while breathing in. Go gently at first, repeating the action with every breath, leaning a bit further on to your fingers each time. The abdominal muscles may seem tight or tender but try to relax fully at the end of each breath while leaning forward. Only do this ten times. You may move your fingers up and down or a little way along your ribs to explore for any tension. Afterwards sit quietly for a minute. You may feel like a good stretch before getting up.

INSOMNIA AND HEADACHES
Work with your fingertips along the base of your skull behind your head where it joins your neck. Feel for any sensitive hollows where your muscles meet the bony ridge and, leaning your head back, let your fingers penetrate. Hold for a few breaths. (If you do this for a friend, support her forehead with one hand and use your other hand to find points with finger and thumb on either side of her neck, pressing inward and upward.) For frontal headaches, lean forward. Let your fingertips support your forehead just below your eyebrows: it may feel tender, but breathe and relax for several seconds. Another useful point for headaches can be found by pressing hard into the fleshy area between your finger and thumb – press towards the edge of the bone on the forefinger side.

Also, work generally along the inside edges and soles of your feet, pressing especially around the inside ankle area.

HOT FLUSHES
The kidneys are the foundation of *yin* and *yang*, responsible for the stages of human development and decline. So it's important to support the kidneys and harmonize the kidney and the heart. It's regarded a bit like fire and water and as the water declines at the time of the menopause the fire begins to flare up: hence the flushes.

As the menopause is considered to be an energetic disharmony of the kidney *chi*, there are two main areas that are worth working on to help alleviate flushing and perspiration.

First, give pressure to points on the heart channel with your thumb held firmly at right angles. There are two or three points on the inside of your wrist, on the little-finger side along a line extending an inch or so up your arm from the wrist crease itself, which is just above the bone. Maintain the pressure for several

158

seconds on each point, breathing and relaxing as you do it. Repeat this on your other wrist.

Then work points along the kidney channel on each foot. Following a line from approximately two inches above your inner ankle, press firmly – inching down between the bone and the Achilles' tendon on to your heel, on around and beneath your ankle bone and along the inside of your foot to the point in the middle of the sole, approximately one-third of the distance back from the toes. (If you look under the sole of your foot while you crunch up your toes, there is a little groove at this point.)

As the kidney is the target area, general massage and thumb or finger pressure around the kidney or the lower back is also useful. Plenty of rest and relaxation to regenerate the energy of the kidneys is also advisable.

If this approach really interests you, there are two particularly good books to read which are mentioned on the reading list on page 295. You could also look for *shiatsu* classes in your area. If you do not know of any, write to the secretary of the Shiatsu Society whose address is listed in Appendix 6 at the back of the book. The Society will send you a list of qualified teachers.

Herbal medicine

Herbal medicine is older and more ubiquitous than any other type of medication on earth: it is as old as food and people, and there is no place which has been inhabited by people and plants that has not had its own herbal medicine. The great majority of plant medicines in use today were discovered by hunter-gatherers and so pre-date history itself. There is very good evidence that in all past and present hunger-gatherer societies, the responsibilities for gathering and learning about plant medicine belonged to women. So perhaps we can trust that, so far as the menopause is concerned, it was the afflicted who discovered their own remedies.

As civilizations emerged, men became involved with agriculture and medicine and tended to form analytical systems. As China, for example, evolved the polar principles of *yin* and *yang*, so European medicine relied on the concepts of *love* and *strife*: these resolved into the four elements which in turn were thought to be represented in the body by the four bodily fluids or *humours*. Many of these concepts still inform the best herbal medical practice in the West today, along with naturopathic ideas, many learned from native North Americans. Like Chinese medicine, European herbal medicine places great emphasis upon diet and exercise and other environmental factors.

THE PRINCIPLES

While herbal medicine aims to treat your current condition, it takes into consideration your past history from the time you were born, and the health of your parents at the time of conception. So, even if your symptoms are the same as your neighbour's, your prescriptions are unlikely to be the same. In other words, while we are all subject to the same biophysical laws, each of us has a unique tissue profile and therefore the treatment (by a once-living plant organism) needs to be unique.

When addressing symptoms of the menopause, the herbal specialist will treat the menstrual cycle: after all, the pituitary gland and the hypothalamus are still functioning, despite the falling levels in oestrogen. Their approach still respects the menstrual cycle, and the herbal remedies aim to reinstate cyclical behaviour. The herbalist wishes to support the adrenal axis and to redress target-organ sensitivity, because that contributes to the menopausal woman's difficulty with heat control. The aim is to enable the woman's body to convert heat into energy, mainly by treating her liver.

THE TREATMENT

The prescription you will receive may consist of a combination of a few or many different herbs. Sometimes you will be given herbs to take at different times of the day; and on occasion, herbs for different times of the month, depending on whether you are perimenopausal or postmenopausal. Some of the herbs used in prescriptions are well known, like *vitex agnus castus*, sage, vervain, St John's wort, mother wort, false unicorn root, hops and French marigold.

Although herbal medicine cannot claim to initiate bone

regeneration – to my knowledge there have been no studies to demonstrate this – they have been shown to help speed up the healing of broken bones, and also to aid *absorption* of minerals from the digestive tract.

If you wish to consult a trained herbalist, you will find the address to contact in Appendix 6.

Homeopathy

Samuel Hahnemann, the founder of homeopathy, developed a system of treating sick people with safe medicine. The word homeopathy comes from two Greek words: *omio* which means 'same' and *pathos* which means 'suffering'. Whereas allopathic medicine (the conventional medicine we know in the West) aims to treat symptoms with a drug that will produce an opposite effect, homeopathy treats 'like with like'. A homeopathic remedy is designed to produce the same symptoms as those you are suffering and in doing so aims to cancel them out. The dosages used are minute and may contain none of the original material. In this latter case, it is thought that the medicine, pill or liquid, contains an energy, or 'spirit', of the original medicine. Even these extreme dilutions have been shown to be effective in many conditions, including arthritis and hayfever. Many people appear to have benefited by their use, including women with menopausal symptoms.

THE PRINCIPLES

Homeopathy is an approach to treatment which aims to assist nature with her own process of healing rather than by-passing her altogether. Like other holistic treatments it treats each person as an individual. A trained homeopath takes an exceedingly thorough history before suggesting the most suitable remedy. It's very much a gentle preventive method of treatment which works best in conjunction with improved dietary and lifestyle measures.

Many people regularly use homeopathic remedies to help themselves, for anything from coughs and colds to menstrual problems. While the British royal family continue to be staunch supporters of homeopathy, it will undoubtedly remain an option for us all. The remedies are widely available, sometimes even on National Health prescriptions, and they are reasonably priced. Sometimes it's trial and error until you find the remedy that suits you, but it may well be worth persisting.

THE TREATMENT
Dr Andrew Lockie and Dr Nicola Geddes wrote an excellent reference book called *The Women's Guide to Homeopathy*. Their view is that menopausal problems represent imbalances which have been present in your body for a long time. As well as recommending homeopathic remedies, they also suggest that women look at their diet, take exercise and correct any PMS symptoms along with the development of a positive attitude and self-value before the onset of the menopause. There are specific remedies to fit symptom pictures and a trained homeopath would be able to decide which remedy is most suited to your needs.

Sepia and sulphur are just two of the many remedies that may be indicated for hot flushes and nightsweats. There is also a wide choice of remedy for poor memory, depression, insomnia, anxiety attacks, irritability, headaches and confusion – in fact, the list is almost endless.

If you want to seek professional help, the addresses of The Faculty of Homeopathy and The British Homeopathic Association are in the Useful Addresses section in Appendix 6. If you are lucky, you may find a qualified medical homeopath in your area or better still in a local NHS practice.

Cranial osteopathy

It's not uncommon, through the wear and tear of everyday life, for subtle back or neck problems to occur. I have seen many resistant, long-standing headaches cured by some good osteopathic manipulation. It is certainly worth having a check-up with a qualified osteopath if you feel tension building up in your back or neck or if you suffer from regular headaches, or you could visit a cranial osteopath.

THE PRINCIPLES

Cranial osteopathy, or cranio-sacral therapy as it is known, is a specialized form of osteopathy and is gentle yet potent. The aim is gently to coax the muscles, tendons, joints and connective tissue to establish correct functions and release restrictions, thus restoring normal circulation, the flow of energy and glandular secretions.

The cranio-sacral mechanism is made up of the cranium (the skull), the sacrum (the bone at the base of the spine), the membranes surrounding the brain, the spinal cord and the fascia of continuous, clingfilm-like sheet that surrounds the muscles, organs, joints and bones. The tension of this fascia, the clingfilm-like lining, is all-important. If you have ever worn an all-in-one pants suit that is too tight or too short, you will have felt uncomfortable. If the tension in the body's fascia becomes too tight, you can't just take it off and it's possible that body functions can be affected in the long-term.

Cranial osteopathy works on two basic principles: first, that structure can affect function, and second, that impairment in the structure, or reduced mobility, will affect blood flow. Blood flow is of supreme importance in osteopathy and the treatment is aimed at improving local circulation and freeing-up the nerve supply.

Everything in the body moves with the cranial rhythm, which is the rhythm of the central nervous system. It's a movement like a breathing rhythm, which is constant, even when we sleep. The movement helps blood flow generally and impaired local circulation after trauma.

If there are restrictions to soft tissue, like muscles, to the fascia or to the membranes, then blood, lymph and cerebral spinal-fluid is restricted; as a result, nutrition to that area is affected.

THE TREATMENT

In the case of hormonal problems, circulation is regarded as being very important. The pituitary gland can be affected in several ways. For example, undue tensions or stresses in the membranes around the pituitary stalk affect the circulation and blood supply, which in turn results in a change of function.

The treatment for women suffering with menopausal symptoms

is often aimed at improving pituitary function and balancing the function of the adrenal glands and the pelvis.

Whichever holistic therapy you choose to explore, it's important to put yourself in the hands of a qualified practitioner. These days, all the recognized 'alternative' therapies have official associations which keep registers of qualified practitioners. It is best to check, as there are, sadly, many non-qualified people who are not to be recommended. You will find the addresses of all the relevant associations on the Useful Address list in Appendix 6.

The holistic approach in practice

From our *Woman's Realm* survey of 500 women we were able to get some insight into the kind of alternative therapies women have turned to, and the degree of success experienced. As you will see from the following chart, even more of the women on HRT had been using alternative therapies than those not using HRT. Seventy-five per cent of the non-HRT users had tried one or more therapy, compared with 80 per cent of those who had used HRT. While the alternative therapies are perfectly compatible with HRT I don't think that explains why more women who had previously tried HRT had also tried more alternative therapy. As over 67 per cent of our sample experienced side-effects with HRT, it's understandable that they then sought alternative help.

HOW POPULAR WERE THE ALTERNATIVE THERAPIES?

Therapy	240 Non-HRT Users	254 HRT Users	Benefit Non-HRT Users	Benefit HRT Users
Vitamin/ Minerals	60%	57.5%	80%	74%
Diet therapy	42%	47%	74%	65%
Homeopathy	10%	14.5%	62.5%	51.5%

Herbal remedies	12.5%	14%	60%	66%
Acupuncture	4%	5.5%	33%	36%
Yoga	9%	10%	68%	62%
Reflexology	4%	6%	40%	47%
Other	11%	7.5%	92%	68%

The only conclusions that we can draw from this is that a lot of women are trying a lot of therapies with some degree of success. In fairness, our survey was not detailed enough to find out specific details about therapies and whether women had a course of treatment or a one-off session. We know that making a few dietary changes may be nowhere near as effective as following a whole programme which has been tailor-made for you.

Fifteen

Banishing Menopausal Symptoms Naturally

We have already discussed *why* diets need to be changed in order to start ameliorating menopausal symptoms; and more specific details will be given on diet in Part Four. The importance of exercise and relaxation has been emphasized as well. So, with the information you already have, and the dietary options to follow, you should be able to make an effective start on banishing your menopausal symptoms in a natural and healthy way.

Flushes

We now know that hot flushes are triggered by a number of factors: external heat like an over-warm room, sunshine, heavy blankets and hot-water bottles, alcohol, tea, coffee and possibly spicy foods. The circulation of women experiencing flushes is much more sensitive to environmental factors, rather than being under their own control, and it is this sensation of being out of control that is one of the most detested phenomena among menopausal women. Flushes are more likely to be troublesome at the start of the climacteric and in some women can persist for many years.

You can help to minimize flushing by implementing some of the following advice:

1 Cut down on the number of hot drinks you consume, especially tea and coffee
2 Don't have a hot drink on an empty stomach
3 Avoid hot, spicy foods

4 Use several thin layers of bedclothes rather than one heavy duvet
5 Avoid spending time out-of-doors in the heat of a summer's day
6 Wear several thin layers of clothing rather than thick clothes, even if it's cold
7 Control the temperature inside your home so that you feel comfortable
8 Keep your alcohol consumption down to a minimum
9 Take some nutritional supplements – Vitamin E, evening primrose oil, ginseng or magnesium (see also Chapter 11).

Make the changes above, follow the dietary changes designed to help you get the best out of natural oestrogens (see page 129), and exercise regularly. Exercise helps to improve your body's control of circulation and smooth out some of the mood swings that occur in women troubled by hot flushes. Don't panic if you do not experience immediate relief: it may take three months for you to feel the full effect of this method of controlling flushes.

Vaginal dryness
This problem is related to oestrogen withdrawal and can be helped by factors other than oestrogen-replacement therapy. Studies published in some respected medical journals have

shown potentially beneficial changes in the cells lining the vagina from a diet rich in soya flour, linseeds and sprouted red clover and from the use of ginseng. Other dietary sources of similar oestrogen-like compounds exist (see page 129).

No nutritional supplements have been put to the test, to my knowledge, but a combination of dietary changes, exercise and the use of the nutritional supplements for other problems associated with the menopause help improve vaginal secretions in some women.

Lubricants are very important. The traditionally recommended KY jelly is a water-based lubricant useful at times of sexual activity. More recently a vaginal gel, Replens, given by use of an applicator, produces effective vaginal lubrication and only needs to be inserted three times each week. It is available over the counter from the chemist.

During the menopause and into the postmenopause sexual stimulation does still increase vaginal moisture. However, instead of taking less than a minute it takes approximately five. So tell your partner that he should whisper sweet nothings into your ear for a little longer!

And try the following:

1 Follow the Option Three diet on page 228 for three months.
2 Include the oestrogen-like foods in your diet as these have been shown to help the vaginal tissues. The list of these foods is on page 129.
3 Take vitamin E or evening primrose oil as well as multivitamins and minerals.
4 Do pelvic-floor exercises regularly and make sure you get three or four good general exercise sessions every week (see Chapter 12).
5 Try some extra foreplay before actual intercourse. If you find it hard to get started, a massage might help. There are some lovely aromatherapy oils available. You only need a few drops of the aromatherapy oil mixed with some almond oil which you can buy at the chemist. Ask your partner to give you a gentle massage – and you might like to return the favour!

6 Don't be afraid to use lubricants like Replens or KY jelly when you feel you need to. If you have enjoyed a fulfilling sex life, do all within your power to preserve it.

Urinary symptoms

The symptoms of urinary frequency, urgency and incontinence become increasingly common in postmenopausal women, which can be both distressing and embarrassing. One group of American experts recently concluded that though HRT seems to help stress-incontinence, the amount of actual fluid lost is no less as a result of treatment. More effective treatments include surgery for those who are severely affected and have a prolapse. Exercises to strengthen the muscles of the pelvic floor can be very effective as is sometimes the use of a ring pessary inserted into the vagina, although this is only suitable for older women.

The symptoms of urinary frequency are often made worse by a high intake of the caffeine in tea and coffee. Urgency and mild discomfort can occasionally be due to dietary factors. The term 'irritable bladder syndrome' is used to describe this problem, providing infection has been ruled out as a cause. We have seen a few such women whose symptoms of urgency and discomfort have improved with the avoidance of a variety of foods in the same way that the symptoms of irritable bowel syndrome can also improve.

So you can try the following:

1 Practise pelvic-floor exercises three or four times each day as described in the general recommendations on page 199.
2 Avoid tea and coffee and use the alternatives suggested on page 198.
3 Try following the Option Three diet on page 228 for three months to see whether it makes any difference.
4 Concentrate particularly on a diet high in phyto-estrogens, those oestrogen-like foods that are listed on page 129.
5 If there is little improvement after three months, then consult your doctor to examine the possibilities of having a surgical repair.

Interestingly, the tissues of the bladder, urethra and vagina are extremely sensitive to oestrogens. As plant phyto-oestrogens are excreted in the urine, they will come into contact with these areas and may therefore be particularly likely to help with these symptoms. Just changing from a high-fat, low-fibre diet to a more healthy one and not using antibiotics helps increase the amount of excreted oestrogens in the urine and reduce the amount lost in the faeces.

Headaches

These are variably reported as being associated with the menopause. Many women find that their migraines lessen or disappear at this time but for some they may get worse and for others tension headaches may begin.

Migraine headaches which are intermittent, often severe, always associated with nausea or vomiting, and usually associated with visual disturbance or light sensitivity can respond well to dietary change. Certain foods rich in the chemical 'amine' are frequent migraine-triggers. Try cutting these foods out of your diet. They include cheese, wine and most other alcoholic beverages, chocolate, yeast extract, pickled foods and oranges.

Tension headaches are less influenced by diet, though tea and coffee sometimes play a part and some women with persistent headaches seem to benefit from cutting out bread and other sources of grain from the diet. Anyone with persistent headaches should always check with their doctor and have their blood pressure checked.

So you can try the following:

1 Cut out the amine-based foods listed above that can trigger headaches.
2 Avoid tea and coffee, bearing in mind that your headaches may get worse while you go through the withdrawal phase, which may last anything from a few days to a few weeks.
3 Try eating some ginger, either root or crystallized, if you feel the headache coming on. During a headache the blood vessels constrict. Ginger, a very old remedy, has the opposite effect:

it makes the blood vessels dilate and therefore can often cancel out the headache altogether. Although I have never seen any clinical trials using ginger for headaches, we have had a lot of success with it over the years, so it must be worth a try.

4 Practise either yoga or relaxation techniques if you feel your headaches are stress related. Learning how to cope with stress can make the world of difference to how you feel. Read the chapter on relaxation on page 145 and work out a programme for yourself to practise on a regular basis.

Depression

Although depression is an associated symptom of the meno-pause, it's one that is likely to be influenced by more than just a change in hormones. Medical opinion is divided as to how often depression is due to hormonal change and how much to other physical and psychological factors.

A youngish woman with an early menopause, severe oestrogen withdrawal and plagued by hot flushes has every reason to feel depressed and will probably feel much better physically and psychologically with HRT. On the other hand, some researchers have related the presence of depression to stresses in the woman's life and in particular the stress of trying to fulfil too many functions. Juggling the identities of mother, lover, wage-earner and carer of ageing parents exacts a toll and for many the result is depression. Lack of exercise can also be depressing. Indeed, a trial on a group of women of one hour's aerobic exercise three times a week for nine weeks had a marked beneficial effect on mood comparable to an antidepressant. (It also helps physical fitness and is likely to help heart-disease risk and bone strength.)

Lack of some nutrients can also be a factor in depression. Studies in depressed adults of both sexes and various ages have revealed that a mild to moderate lack of one or more of the B-group vitamins was present in 50 per cent of them. Women with PMS will probably have a low level of the mineral magnesium, also in over 50 per cent of cases. Supplements of both vitamin B and magne-sium can help improve mood in certain groups though, as yet to our knowledge, postmenopausal women have not been specifically studied. But it would seem worth a try especially if you have one or more of these risk factors:

- A high intake of alcohol: more than fourteen units each week
- Rely upon convenience foods with a poor intake of fresh vegetables, meat or fish or good quality vegetarian proteins
- A history of PMS
- Symptoms such as cracking at the corners of your mouth, a sore tongue, recurrent mouth ulcers or redness and greasiness at the sides of your nose – all possible features of vitamin B deficiency

We have found vitamin B and magnesium sometimes helpful but again they are best considered alongside dietary and exercise measures.

So you can try the following:

1 Take three or four sessions of aerobic exercise per week. If you haven't the time to get out to exercise, then try one of the Y Plan videos at home. There are more details about these in the exercise chapter on page 142.
2 Make time for yourself each day either to take a walk or to practise twenty minutes' relaxation, perhaps creative visualization. See page 154 for details.
3 Follow the Option Three diet on page 228 for three months to see whether your depression is food-related. It may well be that a complete change in diet will help enormously.
4 Take some nutritional supplements that include B vitamins and magnesium for an initial three-month period. An example of this is Gynovite which you can read about on page 126.

Anxiety and insomnia

These symptoms can be related to frequent and severe hot flushes. When this is the case, they can respond to HRT and usually respond well to our programme, as they can be aggravated by certain dietary factors and nutritional imbalances. If hot flushes prevent you from getting a good night's sleep then it's not surprising that your stress-tolerance will be low the next day. So try the following:

1 First follow the recommendations to help hot flushes.
2 If you are still menstruating and your anxiety levels are worse in the run-up to your period, supplements of vitamin B and magnesium may help. If you have finished menstruation, you might find that taking one of the suggested supplements will speed up the recovery process. It is worth a try. The supplements suggested are listed on page 126.
3 Relaxation techniques, yoga and breathing exercises are all potentially helpful. When you are feeling anxious, breathing too rapidly deeply alters the body chemistry by removing too much carbon-dioxide. This has the effect of aggravating anxiety tendencies. Breathing exercises can help.
4 Follow the Option Three diet on page 228 for three months, making sure that you cut out all the stimulants like tea, coffee, chocolate, cola and alcohol. Use the suggested alternatives.
5 Take plenty of exercise, three to four sessions each week to the point of breathlessness. If you can get out to exercise, all well and good. If not, put on an exercise video at home and go for it! See the chapter on exercise on page 131.

Fatigue

This is an even more contentious symptom. While it might improve with HRT, don't count on it unless your symptoms are only associated with nightsweats and the resulting insomnia.

In women who are still menstruating, lack of iron is a common cause of fatigue. In the late-forties age group, anaemia is less of a problem but may still affect 2 to 3 per cent of women. You can still lack iron without being anaemic: this is best detected by measurement of blood level of serum ferritin (protein in the blood, which accurately reflects the level of iron in the body, not just in the haemoglobin or blood pigment). So see your doctor if you are still having periods, especially if they are still heavy. This can be a problem for some 10 per cent of perimenopausal women. Again, lack of vitamin B or magnesium can be a factor so eat healthily and if you fall into one of the risk groups consider taking a supplement.

If you have any other illness or symptoms, see your doctor. Fatigue has so many possible causes that if it is severe a medical check-up is often the best way of finding out if there is anything else wrong. Diet, not just a lack of nutrients, can be a factor. There is some good evidence that undetected food allergies can be associated with fatigue (and headaches and bowel problems). Wheat and the related grains seem to be common culprits. Sometimes fatigue is a symptom of depression or stress so these may need tackling if you think it appropriate.

So try the following:

1 If you have nightsweats and insomnia, follow the recommendations on page 173.
2 If you are still menstruating, ask your doctor to measure your serum ferritin levels, which is a good test for detecting low iron stores.
3 To eliminate the possibility of food allergy being associated with your fatigue, follow the Option Three diet on page 228 for three months to see whether there is any noticeable difference.
4 Take as much regular exercise as you can. If you are really feeling shattered, this may be difficult to start with, but even five minutes every day is better than nothing. You can build up the time as your energy levels improve.
5 Take some of the vitamins and minerals suggested on page 126 to give you a boost.
6 Read a book called *Tired All The Time* by Dr Alan Stewart, and see whether you can pinpoint the underlying cause of your fatigue.
7 If you feel no better after three months, arrange an appointment with your doctor for a thorough check-up.

Aches and pains

Non-specific aches and pains are a common complaint and it's debatable whether they are actual menopause symptoms or to do with a lack of physical well-being. The enthusiasts for HRT would like to claim that it helps aches and pains. The manufacturers, however, are hesitant to do so. Certainly some women experience a substantial improvement in well-being when taking HRT and the improvement of peripheral symptoms seems to be related to the improvement in hot flushes. Interestingly, though, the oestrogen in HRT does cause a slight change in blood chemistry similar to that in pregnancy, with the production of a small amount of pregnancy zone protein (PZP). This has been extracted from the blood of pregnant women, given to non-pregnant women with rheumatoid arthritis and been found to benefit them! Some women do report feeling particularly well during pregnancy.

What is the natural alternative here? Lack of physical fitness has got to be an important factor for some women, so out of your chair and on with your walking shoes. Being overweight won't help either, so you will need to shed some pounds.

A lack of magnesium – yet again – is renowned for causing muscle cramps so follow the dietary recommendations as they are rich in magnesium, potassium and vitamin B, all important for muscle function. Finally, aches and pains often respond to dietary changes with the avoidance of certain foods.

So try the following:

1 Follow the Option Three diet on page 228 for at least three months.
2 If you are overweight you will need to lose weight, which you may well do anyway while on Option Three. If you are not losing weight naturally, you may have to cut your portion sizes or eat from a smaller plate!
3 Take some extra magnesium supplements as well as the suggested multivitamins and minerals. But be careful with extra magnesium because as well as being an important nutrient, it is also a laxative. Unless you are prone to diarrhoea, you should be able to take two or three 200mg tablets each day; if you are constipated, you can increase the dose to four or five tablets and sort out both problems at once.

4 Regular exercise is always important, so take it easy, but make sure you do as much as you can three or four times each week.
5 Massage can soothe away aches and pains. Either treat yourself to a professional massage or persuade your partner to give you a massage several times a week. Use the lovely aromatherapy massage oils I mentioned on page 153.
6 If the aches and pains persist, visit your local cranial osteopath for an evaluation. Underlying mechanical problems can really stop you making progress. Cranial osteopaths offer gentle but effective treatment, and we have had excellent feedback from patients who consulted one.

Weight-gain

Many women attribute weight-gain to the 'change'. Well, it's not really a good excuse. The metabolic rate does drop fractionally at this time but comparison of different age groups shows that on average there is something like a 1 kilo or 2 lb weight gain. A listed side-effect of HRT is weight-gain though some researchers consider this is not really the case. However, fluid retention does seem to be common and in our survey women who had taken HRT reported an average weight-gain of 16 lbs.

In theory, being overweight or, to be more scientific about it, having lots of peripheral fat tissue, will help your body maintain its level of residual oestrogen in the postmenopausal phase. But being too plump is strongly associated with a greater risk of cancer of the womb and a slightly increased risk of breast cancer. There are also all the effects of excess weight on blood pressure, cholesterol, general fitness, mobility and self-esteem. So it doesn't pay to be overweight. Neither does it pay to be too thin. This increases the risk of oesteoporosis and may not be the best for a healthy postmenopausal hormone balance.

Our advice is not to start a strict weight-loss diet just now. You will have enough to do while you are following the option of your choice, in an attempt to control your symptoms. It's important to get those symptoms under control first, before dieting. One of the added bonuses of our programme is that most people lose weight without trying. You might even find, three months down the line, you are somewhat lighter and the need to diet as such has lessened.

We have, of course, included the most important elements of a weight-loss diet into most of the options. These are:

1 Reduce the intake of fatty foods, especially those rich in saturated animal fats.
2 Cut right down on sugar, sweets, chocolate and other foods high in empty calories.
3 Limit your intake of alcohol. It's nutritionally poor and it's an easy way to increase your calories and worsen your hot flushes.
4 Eat plenty of filling, nutritious, low-calorie foods such as fresh fruit, vegetables, lean meats, fish and chicken without their skins, whole-grain or white bread, lower-fat dairy products and vegetarian proteins.

Many women find the support of a slimming group or club is helpful, so find out what is available in your area. Your doctor may have some advice on this. There are many good slimming books, not the least of which is our own *The Vitality Diet*.

Bowel problems

Constipation, bloating, abdominal discomfort and sometimes diarrhoea are common problems in women of all ages. Strictly speaking these are not part of menopausal symptoms proper but deserve a mention here as they are so common. These are the main symptoms of irritable bowel syndrome, where the bowel is over-sensitive resulting in episodes of spasm of the muscles of the bowel wall. Diet and stress are now recognized as the two most important factors in this common condition.

There is now an acknowledged association between bowel problems and a variety of gynaecological problems, including infertility. What happens in the bowel will certainly have some influence on hormone metabolism. Our experience is that women with both PMS and menopausal symptoms seem to fare a lot better if co-existing bowel problems are also tackled simultaneously with their other symptoms.

Anyone with severe pain, blood in the stool, weight-loss or who has only recently developed symptoms should check with their doctor. The advice that follows is suitable for those with constipation or irritable bowel syndrome but not if there is some other problem.

So you could try the following:

1 Cut down on tea, especially if you are constipated: it can slow down the bowel. Coffee can speed it up.
2 Eat plenty of fibre-rich foods, especially fresh fruit and vegetables.
3 Don't eat bran. That's right, don't eat bran. Though it's helpful for some, its effects are too unpredictable. If you can take it, eat oats but not oat bran.
4 Take a fibre supplement. Your doctor may prescribe something but our favourite is linseeds which are available in most healthfood shops. As well as being a good source of fibre they also have some natural oestrogen-like properties. A reasonable daily amount is one or two tablespoons with some breakfast cereal or fruit and yoghurt.
5 If a further laxative is needed, a supplement of magnesium is safe, effective, old-fashioned and has some interesting properties of possible benefit to menopausal symptoms. A reasonable dose is 300 mg increasing to up to 600 mg if necessary. This can be taken in the form of magnesium tablets, liquid milk of magnesia or multivitamins containing magnesium.

More information and advice on tackling irritable bowel syndrome can be found in our book called *Beat IBS through Diet*. If bowel symptoms do not respond to the above measures within four weeks then you should undoubtedly see your doctor.

Skin problems
Skin-thinning does really occur with the menopause and is partly due to the decline in oestrogen. Skin quality is also very much

influenced by diet, circulation and local applications of good moisturizers.

Lack of certain nutrients can influence it in the following ways:

- A lack of vitamin B can result in red, greasy patches at the sides of your nose, peeling of your lips or cracking at the corners of your mouth
- A lack of zinc can also cause red greasy skin with dry scaly patches on your face and body
- Generally dry skin and eczema can be influenced by a lack of certain fats of the type found in evening primrose oil. Some women benefit from its use and this should always be combined with a very healthy diet
- Lack of vitamin C can also lead to skin-thinning, easy bruising and delayed healing. The lack should not occur unless you are eating very little fresh fruit and vegetables. It is more likely to be a problem in smokers and older men.

Anything that stimulates blood-flow to the skin is likely to improve its quality. This could be exercise, a massage, some sun-bathing or just getting out-of-doors on a winter's day to put a bit of colour in your cheeks.

So you can try the following:

1 Follow the option of your choice (see pages 185–234) for three months.
2 Take some vitamins and minerals and if your skin is dry or you suffer with eczema, use Efamol evening primrose oil or Epogam.
3 Take regular exercise.
4 Use a good moisturizer on your face and a lotion enriched with vitamin E on your body. Blackmores Laboratories make an excellent range of reasonably priced creams and lotions which contain only natural ingredients, herbs and vitamins.
5 If the skin on your body is persistently dry, try using some mineral oil in the bath. Alpha Keri is available at the chemist and also on prescription from your doctor.

Thrush

Vaginal infection with the yeast *Candida albicans* is a common problem and most women will have experienced at least one episode of it by the time they reach the menopause. Usually it becomes less of a problem by the time of the menopause but because it's so common and has recently been so widely popularized, it deserves a mention.

There are several types of *candida* but *albicans* is by far the most common. It is also responsible for nappy rash, thrush in the mouth, under the breasts and in other moist dark parts of our bodies. Thrush is not a serious infection but it's very annoying, producing vaginal irritation and a sticky white discharge. About 20 per cent of the normal population carry a small amount of *candida* around with them, usually in their mouths, in their bowels or on the surface of their skin. It's quite happily sitting there doing no harm and only becomes a problem when the body's defences are reduced. This can happen after a course of antibiotics which can kill off the healthy bacteria normally present in the vagina that help protect it from *candida* and other infections.

Diabetes, steroid drugs and the oral contraceptive pill can all increase the risk of *candida*. This was a considerable problem with the early oral contraceptive pill which was high in oestrogen. Today it is hardly a problem with the low- and very-low-dose pills that are available. In theory HRT could increase the risk of thrush but usually this is not the case.

A lot has recently been written about the fact that thrush can also cause a whole range of symptoms including fatigue, headaches, bowel problems, skin problems and more. The scientific evidence for this is very limited. There is reasonable evidence that it can contribute to bowel problems, especially diarrhoea, following treatment with antibiotics, nettle rash and possibly eczema and psoriasis. Some women and men are also predisposed to recurrent problems with thrush because of mild deficiencies in iron, vitamin B and other nutrients. These can reduce the body's defence mechanisms enough to allow infection with *candida*.

If thrush is a problem you can:

1 See your doctor. She can prescribe local treatment with cream or pessary. If this is not enough, treatment with tablets, sometimes for several weeks, can clear thrush and remove any reservoir that may remain in the bowel.
2 Eat a diet low in sugar, sweets and alcohol. This can be a factor for some women. A few women are also sensitive to yeast-rich foods. Cutting down on bread, foods with yeast extract, vinegar, pickles and alcoholic beverages can be very important, especially for those with persistent vaginal irritation or skin problems.
3 Take a multivitamin supplement with iron.
4 There are natural antifungal agents in most fresh vegetables, fruits, herbs and spices. Ensure you have plenty of these in your diet. Avoiding all fruit and other forms of carbohydrate, as has been recommended by some writers, seems to us to be unnecessarily drastic.

One of the reasons why the WNAS programme is successful is that it educates you and subsequently empowers you, with your new-found knowledge, to help yourself to better health. As you are now aware, many of the symptoms that occur at the time of the menopause are not strictly related to oestrogen withdrawal. They are symptoms that would probably have occurred anyway and would have needed to be addressed sooner or later. The programme we have devised not only helps women to overcome their menopause symptoms in the short term; it also addresses other common problems like migraine headaches, bowel problems, mood changes, anxiety syndrome and skin problems, as well as helping to prevent osteoporosis in the longer term.

Our programme, for many women who have been suffering with symptoms for many years, is like the key to the cage in which they have been imprisoned. For the first time for too long they are able to walk free with their health intact and, with relief, contemplate new horizons.

In Part Four I shall give you all the information you need to work out an initial dietary programme for yourself. This, in tandem with the exercise, supplements and relaxation already discussed, is relatively new ground which has been trodden for you by others, who are grateful for the help they have received and have never looked back. The system we have worked out is not exclusive. It is there for the taking, so don't waste any more time in making a start.

Part Four

A DIETARY
SELF-HELP MANUAL

Sixteen
Choosing a Nutritional Plan

As in many other situations in life there are compromises to be made. There is no magic pill that will make menopausal symptoms vanish overnight and prevent osteoporosis for ever more. You will undoubtedly need to make some changes to your diet and your lifestyle to overcome your symptoms and to have the best possible chance of avoiding osteoporosis. We have already outlined some ways in which you might do this. Now we shall concentrate on individual nutritional plans.

If your symptoms are mild to moderate there will be less effort involved than if you have severe symptoms. So that you can select the right programme to suit your individual needs, I have divided the recommendations into three options:

Option 1: General recommendations for mild sufferers
Option 2: A specialized plan for moderate sufferers
Option 3: A tailor-made programme for more severe
          sufferers

You will notice that on the chart that follows you are asked to assess whether your symptoms are mild, moderate or severe. Each category has a numerical score as follows:

0 = None
1 = Mild
2 = Moderate
3 = Severe

Menopause Symptom Questionnaire

Do you suffer from any of the following? Please ensure each symptom is only ticked *once*.

MOIRA	*How many times per month	None	Mild	Moderate	Severe
1 Hot/~~cold~~ flushes*	? often		✓		
2 Facial/~~body~~ flushing* neck	?		✓		
3 Nightsweats*	?.		✓		
4 Palpitations*	?		✓		
5 Panic attacks*	? not very often now		✓		
6 Generalised aches and pains			✓		
7 Depression			✓-	✓+	
8 Perspiration			✓		
9 Numbness/skin tingling in arms and legs in hands not bad now			✓		
10 Headaches			✓		
11 Backache				✓+	
12 Fatigue			✓		
13 Irritability				✓	
14 Anxiety				✓	
15 Nervousness				✓+	
16 Loss of confidence					
17 Insomnia			✓		
18 Giddiness/dizziness floating feeling			✓		
19 ~~Difficulty~~/frequency in passing water			✓		
20 Water retention	Have had some in past				

21	Bloated abdomen	✓	
22	Constipation	✓	
23	Itchy vagina	✓	✓
24	Dry vagina		✓+
25	Painful intercourse *Haven't had any for 3½ years*		
26	Decreased sex drive	✓	
27	Loss of concentration	✓	
28	~~Confusion~~/Loss of vitality		✓+

Have you noticed since the onset of the menopause:

1 Loss of height   Yes/~~No~~

2 Difficulty in bending   Yes/~~No~~ *but not severe*

3 Increased curvature of back   Yes/~~No~~

Are any of the above symptoms cyclic? (i.e. come in cycles, for example on a monthly basis) *Not as far as I've noticed*

Have you gained weight since you started the menopause?   Yes/~~No~~ If yes, how much *about 12 Lbs - 1 stone*

Do you have any other menopausal symptoms not mentioned above? ___

How long have you had menopausal symptoms? *going on for 15 years*

Did you suffer from pre-menstrual tension prior to the menopause? ~~Yes~~/No   If yes, for how long?

187

Menopause Symptom Questionnaire

Do you suffer from any of the following? Please ensure each symptom is only ticked *once*.

	How many times per month	None	Mild	Moderate	Severe
1 Hot/cold flushes*					
2 Facial/body flushing*					
3 Nightsweats*					
4 Palpitations*					
5 Panic attacks*					
6 Generalised aches and pains					
7 Depression					
8 Perspiration					
9 Numbness/skin tingling in arms and legs					
10 Headaches					
11 Backache					
12 Fatigue					
13 Irritability					
14 Anxiety					
15 Nervousness					
16 Loss of confidence					
17 Insomnia					
18 Giddiness/dizziness					
19 Difficulty/frequency in passing water					
20 Water retention					

21	Bloated abdomen			
22	Constipation			
23	Itchy vagina			
24	Dry vagina			
25	Painful intercourse			
26	Decreased sex drive			
27	Loss of concentration			
28	Confusion/Loss of vitality			

Mild	means that symptoms are present but they do not interfere with your activities. You feel all right, but are aware that some physical and emotional changes are taking place which make you feel below par.
Moderate	means that symptoms are present and they do interfere with some activities, but they are not disabling. You feel below par and maybe even cancel arrangements. Family and close friends are aware that you are not your usual self.
Severe	means that symptoms are not only present, they interfere with all activities. They are severely disabling and life is hard to cope with while you are experiencing them.

I have used Moira's first menopause symptom questionnaire on page 186 to demonstrate how the chart looks when it's completed. You simply decide on the severity of each symptom and tick the appropriate box. Ideally you should complete a new chart each month so that you can compare them. (There's a blank version of this chart on page 188 for you to fill in.)

You also need to keep a daily symptomatology diary, like the one on page 318. This covers a month, and each evening before you go to bed, you should fill in one column with a number ranging from 0–3 depending on the severity of each symptom that day. This on-going record becomes very important, particularly if you are reintroducing foods to your diet in Option Three.

Read through the three options before deciding which one to follow. Make a note of your decisions on your personal nutritional programme on page 194.

How to begin
Once you have chosen the programme to follow you will need to sort out your record-keeping. It's important to keep accurate records as you go along as they will prove to be an immensely useful reference.

Complete the blank Menopause Symptom Questionnaire on page 188 before you begin so that you have a clear picture of your symptoms.

- Follow the specialized regime for a period of three months
- Keep a daily symptomatology diary of all your symptoms. A chart is provided on page 192 and at the end of the book
- Keep daily diaries of what you eat and drink, of exercise taken, and relaxation. Charts for these are supplied at the end of the book (pages 320–23).
- Complete another Menopause Symptom Questionnaire after three months. This can then be compared with your first chart to measure your progress. You can see how the ladies who have told their stories fared before and after on pages xv, 22, 146 and 186.

Menopause Symptomatology Daily Diary

Grading of symptoms

0 None
1 Mild – present but does not interfere with activities
2 Moderate – present and interferes with activities but not disabling
3 Severe – disabling. Unable to function

Date													
Hot/cold flushes													
Facial/body flushing													
Nightsweats													
Palpitations													
Panic attacks													
Generalised aches and pains													
Depression													
Perspiration													
Numbness/skin tingling in arms and legs													
Headaches													
Backache													
Fatigue													
Irritability													
Anxiety													
Nervousness													
Loss of confidence													

Insomnia																											
Giddiness/dizziness																											
Difficulty/frequency in passing water																											
Constipation																											
Itchy vagina																											
Dry vagina																											
Painful intercourse																											
Decreased sex drive																											
Loss of concentration																											
Weight in pounds																											

Notes

193

Personal Nutritional Programme
Summary of Recommendations

DIET

1

2

3

4

5

6

7

8

9

10

11

12

SUPPLEMENTS

1

2

3

4

EXERCISE AND RELAXATION

1

2

3

4

When you have finished preparing this chart, pin it up somewhere highly visible like on the outside of your fridge or on your kitchen noticeboard and refer to it daily.

Seventeen

Option One: General Recommendations for Mild Sufferers

If you suffer from mild symptoms, or need a preventive programme to follow before your menopause, you should follow these general dietary guidelines rather than make any radical changes.

General dietary guidelines

- Concentrate on eating foods that contain phytoestrols or phyto-oestrogens, the oestrogen-like properties. You will find a list of these on page 129
- Reduce your intake of sugar and junk foods. This includes sugar added to tea and coffee, and that in sweets, cakes, biscuits, chocolate, jam, puddings, marmalades, soft drinks containing phosphates, ice-cream and honey. Consumption of these may cause water retention and impede the uptake of essential minerals
- Reduce your intake of salt, both added to cooking and at the table. Avoid salted foods such as salted nuts, kippers and bacon. Salt causes fluid retention and induces calcium loss from the body in the urine. Use flavour enhancers such as garlic, onion, kelp powder, fresh herbs, sesame powder or other mild spices instead of salt. But avoid *over*-spicy foods as these can cause hot flushes.
- Eat vegetables and salads daily. Three portions of vegetables and a salad should be eaten every day, as they contain plenty of essential nutrients. Where possible use good quality vegetables,

196

possibly organic, or try growing your own. Eat a combination of green leafy vegetables, peas, beans and lentils. These are all good sources of fibre, calcium, magnesium and other minerals.

- Eat plenty of fresh fruit, at least two servings each day. Fruit is a good source of important nutrients and a healthy way to satisfy a sweet tooth

- Millet, buckwheat, rye and barley are high in magnesium and fibre. Oatmeal is a good source of complex carbohydrates and fibre. Eat at least one serving of cereal each day, as long as you do not get abdominal bloating as a result

- Limit your consumption of red meat to one or two portions each week. Substitute meat with fish, poultry, peas, beans and nuts. Rice and beans also combine to form a complete protein. Meat-eaters have a lesser bone density than women who are vegetarian: animal proteins can take calcium and other minerals from bones which can then increase your chances of osteoporosis

- Dairy products, such as milk and cheese, are excellent sources of calcium. Use low-fat versions if you need to lose or watch your weight. Drink up to one pint of milk every day. If you drink less than this, you will need to eat plenty of other calcium-rich foods. Good non-dairy sources of calcium include tinned bony fish such as sardines and salmon. Mash up the fish so that you can eat the little bones, which are extremely rich in calcium. All green vegetables, peas, beans, lentils, nuts, especially brazils, almonds and cashews and most seeds such as sesame, sunflower and pumpkin are also good sources of calcium and other minerals.

- Limit your intake of fats to 30 per cent of the total calories you consume every day. For most of us this means reducing our fat intake by about a quarter. Avoid the use of lard and excessive amounts of butter and hydrogenated vegetable oil such as shortening and hard margarines. Instead, use cold pressed safflower, olive, sesame and sunflower oils. For example, use safflower oil in mayonnaise, olive oil for salads and all four oils for cooking.

- Drink plenty of liquids. Drink three to six large glasses of water daily, preferably filtered or bottled. You might like to add lemon juice to taste. Tap and mineral water can contain some calcium and magnesium. If you must drink tea and coffee use decaffeinated or, better still, herb teas or coffee substitutes. When giving up caffeine remember you may suffer headaches for a few days. See also the lists below.

- Keep the consumption of alcohol to a maximum of three to four drinks each week. Alcohol knocks most nutrients sideways and may aggravate hot flushes.

- If you smoke, try to cut down gradually as smoking can aggravate some symptoms especially hot flushes and night-sweats. Pace yourself during the day, waiting for longer periods of time between each cigarette.

- Arm yourself with nutritious snacks to eat in-between meals if you are hungry. Nuts and raisins and fresh or dried fruit are fine. If you keep your blood-sugar levels constant there is less chance of you dipping into the biscuit tin.

COFFEE SUBSTITUTES

There are a number of coffee substitutes you can try. It you are avoiding grains as you might have to (see Option Three), you will be restricted to Dandelion coffee, instant (which is quite sweet) or dandelion root, which you can boil or put through a coffee filter – it makes a nice malted drink – or alternatively a chicory drink. There is a wider choice if you remain on grains, or when you re-introduce them to your diet. You can try Barley cup which is a very acceptable cereal-based alternative, or Bambu or Caro. All these are available in healthfood shops. You can have up to two cups of decaffeinated coffee each day, either instant or filter.

Herbal teas and tea substitutes

Rooibosch Eleven O'Clock Tea is the most tea-like alternative. It comes in teabags and can be made with or without milk. Interestingly it contains a mild, natural muscle relaxant which may help alleviate tension and ease period pains if you are still menstruating. It is favoured by many of our patients and is definitely worth a try. Other suggestions are ginseng tea, fennel tea, raspberry and ginseng tea, mixed berry tea, lemon verbena tea and wild strawberry tea. These days most healthfood shops sell single sachets so that you can 'buy and try' without being saddled with a whole box of teabags you absolutely detest.

Cold drinks
Soft drinks should be non-carbonated, sugar free, phosphate-free and decaffeinated. As the phosphorus in fizzy drinks blocks the uptake of magnesium and calcium by bone tissue, it is better if you keep fizzy drinks to a minimum. Drink plenty of still water, either bottled or filtered, with or without fruit juice and have small quantities of mineral water, Appletise, Aqua Libra and other water- and fruit-juice-based drinks. Avoid cola drinks and other canned and bottled drinks that contain anything other than natural ingredients. Read the labels carefully before buying.

Other useful self-help tips

- Wear several layers of thin comfortable clothing during the day so that you can peel them off should the need arise.
- Use lightweight layers of bed clothes so that you can adjust them according to your temperature. Wear cotton night-dresses instead of manmade fibres.
- Carry some cool wipes in your handbag until the flushes have abated.
- Take extra care of your hair, skin and nails. Use rich hair conditioner, good moisturising lotions for your skin and nail strengtheners.
- Do toning pelvic floor exercises once or twice a day in your spare time. Draw the vaginal muscles in and hold while you count to ten. Release them slowly. Repeat this ten times.
- Spend time learning to relax if you have not already mastered the art. Get your partner to give you a massage if you are feeling tense, or treat yourself to one on a regular basis. See also Chapter 13.
- Learn some simple yoga exercises and make some time to put them into practice each day, even if you can only manage them for ten to fifteen minutes. Remember: relaxation and rest tend to minimize flushes whereas constant activity and stress tend to make them worse.

Eighteen

Option Two:
A Specialized Plan
for Moderate Sufferers

As well as following the general recommendations for mild sufferers from option one, you will need to choose specific nutrients, according to your symptoms, by referring to the following chart. You can do this initially in two ways. First, refer to the section on the nutritional content of foods on pages 204–212. Choose the foods you like that contain substantial amounts of the nutrients you need. Second, take extra nutritional supplements where you feel it's appropriate (see page 126 for our recommendations).

Nutrients for menopausal symptoms
In conjunction with other dietary measures, plus moderate exercise and regular periods of relaxation, you will find the following nutrients make an enormous difference to specific symptoms, as well as help prevent osteoporosis:

General symptoms
Concentrate on taking magnesium, calcium and the B vitamins.

Hot flushes
Concentrate on taking vitamin E, essential fatty acids and ginseng.

Anxiety attacks
B vitamins and magnesium help to relieve anxiety attacks.

Depression
Concentrate on taking B vitamins, vitamins C and E and magnesium.

Lack of libido
Magnesium, zinc, iron and B vitamins will all help you to regain your libido.

Heavy periods
Concentrate on taking an iron-rich diet.

Skin problems
Concentrate on taking zinc and B vitamins.

Prevention of oesteoporosis
Concentrate on taking calcium, magnesium, and essential fatty acids in Evening Primrose Oil and fish oil.

Make a note of the nutrients that you feel you need to concentrate on and look them up in the nutritional content of foods on the following pages. From these lists you can select the foods and drinks you wish to include in your daily diet. I have suggested a one-week sample menu, which is generally high in important nutrients, to give you some ideas. You can either follow the menu exactly to get yourself started, or you can use it as a guideline and adapt it to suit your tastes and needs.

Don't eat too much red meat at the time of the menopause, as it is acknowledged that vegetarians have an easier menopause. This is why I have included only a couple of meat dishes. There are some fish dishes here, and plenty of vegetarian options.

BUYING FOOD
I shall suggest that you eat plenty of salads, vegetables and fruit, no matter which option you choose, but you will have realized that many of these foods are contaminated with chemicals. Fortunately, most of the large supermarkets now stock organic produce. Although this is a little more expensive, do try to buy at least some organic produce – unless you grow your own, which makes even more sense.

While I have included many vegetarian suggestions and recipes, I have also catered for meat- and fish-eaters. Again, because of the chemicals and hormones in meat, I would suggest you try to find a

Vitamins and Minerals – do you lack them?

	Food sources	What they do
Vitamin B6	Meat, fish, nuts, bananas, avocados, wholegrains	Essential in the metabolism of protein and the amino acids that control mood and behaviour. Affects hormone metabolism
Vitamin B1 Thiamin	Meat, fish, nuts, wholegrains and fortified breakfast cereals	Essential in the metabolism of sugar, especially in nerves and muscles
Vitamin C Ascorbic acid	Any fresh fruits and vegetables	Involved in healing, repair of tissues and production of some hormones
Iron	Meat, wholegrains, nuts, eggs and fortified breakfast cereals	Essential to make blood-haemoglobin. Many other tissues need iron for energy reactions
Zinc	Meat, wholegrains, nuts, peas, beans, lentils	Essential for normal growth, mental function, hormone production and resistance to infection
Magnesium	Green vegetables, wholegrains, Brazil and almond nuts, many other non-junk foods	Essential for sugar and energy metabolism, needed for healthy nerves and muscles

	Deficiencies	
Who is at risk	Symptoms	Visible signs
Women, especially smokers, 'junk-eaters'	Depression, anxiety, insomnia, loss of responsibility	Dry/greasy facial skin, cracking at corners of mouth
Alcohol consumers, women on the pill, breast-feeding mothers, high consumers of sugar	Depression, anxiety, poor appetite, nausea, personality change	None usually! Heart, nerve and muscle problems if severe
Smokers particularly	Lethargy, depression, hypochondriasis (imagined illnesses)	Easy bruising, look for small pinpoint bruises under the tongue
Women who have heavy periods (e.g. coil users), vegetarians, especially if tea or coffee drinkers, women with recurrent thrush	Fatigue, poor energy, depression, poor digestion, sore tongue, cracking at corners of mouth	Pale complexion, brittle nails, cracking at corners of mouth
Vegetarians, especially tea and coffee drinkers, alcohol consumers, long-term users of diuretics (water pills)	Poor mental function, skin problems in general, repeated infections	Eczema, acne, greasy or dry facial skin
Women with PMS! (some 50 per cent may be lacking), long-term diuretic users, alcohol consumers	Nausea, apathy, loss of appetite, depression, mood changes, muscle cramps	Usually NONE! so easily missed; muscle spasms sometimes

butcher who sells additive-free meat. Some supermarkets now sell it, as do the small organic farms dotted around the UK.

Changing to a full range of organic produce is probably impossible at the moment. Currently the demands by the retailers for organic produce cannot be met. But as more and more farmers switch over, there will be plenty to go round.

VEGETARIANS

If you have been eating a good vegetarian diet for some time in theory you should by now be reaping the benefits. Vegetarians do need to pay particular attention to certain aspects of their diet, so that they do not become nutritionally deficient. Although many vegetarians and vegans take great care with their diet, there are still too many who try to exist on lettuce leaves. Apart from all the recommendations made so far, vegetarians and vegans should concentrate on making sure they have an adequate balance of proteins in their diet. No single vegetarian protein contains all the appropriate nutrients required, so it's important to combine the different types of vegetable proteins. These include nuts, seeds, peas, beans, lentils, whole grains, brown rice, sprouted-bean and soya-bean products and are particularly important for menopausal women.

Although beans are particularly nutritious, they often cause abdominal wind. Soaking them for twenty-four hours before cooking them, and dehusking them, may reduce the problem.

There are many vegetarian suggestions in the body of the menus. You can use these, and you will also find a one-week suggested vegetarian menu on page 215.

Nutritional content of foods

The following lists detail the foods that contain good amounts of each of the vitamins and minerals that will help combat your menopause. Read the lists through carefully to see which nutrients your favourite foods contain. You can then concentrate on foods with good quantities of the right nutrients in your diet.

FOODS CONTAINING **CALCIUM** (PER 100 G/4 OZ)

	mg		mg
Cereals		Rhubarb (stewed)	93
Brown flour	150	Tangerines	42
Oatmeal (uncooked)	55		
Soya flour	210	**Dairy**	
Wholemeal (wholewheat) bread	23	Milk	120
		Milk, dried (skimmed)	1190
Brown bread	100	Cheddar cheese	800
Muesli	200	Parmesan cheese	1220
		Cottage cheese	800
Fish		Yoghurt (natural)	180
Haddock (fried)	110		
Pilchards (canned in tomato sauce)	300	**Vegetables and pulses**	
		Carrot (raw)	48
Sardines (canned in oil)	460	Celery (raw)	52
Sprats (fried)	710	Parsley (raw)	330
Tuna (canned in oil)	7	Spinach (boiled)	600
Shrimps (boiled)	320	Watercress	220
Whitebait (fried)	860	Turnips (boiled)	55
Salmon (canned)	93	French beans (boiled)	39
Kipper (baked)	65	Haricot beans (boiled)	65
Plaice (steamed)	38	Broccoli florets (boiled)	61
		Spring greens (boiled)	86
Fruit			
Apricots (dried)	92	**Nuts**	
Blackberries (raw)	63	Almonds	250
Figs (dried)	280	Brazil nuts	180
Lemons (whole)	110	Peanuts	61

FOODS CONTAINING **MAGNESIUM** (PER 100 G/4 OZ)

	mg		mg
Cereals		**Dairy**	
Wheat bran	520	Dried skimmed milk	117
Wholemeal flour	140	Fresh whole milk	12
Oatmeal (raw)	110		
Porridge (rolled) oats	30	**Meat**	
Soya flour	290	Beef (lean cooked)	11
Wholemeal bread	230	Lamb (lean cooked)	12
Muesli	100	Chicken meat (roast)	24
Fish		**Nuts**	
Cod (baked)	26	Almonds	260
Herring (grilled)	32	Brazil nuts	410
Kipper (baked)	48	Walnuts	130
Pilchards (canned)	39	Peanuts	180
Salmon (steamed)	29		
Sardines (canned in oil)	52	**Vegetables and Pulses**	
Winkles (boiled)	360	Butter beans (boiled)	33
Crab (boiled)	48	Haricot beans (boiled)	45
		Mung beans (raw)	170
Fruit (raw)		Chick peas (cooked)	67
Pineapple (fresh)	17	Spinach (boiled)	45
Apricots (fresh)	12	Potatoes (baked with skins)	24
Apricots (dried)	65	Avocado	29
Bananas	42		
Blackberries	30	**Beverages/drinks**	
Dates (dried)	59	Herbal tea bag	6
Figs (dried)	92	Indian tea	250
Raisins	42		
Passion-fruit	39	**Other**	
Sultanas	35	Black treacle	140
Prunes	27		

FOODS RICH IN VITAMIN B

Cereals
Wholemeal flour
Wheat bran
Soya flour
Brown rice
Corn flakes

Meat
Lamb's liver
Pig's liver
Bacon (lean)
Gammon (lean)
Beef (lean)
Minced beef
Lamb breast (lean)
Veal
Chicken
Duck
Turkey
Steak
Pork chop
Rabbit

Fish
Cod
Salmon
Plaice
Herring
Kipper
Mackerel
Pilchards
Tuna

Fruit
Bananas
Apricots (dried)
Prunes
Raisins

Vegetables and pulses
Spinach
Butter beans
Haricot beans
Mung beans
Red kidney beans
Chick peas
Peas
Broccoli florets
Brussels sprouts
Cabbage (red)
Cauliflower
Avocado
Leeks
Potatoes

Nuts
Hazelnuts
Peanuts
Walnuts

Other
Tomato purée
Bovril
Marmite
Beef extract
Milk (skimmed)
Milk (fresh whole)

FOODS CONTAINING **VITAMIN E** (PER 100 G/4 OZ)

	mg		mg
Oils		**Nuts**	
Cod liver oil	20.0	Almonds	20.0
Sunflower oil	48.7	Brazil nuts	6.5
Peanut oil	13.0	Hazelnuts	21.0
Olive oil	5.1	Peanuts	8.1
Meat		**Fruit**	
Lamb (cooked)	0.18	Blackberries (raw)	3.5
Lamb kidney	0.41	Blackcurrants	1.0
Pork (cooked)	0.12		
Chicken (roast meat)	0.11	**Vegetables**	
		Asparagus (boiled)	2.5
Eggs		Broccoli florets (boiled)	1.1
Eggs (boiled/poached)	1.6	Brussels sprouts (boiled)	0.9
		Parsley	1.8
Fish		Spinach (boiled)	2.0
Cod (baked)	0.59	Avocado	3.2
Halibut (grilled)	0.90		
Herring (grilled)	0.30		
Mussels (boiled)	1.2		
Salmon (canned)	1.5		
Tuna (canned in oil)	6.3		

FOODS CONTAINING IRON (PER 100 G/4 OZ)

	mg		mg
Cereals		**Nuts**	
Bemax (wheatgerm)	10.0	Almonds	4.2
Wheat bran	12.9	Brazil nuts	2.8
Rice	0.5	Coconut (fresh)	2.1
Meat		**Dairy**	
Beef (lean cooked)	1.4	Cheddar cheese	0.40
Rumpsteak (boneless			
sirloin) (lean, grilled)	3.5	**Vegetables and pulses**	
Lamb (lean, roast)	2.5	Haricot beans (boiled)	2.5
Lamb kidney	12.0	Mung beans (raw)	8.0
Pork (lean, grilled)	1.2	Red kidney beans	6.7
Pig liver (stewed)	17.0	Avocado	1.5
Veal	1.2	Lentils (boiled)	2.4
Chicken (dark meat)	1.0	Butter beans (boiled)	1.7
Chicken liver (fried)	9.1	Parsley	8.0
Bovril	14.0	Spring greens (boiled)	1.3
		Leeks (boiled)	2.0
Eggs			
Eggs, whole (boiled)	2.0	**Fruit**	
Egg yolk (raw)	6.1	Apricots (fresh)	0.4
		Bananas	0.4
Fish		Blackberries	0.9
Mackerel (fried)	1.2	Dates (dried)	1.6
Sardines (canned in oil)	2.9	Figs (dried)	4.2
Trout (steamed)	1.0	Sultanas (dried)	1.8
Crab (boiled)	1.3	Prunes	2.9
Prawns (boiled)	1.1	Raisins	1.6
Cockles (boiled)	26.0	Strawberries	0.7
Mussels (boiled)	7.7		
Oysters (raw)	6.0		
Scallops (steamed)	3.0		

FOODS CONTAINING **VITAMIN C** (PER 100 G/4 OZ)

	mg		mg
Dairy		**Fruit** (raw unless otherwise	
Fresh whole milk	1.5	stated)	
Natural yoghurt	0.4	Apples	10
		Apples (baked with sugar)	14
Vegetables		Apricots (fresh)	7
Asparagus (boiled)	20	Banana	10
Runner beans (boiled)	5	Blackberries	20
Broad beans (boiled)	15	Blackcurrants	200
Broccoli florets (boiled)	34	Gooseberries (stewed)	31
Brussels sprouts (boiled)	40	Grapes (white)	4
Cabbage, red (raw)	55	Grapefruit	40
Radishes	25	Guavas (canned)	180
Spinach (boiled)	25	Lemons (whole)	80
Peppers, green (boiled)	60	Lychees	40
Potatoes (baked)	5–16	Oranges	50
Watercress	60	Orange juice (fresh)	50
Cauliflower (boiled)	20	Peaches (fresh)	8
Spring greens	30	Pears (eating)	3
Avocado	15	Pineapple (fresh)	25
Leeks (boiled)	15	Plums	3
Lettuce	15	Raspberries	25
Mustard and cress	40	Rhubarb (stewed)	8
Onions (raw)	10	Strawberries	60
Spring onions (raw)	25	Coconut (fresh)	2
Parsley	150	Grapefruit juice	
Parsnips (boiled)	10	(unsweetened)	28
Peas, fresh (boiled)	10		

Meat
Lamb's kidney   9.0

Note: Nuts generally contain only a trace of vitamin C

FOODS CONTAINING **ZINC** (PER 100 G/4 OZ)

	mg		mg
Cereals		**Nuts**	
Wheat bran	16.2	Almonds	3.1
Wholemeal (wholewheat)		Brazil nuts	4.2
flour	3.0	Hazelnuts	2.4
		Peanuts	3.0
Dairy		Walnuts	3.0
Whole fresh milk	0.35		
Dried whole milk	3.2	**Fish**	
Dried skimmed milk	4.1	Cod (baked)	0.5
Cheddar cheese	4.0	Plaice (fried)	0.7
Parmesan cheese	4.0	Herring (grilled)	0.5
Yoghurt	0.60	Mackerel (fried)	0.5
		Salmon (canned)	0.9
Eggs		Sardines (canned in oil)	3.0
Eggs (boiled)	1.5		
Egg yolk (raw)	3.6	**Vegetables and pulses**	
Egg (poached)	1.5	Butter beans (boiled)	1.0
		Savoy cabbage (boiled)	0.2
Meat		Cabbage, red (raw)	0.3
Bacon (cooked)	0.8	Lentils, split (boiled)	1.0
Beef (lean roast)	6.8	Peas, fresh (boiled)	0.5
Lamb (cooked)	1.4	Lettuce	0.2
Lamb chops (lean only,		Spinach (boiled)	0.4
grilled)	4.1	Sweetcorn (boiled)	1.0
Pork (lean only, grilled)	3.5		
Chicken (roast meat)	1.4	**Other**	
Turkey (roast meat)	2.4	Ginger (ground)	6.8
Liver (fried)	6.0		

FOODS CONTAINING **CHROMIUM** (PER 100 G/4 OZ)

	micrograms		*micrograms*
Meat		**Fruit**	
Calves' liver	55	Apple	14
Chicken	15	Banana	10
Lamb chops	12	Orange	5
Pork chops	10	Strawberries	3
Eggs		**Vegetables**	
Hens' eggs	16	Cabbage	4
		Carrots	9
Fish		Fresh chilli	30
Scallops	11	Green beans	4
Shrimps	7	Green peppers	19
		Lettuce	7
Cereals		Mushrooms	4
Rye bread	30	Parsnips	13
		Potatoes	24
Dairy		Spinach	10
Milk	1		
Butter	13	**Other**	
		Brewer's yeast	112

FOODS CONTAINING **ESSENTIAL FATTY ACIDS**

Certain foods contain essential oils, which are helpful in maintaining skin quality and may also be of value in preventing heart disease and osteoporosis.

Omega-3 EFAs

Herring	Sardines	Walnuts
Mackerel	Sprats	Rape seed oil
Pilchard	Whitebait	Green vegetables
Salmon		

Omega-6 EFAs

Sunflower oil	Almonds	Some margarines
Safflower oil	Brazil nuts	
Corn oil	Walnuts	

ONE-WEEK SAMPLE MENUS
Dishes marked * are given in the recipe section.

DAY ONE
Breakfast
Jordans' Special Muesli or cornflakes with semi-skimmed
milk, and chopped banana or
other fruit
1 tablespoon Linusit Gold
Rooibosch Eleven O'Clock Tea

Lunch
Smoked mackerel pâté with
watercress, fennel and lemon
salad
Ryvita
Portion of grapes
Fennel tea

Dinner
Tofu, bean and herb stir-fry*
Tropical rice salad*
Broccoli and cauliflower
Rhubarb fool*
Raspberry and ginseng tea

DAY THREE
Breakfast
Oats (soaked overnight) with
sliced apple or chopped fresh
fruit and semi-skimmed milk
Oatcakes and low-sugar jam or
marmalade
Dandelion coffee

DAY TWO
Breakfast
Scrambled eggs or 2-egg omelette
with tomato and mushrooms
Ryvita and low-sugar jam
Barley cup

Lunch
Chickpea dips* with a selection
of fresh vegetable crudités and
wholemeal pitta bread
Slice of melon
Raspberry and ginseng tea

Dinner
Fish crumble* with braised fen-
nel, celery and mangetout
Rum and Raisin cheesecake*
Dandelion coffee

DAY FOUR
Breakfast
Wholewheat or corn and rice
pancakes* with dried fruit con-
serve*
Rooibosch Eleven O'Clock Tea

Lunch
Tuna jackets* with celery, fennel
    and walnut salad*
Fresh apple with honey
Lemon verbena tea

Dinner
Nut and vegetable loaf* with
    mustard sauce*
Courgette and cauliflower
Baked parsnips
Rhubard and Oat crumble*
Fennel tea

DAY FIVE
Breakfast
Glass of orange juice
Poached egg on toast with grilled
    tomatoes and mushrooms (or
    boiled egg followed by toast and
    low-sugar jam or marmalade)
Barley cup

Lunch
Asparagus consommé* with
    French bread
Beansprout salad*
Grilled grapefruit with brown-
    sugar topping
Fennel tea

Dinner
Snow peas with tiger prawns* and
    noodles, spring greens and baby
    sweetcorn
Caramel Custard*
Raspberry and ginseng tea

Lunch
Stir-fry vegetables* and rice
Live yoghurt with chopped pear
Ginseng tea

Dinner
Fragrant lamb*
Spring greens, green beans and
    rice or noodles
Banana and tofu cream*
Raspberry and gingseng tea

DAY SIX
Breakfast
Live yoghurt with chopped
    almonds and pecan nuts, raisins
    and grapes and 1 tablespoon
    linseeds
Toast with low-sugar jam
Rooibosch Eleven O'Clock Tea

Lunch
Liver pâte* with hot toast
Bean salad*
Peach or plums
Barley cup

Dinner
Crispy fried vegetables with garlic
    mayonnaise*
Brown rice and celery, fennel and
    walnut salad*
Carrot and date cake*
Fennel tea

DAY SEVEN
Breakfast
Fruit compote* or fresh fruit
   salad*
Toast and low-sugar marmalade
Fennel tea

Lunch
Oaty cheese quiche*
Ginger and carrot salad*
Green salad
Slice of melon
Rooibosch Eleven O'Clock Tea

Dinner
Chicken with ham and fennel*
   with noodles, Brussels sprouts,
   leeks and carrots
Rhubarb and ginger mousse*
Raspberry and ginseng tea

ONE-WEEK SAMPLE MENUS FOR VEGETARIANS
Dishes marked * are given in the recipe section.

DAY ONE
Breakfast
Glass of orange juice
Pancakes* with dried fruit con-
   serve*
Rooibosch Eleven O'Clock Tea

Lunch
Tofu with beansprout salad*
Pitta bread, Ryvita or alternative
   crackers
Fresh pineapple with soya yoghurt
Barley cup

DAY TWO
Breakfast
Jordans' Oat Crunchy with
   chopped banana, 1 tablespoon
   Linusit Gold and semi-
   skimmed milk
Dandelion coffee

Lunch
Herb tofu* with green beans and
   green salad
Fresh pear
Ginseng tea

215

Dinner
Crispy fried vegetables with garlic mayonnaise* and brown rice
Celery, fennel and walnut salad*
Carrot and date cake*
Barley cup

DAY THREE
Breakfast
Live yoghurt with chopped almonds and pecan nuts, raisins, grapes, sunflower seeds and 1 tablespoon linseeds
Rooibosch Eleven O'Clock Tea

Lunch
Chilled cucumber and ginger soup*
Bean salad*
Fresh orange
Raspberry and ginseng tea

Dinner
Vegetable lasagne*
Spring greens with mixed salad
Rhubarb fool*
Raspberry and ginseng tea

DAY FIVE
Breakfast
Oats (soaked overnight) with chopped mixed fresh fruit and nuts and semi-skimmed milk
Oatcakes and low-sugar jam

Dinner
Nut and vegetable loaf* with mustard sauce*
Braised fennel and celery with baked parsnips
Pistachio cream*
Fennel tea

DAY FOUR
Breakfast
Fruit compote* with soya yoghurt
Ryvita and low-sugar jam
Barley cup

Lunch
Chickpea dips* and a selection of raw vegetable crudités and corn chips (Nachips)
Fresh apple and honey
Fennel tea

Dinner
Nutty Quorn risotto*
Ginger and carrot salad* and braised celery
Walnut cheesecake*
Dandelion coffee

DAY SIX
Breakfast
Glass of orange juice
Cornflakes, chopped nuts, sliced pear and 1 tablespoon linseeds with semi-skimmed milk

Dandelion coffee

Toast or Ryvita and low-sugar marmalade
Rooibosch Eleven O'Clock Tea

Lunch
Cheese omelette
Beansprout salad*
Ryvita
Portion of grapes
Rooibosch Eleven O'Clock Tea

Lunch
Brown lentil Scotch eggs* with endive, fruit and nut salad*
Fruit compote* with soya yoghurt
Barley cup

Dinner
Tofu, bean and herb stir-fry*
Tropical rice salad* with broccoli and cauliflower
Caramel custard* with fresh strawberries
Raspberry and ginseng tea

Dinner
Red lentil and coconut smoothy*
Brown rice with baby sweetcorn, green beans or okra
Banana and tofu cream*
Raspberry and ginseng tea

DAY SEVEN
Breakfast
Fresh fruit salad*
Puffed rice, sunflower seeds, almonds and 1 tablespoon linseeds
Soya yoghurt
Dandelion coffee

Lunch
Cheese pots*
Celery, fennel and walnut salad*
Slice of melon
Fennel tea

Dinner
Bean and tomato hotpot*
Cabbage, leeks and carrots
Walnut, apple and brandy roulade*
Ginseng tea

EASY-OPTION LUNCHES (NOT AVOIDING GRAINS)
Sardines on toast
Peanut butter sandwich and fruit salad
French stick with mackerel and salad
Cheese sandwich and mixed salad
Raw vegetables with pitta bread and humus
Beans on toast and salad
Jacket potato with cheese or beans and salad
Mixed bean salad
Turkey salad sandwich
Stir-fry vegetables and rice
Soup and a salad
Omelette and salad
Fruit and nut salad and live yoghurt

EASY-OPTION DINNERS (NOT AVOIDING GRAINS)
Broccoli and cauliflower cheese with jacket potato
Grilled mackerel and salad
Pasta with tomato sauce, fresh herbs, pine kernels and Parmesan
    cheese
Grilled lamb or pork chops with vegetables
Fresh grilled sardines and salad
Stir-fry Quorn and vegetables with rice
Steak, chips and salad
Stir-fry vegetables and almonds with noodles
Stir-fry vegetables with prawns and rice
Hard-boiled egg and grated cheese salad
Mixed bean salad with wholemeal pitta bread
Tofu burgers and salad
Mackerel coated with rolled oats and grilled with green vegetables
    and salad

SNACK LIST
Ryvita and peanut butter or low-sugar jam

Fresh fruit, nuts and seeds
Nuts and raisins
Yoghurt (live or soya)

Fruit

Jordans' Oat and Nut Frusli Bars
Dried fruit bars like Granovita
La Fruit – dried fruit cubes

Raw vegetables and dips like humus or taramasalata
Pitta bread

Pasta or bean salad

BEVERAGE LIST

Hot
Rooibosch Eleven O'Clock Tea
Barley cup
Dandelion coffee (instant or root)
Fennel tea
Ginseng tea
Raspberry and ginseng tea

Other herbal teas and coffee
substitutes

No more than two cups of decaffeinated drinks per day.

Cold
Tap water or still bottled water
Small amount of carbonated water
Fruit juice watered down to taste
Small amounts of Appletise or similar drinks
Mixed fruit cocktails

Only very small amounts of alcohol as it may aggravate flushing
and impedes the absorption of most nutrients.

Nineteen

Option Three:
A Tailor-made Programme
for Severe Symptoms

Once you have chosen your programme you will need to follow it. That may sound a bit obvious, but it does take time to adjust to a new way of eating. Changing the habits of a lifetime is not always easy and initially you will need a good deal of discipline and will-power. If you choose Option 3, presumably it will be because you are suffering severely. In my experience of dealing with severe sufferers, their very suffering is enough to motivate them initially. When the symptoms get bad, most people are willing to make short-term sacrifices. It is the first month that is usually the most difficult. Not only do you have to discipline yourself to follow a new and different regime while you are still feeling rough, but also you may well encounter some withdrawal symptoms to foods and drinks that have become a habit.

Withdrawal symptoms may occur during the first few days on the programme and can sometimes last for as long as two weeks. Although you shouldn't definitely expect these, it's worth remembering that they are very common. Depriving the body of things it has grown used to sometimes causes it to 'bite back'. It may seem strange that this should occur as a result of dietary changes, but it's similar to the mechanism of withdrawing from drugs or alcohol. Because of this it's best to start your programme when you have a few quiet days or, better still, a quiet week. If you experience headaches or extra nervous tension or fatigue, you will be able to relax or lie quietly in a cool, darkened room.

Giving up tea and coffee, for example, may trigger off a

220

number of changes in your body. These may make you feel tired or uptight, anxious and on edge. Headaches may occur and, more often, the desire to eat seems to persist. You will be pleased to hear that all this settles down within days, certainly within a few weeks. Once you have passed through this stage, if it happens to you at all, life becomes much easier and before long you will notice new habit patterns forming. So much so that patients often prefer not to return to some of their former habits, simply because their tastes have changed! For example, they lose their desire for salty food and regular cups of strong coffee.

It is certainly worth persevering for there is light at the end of the tunnel. Our research proves this very strongly. We analysed the results of a group of fifty menopausal women who went through our four-month nutritional programme, making the recommended dietary changes and taking regular weight-bearing exercise. They also took the vitamin and mineral supplement Gynovite Plus. This particular nutritional supplement contains substantial quantities of the essential vitamins and minerals, particularly calcium and magnesium. The results of the analysis showed that just over 80 per cent of the women felt that their symptoms had been completely controlled or much improved by the nutritional programme. Only one woman in the sample felt that her symptoms had not been helped at all.

If I haven't put you off – let's get down to it! First, prepare a personal nutritional programme (see page 194). Read through the nutritional content of food lists starting on page 204 and, with the exception of any food or drink you decide to steer clear of, you can choose the foods and drinks you like, knowing they are high up in the important nutrients. As your symptoms are severe it would probably be a good idea initially to incorporate foods from all the nutrient lists. Then refer again to the chapters on supplement recommendations, exercise and stress and relaxation on pages 116, 131 and 145. Add on to your personal chart the supplements you decide to take and make a note of the exercise you intend to carry out each week. Note the actual exercise schedule as well as the *type* of exercise.

I have laid out sample menus and recipes for you to follow for one week. I have also outlined some simple alternatives in case you do not feel like cooking or have a hectic lifestyle. Many of the easy options are quick to prepare and are portable if you are eating lunch at work or away from home. If you are careful, you should be able to eat your way around most restaurant menus, but it may take you a while to get used to doing so.

Sensitivity to grains

There is evidence to show that many menopausal symptoms may be related to food sensitivity. Research suggests that a significant percentage of the population produce antibodies to some foods. In our experience, this may be only a temporary state of affairs that occurs when we are not in very good nutritional shape. Finding the right kind of diet for your body will help to overcome your symptoms. It's therefore worth avoiding certain groups of foods temporarily if you suffer with the symptoms in this section. Try to follow the recommendations closely: you will reap the benefit.

The most common sensitivity is to wholewheat and gains, and many symptoms such as irritability, abdominal bloating, constipation, diarrhoea, excessive wind, irritable bowel, fatigue and depression can be aggravated by eating foods containing them. Certain people react to wheat, oats, barley and rye and all foods made from or containing them. They are therefore better off avoiding them altogether initially until the symptoms are under control. It sounds a bit drastic, but there are many alternative foods that can be used instead.

BREAD
Both chemists and healthfood shops usually have some stocks of alternative grain products; in our experience, chemists are usually the most reasonably priced. They will usually hold a stock of products for people with gluten allergy.

Look out for some of the following products:

- Ener G white or brown rice bread (which toasts nicely)
- Glutafin wheat-free bread and rolls and Glutafin crackers
- Rice cakes

Home-made bread
Although I have not been very successful in making bread with
alternative flours, some of our patients have successfully experi-
mented. Recipes for potato and rice bread and for buckwheat
and rice bread are on pages 274–75.

PASTA
Although you will need to avoid pasta made with wheat, there
are many reasonable alternatives. Most of these are available
from healthfood shops, the Chinese supermarket or the pharma-
cist.

  Pastariso make brown rice spaghetti which is very acceptable slightly undercooked. They also make a range of other pastas. Although some healthfood shops do stock it, it is easier to order it from the chemist.

Glutafin have a range of pasta which is sometimes available in healthfood shops, and can also be ordered from the chemist.

Rice noodles are available in a wide variety from Chinese supermarkets. There are wide, flat rice noodles that resemble tagliatelli, spaghetti-like noodles, and the very skinny variety that only need soaking in a covered pan in boiling water for a few minutes. You will probably find that these are cheaper than the alternative pastas available from healthfood shops and chemists.

BREAKFAST CEREAL

Any rice or corn cereals will be fine, even the ordinary Rice Krispies and cornflakes from the supermarket, or the health food shop equivalent. Add some chopped fruit and crumbled nuts, perhaps a few seeds and a little dried fruit to make it a bit more wholesome. There are some alternative mueslis available, but they are usually very expensive for only a small packet.

HOME-BAKED FOODS

If you enjoy cooking there are plenty of very acceptable biscuits, cakes, pastries, sponges and pancakes you can make using alternative flours. If you have never used any of these before it may take you a little time to find the consistency that you like.

Sponge

Brown rice flour is probably the best for making sponge. Make it up to the weight given in the recipe by mixing it with a little ground almond and a raising agent (cream of tartar and bicarbonate of soda).

Raising agents

As baking powder contains wheat, you will need to use an alternative. Either use a combination of one part of bicarbonate of soda to two parts of cream of tartar, or use Glutafin wheat-free baking powder.

Savoury pancakes
These can be made with pure buckwheat flour. Buckwheat is part of the rhubarb family, and the flour tends to be quite heavy, but it can be mixed with a little white rice flour, which is very light.

Sweet pancakes
These are best made with a combination of brown rice flour or ground rice (purchased from a healthfood shop or Chinese supermarket) and cornflour. Use half cornflour and half rice flour to replace the normal quantity of flour in the ordinary pancake recipe.

Breadcrumbs or batter
A crisp coating for fish or meat can be made with maize meal, sold in healthfood shops. Coat the fish or meat with maize meal, then with beaten egg and once again with maize meal. You can then bake, grill or even fry the food which should emerge with a crispy coat.

Biscuits
There are varieties of biscuits that you can make using brown rice flour or ground rice and ground nuts or coconut. If you make plain biscuits you can flavour them with lemon or ginger. Our recipes for almond macaroons and coconut biscuits are very acceptable and at the same time more nutritious than the average biscuit as they are full of eggs and nuts. Make some and keep them in the freezer so that you can take a few out when you need something sweet to eat.

Other flours
There are many other flours you can use in your cooking. Gram flour made from chickpeas, potato flour, soya flour, tapioca flour and millet flour are all good examples. Glutafin make flour mixes for bread, pastry and cakes, as do True Free,

and these are available in some healthfood shops.

SHOP-BOUGHT BAKED GOODS
Acceptable cakes and biscuits can now be purchased in health-food shops and ordered from most chemists' shops. Glutafin have a range of biscuits, including digestives, and Rite-Diet have a range of biscuits and cakes. The coconut biscuits are the least sweet and the banana or lemon cakes are also worth trying, as are Granny Ann protein biscuits.

SNACKS
It's nice to have something to crunch on when you are avoiding wheat. There are lots of corn products available, but do remember to read the labels as some have added wheat. Try corn chips (Nachips), crisps and wafers and look in the Mexican section of the supermarket.

Assessing for grain sensitivity
You will need to become a nutritional detective by doing the following:

- Stop eating all the grains mentioned above (wheat, oats, barley, rye) for at least four, preferably six, weeks. You can eat one slice of French bread made with French flour each day if you are desperate! This may seem strange, as refined bread is nowhere near as nutritious as wholemeal. However, during the refining process most of the grain has been removed, so the degree of aggravation caused by this is far less than by a wholegrain loaf. It's better to manage on rice cakes or Glutafin crackers.
- After four or six weeks, or longer, when you feel that your symptoms have diminished, introduce the various grains one-by-one back into your diet. Begin just after your period, so that you don't confuse any reaction with menopausal symptoms. Choose one grain, like rye in the form of Ryvita. Introduce this into your diet and eat it for several days. If you have no reaction after five days, choose another grain and repeat the process. *Do not mix the grains* initially because if

226

you do get a reaction you won't know exactly what you have reacted to! Continue to do this with all the grains, providing you don't have reactions to any one of them. Try wheat last, as this grain causes most problems.

- Once you get used to using the alternatives you shouldn't find the diet difficult to maintain. If you are going to avoid certain groups of foods for any length of time, it's important to arm yourself with all the alternative foods you can muster. It's not a weight-loss diet (although you may lose weight on it if you are overweight) and you can literally eat as much as you like of the foods on your list. Never allow yourself to get hungry and never miss a meal. It's important to eat a steady flow of good nutrients to allow your hormone- and brain-chemical metabolism to function at its best.

WHAT TO DO IF YOU HAVE A REACTION
The reactions may include diarrhoea or constipation, excessive wind, abdominal bloating, headaches, weight-gain, fatigue, confusion, depression, mouth ulcers, skin rash, irritability and palpitations.

1 Once you have established what you have reacted to, make a note of it and avoid eating this food at all for the moment. This doesn't mean that you won't ever be able to eat this food again but it's best avoided for now.
2 Wait until your body has settled down again and then try another grain.

FOODS CONTAINING GRAINS
It's surprising how many foods contain grains. Before I began 'label-reading' I would never have believed the extent to which grains are used. It's a good exercise to go around the supermarket reading labels on packets to get an idea of this for yourself. Sometimes labels aren't as explicit as they might be and they just contain the words 'edible starch'. Regard this with suspicion if you are on a grain-free diet. The labelling of food in healthfood shops is usually more reliable and precise.

Wheat
The most obvious foods containing wheat are bread, biscuits, cakes, pasta, cereals, pastries and flour made from wheat, etc., but wheat is often present in prepared sauces, soups and processed foods in general, including sausages. Gluten-free products are not particularly recommended on a wheat-free diet, as some of them still contain wheat.

Oats
Porridge, oat cookies, oatcakes and oat flakes.

Rye
Rye bread (which may also contain wheat), Ryvita and pumpernickel.

Barley
Often found in packet or tinned soups and stews, and in barley beverages.

There are many lovely recipe books available with lots of ideas. These are listed in the recommended reading section on page 296. I have also prepared some sample menus to give you an idea of the scope possible. There are also a few guideline recipes included in the recipe section on page 235.

ONE-WEEK GRAIN-FREE SAMPLE MENUS
wheat, oats, barley and rye free
Dishes marked * are given in the recipe section, but many others are marked WOBR.

DAY ONE
Breakfast
Cornflakes or millet flakes with crumbled pecan nuts and raisins, chopped pear, 1 tablespoon Linusit Gold and semi-skimmed milk
Rice cakes and low-sugar jam
Rooibosch Eleven O'Clock Tea

DAY TWO
Breakfast
Puffed rice, chopped almonds, chopped banana and raisins with 2 tablespoons live yoghurt and semi-skimmed milk
Dandelion coffee

Lunch
Tuna jackets*
Mixed salad
Portion of grapes or fresh sliced
  apple with honey
Fennel tea

Dinner
Crispy fried vegetables with garlic
  mayonnaise*
Celery and alfalfa salad
Banana and tofu cream*
Raspberry and ginseng tea

DAY THREE
Breakfast
Scrambled eggs or 2-egg omelette,
  with tomatoes and mushrooms
Glutafin crackers and low-sugar
  jam
Chicory drink

Lunch
Chilled cucumber and ginger
  soup*
Bean salad*
Fresh orange
Raspberry and ginseng tea

Dinner
Chicken with almonds*
Sauté potatoes, spring onions and
  carrots
Fruit compote* with yoghurt or
  soya ice cream
Raspberry and ginseng tea

Lunch
Cream of watercress soup*
Ginger and carrot salad*
Beansprout salad*
Fresh fruit salad*
Rooibosch Eleven O'Clock Tea

Dinner
Plaice with oranges*, with mashed
  swede, braised celery and carrot,
  turnip and broccoli
Rhubarb and ginger mousse*
Fennel tea

DAY FOUR
Breakfast
Fresh fruit salad* with chopped
  nuts, raisins and linseeds with
  live yoghurt
Fennel tea

Lunch
Cheese pots*
Mixed salad
Slice of melon
Dandelion coffee

Dinner
Salmon steaks with ginger*
Braised fennel, peas and new pota-
  toes
Rhubarb fool*
Raspberry and fennel tea

DAY FIVE
Breakfast
Corn and rice pancakes* with dried fruit conserve* or stewed apple and live yoghurt
Dandelion coffee

Lunch
Fish soup*
Watercress, fennel and lemon salad

Slice of melon
Fennel tea

Dinner
Nut and vegetable loaf* with mustard sauce*
Broccoli and braised fennel
Corn and rice pancakes with raspberries
Raspberry and ginseng tea

DAY SEVEN
Breakfast
Boiled or poached egg
Alternative toast and low-sugar marmalade
Rooibosch Eleven O'Clock Tea

Lunch
Asparagus consommé*
Tropical rice salad*
Fresh orange
Fennel tea

Dinner
Noisettes of lamb with cumin and garlic*

DAY SIX
Breakfast
Live yoghurt with chopped fruit and nuts and linseeds
Chicory drink

Lunch
Brown lentil Scotch eggs*
Endive, fruit and nut salad*
Fresh apple and honey
Fennel tea

Dinner
Prawn provencale* with rice noodles, spinach and cauliflower
Walnut, apple and brandy roulade*
Dandelion coffee

Brussels sprouts, leeks, turnip and
  baked parsnips
Cinnamon rhubarb*
Raspberry and ginseng tea

EASY-OPTION LUNCHES (WHEAT, OATS, BARLEY AND RYE FREE)
Raw vegetables and dips e.g. humus, taramasalata
Jacket potato with cheese and salad
Tinned mackerel and salad
Cold meat and salad
Beans on alternative toast
Stir-fry vegetables and rice
Soup and salad
Omelette and salad
Rice salad with nuts
Fruit and nut salad with live yoghurt
Mixed bean salad

EASY-OPTION DINNERS (WHEAT, OATS, BARLEY AND RYE FREE)
Grilled mackerel with salad
Corn pasta with tomato sauce, pine kernels and fresh herbs
Grilled lamb or pork chops with vegetables
Grilled fresh sardines with salad
Stir-fry Quorn and vegetables with rice
Stir-fry vegetables and almonds with rice noodles
Stir-fry prawns and vegetables with rice
Hard-boiled egg and grated cheese salad
Greek salad with pine nuts
Steak, chips and salad
Mixed bean salad with rice salad
Prepared Quorn and sweetcorn escalopes (frozen) with vegetables
Salmon with new potatoes and salad
Broccoli and cauliflower cheese (made with cornflour) and
  jacket potato
Grilled gammon and pineapple and vegetables

SNACK LIST (REDUCED-GRAIN)
Rice cakes or Glutafin crackers and peanut butter or low-sugar jam

231

Fresh fruit, nuts and seeds
Nuts and raisins
Yoghurt (live or soya)
Fruit

Dried fruit bars like Granovita
La Fruit – dried fruit cubes

Raw vegetables and dips like humus or taramasalata with corn
  wafers (Nachips)

Corn pasta or rice salad

BEVERAGE LIST (REDUCED GRAINS)

Hot
Rooibosch Eleven O'Clock Tea
Dandelion coffee (instant or root)
Fennel tea
Ginseng tea
Raspberry and ginseng tea
Chicory drink

Other herbal teas

Cold
Bottled water
Fruit juice
Aqua Libra or Amé
Small amounts of carbonated water with fruit juice, like Irish
  Spring, Appletise etc.

Will you be on a restricted diet for ever?
There seems to be a definite difference between a 'food allergy'
and a 'food sensitivity'. We often find that severe menopause
cases are suffering from food sensitivity rather than actual
allergy, although there are cases where women are violently
allergic to certain types of food.

Realistically, if you are suffering with severe symptoms, you need to give your body a complete rest for a minimum of two to three months. We often find it takes as much as six months to a year before the body is really back to normal and can once again cope fully with foods that have been eliminated.

If you notice unpleasant side-effects occurring when you begin to reintroduce the grains, one-by-one, discontinue them for another month or two before attempting to reintroduce them again. Usually, the very fact that there is so much progress occurring is an incentive to continue with the nutritional programme.

Occasionally we have found that some women have what seems to be a permanent allergy to a particular food which when reintroduced continues to make them feel very unwell. In these cases the women themselves usually decide that it's better to be well and do without the food in question than to suffer unnecessarily.

All the women who go through the programme cheat at some point. Not only do we expect it, we also think it's a positive step. It's only when you have put the system to the test yourself that you really begin to follow it because you believe in it rather than because someone else said it might work.

You begin to feel so well on the diet that you start to doubt that you really have food sensitivities. So you decide to blow the diet. You eat and enjoy one or two days' helpings of the 'forbidden fruit'. Sometimes the symptoms return within an hour or two, sometimes they creep on within a day or so; either way, you have the symptoms back again and you remember what it was like to feel so unwell. You now realize that dietary factors and your symptoms are clearly related. So it's back on the diet with a far more self-determined resolution not to cheat.

What about the long term?
Once you have followed the dietary and supplement recommendations closely for three or four months and you have noticed a substantial improvement, you can then start to relax a bit. As long as you follow the basic recommendations most of the time,

the occasional indulgence should not hurt. Make sure it's only occasional to begin with and preferably not when you have a heavy schedule or pressing engagements. The dietary regime should be followed and the supplements taken until you feel your symptoms are well under control, which may take as little as three or four months or as long as nine months to a year. Once your menopause symptoms are under control, if you cannot or do not intend to take HRT, then you should continue with the supplements that are intended to help bone-regeneration. It's important to ease off the diet slowly, as a sudden withdrawal can often lead to recurrence of the symptoms.

Occasionally, months after completing your programme, symptoms may recur. If you suspect they are, take some speedy action to get them under control again. Times of great stress and general illness may, in some circumstances, place extra nutritional demands on your body and this may bring on some of the old symptoms. Should this happen, return to the basic diet for a few months until things have settled down.

Twenty

Nutritious Recipes

It is important to think carefully about the method of cooking, as so many vital nutrients may be lost in the cooking process.

- Steam, stir-fry or grill for preference, and with as little extra fat as possible. Shallow- and deep-frying are the least healthy cooking methods as they use a lot of fat
- Boiling is another method to be avoided if you can. With vegetables in particular, you can expect to lose over 50 per cent of the nutrients in the water
- Vegetables are a special case: steam them *over* boiling water, or cook gently in a very little water
- If you cook vegetables in *boiling* water from the start, you will lose less nutrients than if you started with cold water
- Baking, braising and roasting are also acceptable ways of cooking. Again, use as little fat as possible
- Braise prepared vegetables, on top of the stove or in the oven, in as little liquid as possible, only until they are al dente. You can add flavourings (such as garlic, onion, herbs, spices, seeds etc.) if you like
- One way of preserving most of a food's nutrients is by using a pressure-cooker

The recipes following include a selection of soups, salads, fish, meat and poultry, cheese and vegetables, desserts, and some breads and cakes. They should give you a fair idea of the sort of things you can still enjoy even when you are cutting down on or eliminating certain foods. All are suitable for those of you who are moderate sufferers; if you are cutting out grains, you can tell at a glance the recipes which are suitable for you. These are marked with the code WOBR, or similar. This means that the recipe is Wheat, Oat, Barley and/or Rye free.

SOUPS

Chilled Cucumber and Ginger Soup WOBR
SERVES 4

1 cucumber
4cm (1¹/₂ inch) piece of peeled fresh ginger
1 spring onion, white part only
300ml (¹/₂ pint) milk
900ml (1¹/₂ pints) vegetable or chicken stock
freshly ground pepper

Garnish
Cucumber slices

1. Chop the cucumber into chunks.
2. Grate the ginger and slice the spring onion.
3. Put all the ingredients except for the pepper into a blender, and process until smooth.
4. Season to taste and chill.
5. Serve garnished with slices of cucumber.

Variation
100g (4oz) of white crab meat can be stirred in just before serving to give an oriental flavour to this light spicy soup.

Asparagus Consommé
SERVES 4–6

WOBR

olive oil for frying
1 small Spanish onion, peeled and sliced
675g (1¹/₂lb) green asparagus
2¹/₂ tablespoons coriander seeds, crushed
1 litre (1³/₄ pints) good chicken stock
salt and freshly ground pepper
lemon juice
finely grated Parmesan cheese

1. Heat a little olive oil in a large saucepan, add the onion and cook gently until soft but not coloured.
2. Cut the tips from the asparagus and reserve.
3. Chop the rest of the asparagus spears and add to the saucepan with the coriander seeds. Cover the saucepan and stir occasionally for 4–5 minutes then stir in the stock and 300ml (¹/₂ pint) water.
4. Simmer gently for about 10–20 minutes until the asparagus is tender.
5. Purée the soup then pass through a sieve. Leave to cool, then cover and chill.
6. Taste, adjust seasoning and add a little lemon juice to 'lift' the flavour. Chill again.
7. Steam the reserved asparagus tips until tender.
8. Serve the soup spooned over the asparagus tips in chilled shallow bowls, with just a little freshly grated Parmesan sprinkled over.

Cream of Watercress Soup WOBR
SERVES 4–6

2 bunches watercress
1 leek
25g (1oz) butter
600ml (1 pint) light stock (or water and a chicken stock cube)
salt and cayenne pepper
25g (1oz) cornflour
5 tablespoons double or whipping cream
croûtons

1. Wash the watercress, and remove the stalks.
2. Chop the leek and sauté in the butter for 10 minutes. Do not brown. Add the watercress and saute for 2–3 minutes.
3. Add the stock and seasonings, and simmer for 30 minutes.
4. Mix the cornflour with a little water, and stir carefully into the soup to thicken it a little.
5. Liquidize the soup and then reheat to serve. Adjust seasonings.
6. Add the cream, but do not reboil. Serve with croûtons.

Fish Soup WOBR
SERVES 6

1.8 litres (3 pints) fish stock
4 medium onions, peeled and finely chopped
freshly ground black pepper
1 tablespoon paprika
900g (2 lb) filleted white fish cut into 5cm (2 inch) pieces
1 red chilli, seeded and finely chopped
1 medium green pepper, seeded and thinly sliced
5 tablespoons soured cream

1. Bring the fish stock to the boil.
2. Reduce the heat, add the onions, pepper and paprika, and stir well.
3. Cover the pan and simmer the mixture for an hour, or until the onions are soft.

4. Remove the pan from the heat and strain the mixture. Discard any pulp left in the strainer.
5. Add the fish to the strained stock and bring to the boil. Add the chilli and green pepper, reduce the heat and simmer for 15–20 minutes or until the fish flakes easily when tested with a fork.
6. Transfer the soup to a warmed tureen. Stir in the soured cream and serve immediately.

SALADS

Watercress, Fennel and Lemon Salad   WOBR
SERVES 4

1 large fennel bulb, thinly sliced
1 small bunch watercress, washed and trimmed
a handful of fresh parsley, washed, dried and finely chopped
freshly ground black pepper
1 tablespoon lemon juice
1/2 lemon, thinly sliced

1. Mix together the fennel, watercress and chopped parsley.
2. Add the black pepper and the lemon juice.
3. Cut each lemon slice into segments, and add to the salad.

Celery, Fennel and Walnut Salad   WOBR
SERVES 2

3 celery sticks
1 fennel bulb
50g (2oz) shelled walnuts
dressing of choice (see method)
freshly ground black pepper

1. Chop the ingredients, then mix them together.
2. Sprinkle with oil and fruit dressing (see page 242), or with walnut oil. Season with black pepper to taste.

Endive, Fruit and Nut Salad   WOBR
SERVES 4–6

2 heads curly endive (frisée)
3 oranges
25g (1oz) flaked almonds
25g (1oz) shelled walnuts, chopped
2 apples, cored and sliced into small segments
75g (3oz) seedless grapes
1 tablespoon lemon juice
dressing of choice (or see page 242)

1. Separate the endive leaves, wash and dry thoroughly. Tear the leaves into pieces and place in a salad bowl.
2. Grate the rind of one of the oranges into a bowl. Remove the peel and pith from all the oranges, divide them into segments and place in a separate bowl.
3. Mix together the almonds, walnuts, apple, grapes and lemon juice, and add to the oranges. Mix well.
4. Place the fruit and nut mixture in the bowl on top of the endive. Chill before serving with a dressing of your choice, sprinkled with the grated orange rind.

Bean Salad   WOBR
SERVES 4 AS A SIDE SALAD

100g (4oz) podded broad beans
100g (4oz) canned red kidney beans
100g (4oz) haricot beans, soaked overnight
100g (4oz) chickpeas, soaked overnight
1 bay leaf
2 sprigs fresh thyme
1 clove garlic, peeled and crushed (optional)
2 tablespoons cold-pressed olive or vegetable oil
2 tablespoons finely chopped parsley
1/2 teaspoon cumin seeds, ground
1 medium onion, peeled and finely chopped

1. Cook the broad beans for 5 minutes, then drain and cool. If large, take off the outer skin to reveal the green inner bean. Rinse and drain the kidney beans.
2. Drain the haricot beans and chickpeas and cover with water in a saucepan. Boil for 10 minutes and then add the bay leaf and sprigs of thyme and simmer for 1–1½ hours. Drain and leave to cool.
3. Mix the garlic with the oil and kidney and broad beans. Pour over the remaining beans.
4. Add and mix in the parsley, cumin seeds and onion.

Beansprout Salad   WOBR
SERVES 4 AS A SIDE SALAD

175g (6oz) beansprouts
100g (4oz) red pepper, seeded and sliced
100g (4oz) canned sweetcorn, drained
50g (2oz) sprouted alfalfa
2 apples, shredded or grated
50g (2oz) sprouted soya beans
4 spring onions

1. Toss all the ingredients together lightly in a salad bowl.

Tropical Rice Salad   WOBR
SERVES 4–6

175g (6oz) American long-grain rice
½ teaspoon ground turmeric
450ml (¾ pint) vegetable stock
2 ripe bananas
2 tablespoons lemon juice
½ pineapple, peeled, cored and chopped
100g (4oz) sultanas
½ cucumber, cubed

1. Put the rice, turmeric and vegetable stock in a saucepan and bring to the boil. Reduce the heat and simmer for 10–15 minutes. Drain thoroughly and allow to cool.
2. Peel and slice the bananas and toss in the lemon juice.
3. Mix the rice, bananas, pineapple, sultanas and cucumber together, and put in a salad bowl.

Ginger and Carrot Salad WOBR
SERVES 4 AS A SIDE SALAD

175g (6oz) carrots, grated
2 medium apples, grated
1 teaspoon ground ginger
1 celery stick, chopped

1. Toss together and serve.

Basic Dressing WOBR

2 tablespoons red or white wine vinegar
salt and freshly ground black pepper
4 tablespoons good olive oil

1. Mix the vinegar with seasonings to taste, and then whisk in the olive oil, until the simple dressing is well emulsified.

Oil and Fruit Dressing WOBR
MAKES 75ML (2½ FL OZ)

2 tablespoons olive oil
1 tablespoon sesame oil
1 teaspoon mayonnaise
1 teaspoon mustard
juice of 1 lemon or 1 tablespoon white wine vinegar
1 teaspoon concentrated apple juice (optional)
freshly ground black pepper to taste

1. Blend all the ingredients together until smooth.
2. This dressing keeps well in the fridge in a sealed container.

FISH, POULTRY AND MEAT

Salmon Steaks with Ginger   WOBR
SERVES 2

2 salmon steaks
2 tablespoons lemon juice
2.5cm (1 inch) square of fresh ginger, peeled and finely chopped
freshly ground black pepper to taste

1. Place each salmon steak on a large piece of foil. Add 1 tablespoon lemon juice and half the chopped ginger to each steak. Season with a little black pepper.
2. Wrap the steaks individually in foil to make two parcels and bake in a preheated oven at 180°C (350°F) Gas 4 for 20 minutes. Serve hot with vegetables or cold with salad.

Plaice with Orange   WOBR
SERVES 2

1 large plaice, filleted
salt and freshly ground pepper
juice of 1/2 lemon
2 oranges
25g (1oz) margarine
150ml (1/4 pt) mayonnaise
paprika
1/2 tin anchovy fillets
watercress

1. Cut the fillets in half lengthwise (i.e. 4 pieces of fish). Season with salt, pepper and lemon juice.
2. Finely grate rind of 1/2 orange over fish.
3. Fold fillets over and put into a buttered Pyrex dish. Squeeze

the juice of the ½ orange over. Cover. Bake in the oven preheated to 180°C (350°F) Gas 4 for 10–15 minutes. Leave to become cold.

4. Add the finely grated rind and juice of the second ½ orange to the mayonnaise (drip the juice in slowly).
5. Place the fillets on to a serving dish, and coat with the orange mayonnaise.
6. Wash the anchovies to remove oil and excess salt. Garnish the fish with the anchovies, the remaining orange cut in slices, and the watercress.

Fish Crumble   OBR
SERVES 2

200g (7oz) cod fillet
1 small onion, peeled and sliced
1 carrot sliced
75g (3oz) green beans, sliced
3 fresh tomatoes, skinned and sliced
1 clove garlic, peeled and finely chopped
½ teaspoon chopped fresh basil
1 teaspoon chopped fresh parsley
freshly ground black pepper
1 tablespoon cornflour
1 tablespoon water

Crumble
25g (1oz) wholemeal flour
25g (1oz) plain flour
4 teaspoons margarine

1. Remove the skin from the fish, and cut the fish into strips about 3.5cm (1½ inches) across.
2. Place the onion, carrot, beans, tomatoes, garlic, basil and parsley in a saucepan. Add the fish and pepper to taste.
3. Bring the mixture to the boil, cover and reduce the heat. Simmer for 12–15 minutes.

4. Blend the cornflour to a paste with the water and stir into the fish mixture. Bring to the boil, then transfer to a deep ovenproof dish.
5. To make the crumble topping, rub the two flours and margarine together until the mixture resembles breadcrumbs.
6. Sprinkle the crumbs over the fish mixture and bake for 20–25 minutes at 180°C (350°F) Gas 4.

Snow Peas with Tiger Prawns WOBR
SERVES 4

450g (1lb) snow peas (mangetout)
450g (1lb) uncooked tiger prawns
375g (13oz) broad oriental rice noodles
1 teaspoon finely chopped root ginger
3 tablespoons sesame oil
2 tablespoons oyster sauce
1 teaspoon sugar
1 tablespoon sherry or white wine
fresh coriander leaves

1. Top and tail the snow peas and wash them.
2. Clean and wash the prawns and pat them dry with kitchen paper.
3. Place the noodles in boiling water and simmer gently for 3 minutes, until slightly undercooked.
4. Place the ginger and the oil in a wok and heat. Fry the snow peas briefly in the hot oil, stirring constantly. Remove and place on a warmed dish.
5. Place the tiger prawns in the wok and cook until they become pink.
6. Drain the noodles and rinse with cold water to remove the starch.
7. Return the snow peas to the wok with the prawns, add the oyster sauce and the sugar, and simmer for another minute or two.

8. Gently pour the sherry or white wine around the circumference of the wok, and then remove peas and prawns from the wok with a slotted spoon and transfer to a dish.

9. Place noodles in the wok and quickly stir-fry them in the remaining oil, turning constantly. Turn out on to a flat platter and place the snow peas and prawns on the top. Decorate with fresh coriander and serve immediately.

Variation
If you like spicy food, before stir-frying the noodles, mix 1 teaspoon chilli sauce with the hot oil and then place the noodles in the wok.

Prawn Provençale   WOBR
SERVES 4

675g (1¹/₂lb) peeled prawns
50g (2oz) margarine
2 tablespoons olive oil
4 shallots, peeled and finely chopped
1 garlic clove, peeled and crushed (optional)
6 tomatoes, blanched, skinned and chopped
50g (2oz) tomato purée
1 teaspoon dried thyme
1 pinch dried basil
freshly ground black pepper

1. In a large frying pan heat the margarine with the oil. Add the shallots and garlic and fry them for 4 minutes.

2. Add the skinned tomatoes, tomato purée, thyme, basil and pepper to taste. Cover the pan, reduce the heat to low and simmer for 20 minutes.

3. Stir in the prawns and cook uncovered for a further 4 minutes. Remove from the heat and serve at once.

Tuna Jackets   WOBR
SERVES 4

1 tablespoon sunflower oil
1 red, 1 yellow and 1 green pepper, cored, seeded and diced
4 tablespoons white wine vinegar
2 tablespoons wholegrain mustard
1 x 200g (7oz) can tuna in oil, drained and flaked
1 x 100g (4oz) can sweetcorn, drained
4 hot baked potatoes
freshly ground black pepper

1. Heat the oil in a pan, add the diced pepper and sauté for 5 minutes.
2. Add the vinegar and mustard and cook for 5 minutes, stirring. Stir in the flaked tuna and sweetcorn.
3. Cut the tops off the potatoes and scoop out the centres. Chop the potato centres and stir into half the pepper relish mixture. Season with black pepper to taste.
4. Spoon the potato mixture back into the potato jackets. Serve the remaining relish separately.

Smoked Mackerel Pâté   WOBR
SERVES 4

50g (2oz) vegetable margarine
225g (8oz) smoked mackerel fillets, skinned and any bones removed
juice of 1/2 orange
1 teaspoon tomato purée
1 teaspoon white wine vinegar
freshly ground black pepper to taste

1. Beat the margarine until very soft, then put in a blender or food processor with the remaining ingredients. Purée until smooth.
2. Spoon the pâté into 4 individual dishes or ramekins and chill before serving with pitta bread or crudités.

Chicken with Almonds   WOBR
SERVES 4

4 chicken breasts
15g (¹/₂oz) butter or margarine
150ml (¹/₄ pint) water
a few black peppercorns
75g (3oz) flaked almonds

1. Skin the chicken and brush with melted butter or margarine.
2. Place water and peppercorns in an ovenproof dish. Place the chicken in the water and cover with foil. Bake for 15 minutes in the preheated oven at 180°C (350°F) Gas 4.
3. Remove the foil and sprinkle with flaked almonds. Return to the oven for a further 15 minutes, or until the chicken is tender and the almonds have browned.
4. Serve with steamed vegetables, e.g. new potatoes and broccoli.

Chicken with Ham and Fennel   WOBR
SERVES 4

1.6kg (3¹/₂lb) oven-ready chicken
1 fennel bulb
10 fresh bay leaves
50g (2oz) butter, softened
2–3 garlic cloves, peeled
1 strip lemon zest
175g (6oz) cooked ham, cut into fingers
1¹/₂tablespoons black peppercorns, coarsely crushed
salt
4 tablespoons brandy

1. If using a clay pot, soak it in water for 15 minutes.
2. Separate the layers of fennel roughly. Place fennel and 6 of the bay leaves in the clay pot or a casserole.
3. Rub the chicken with butter, and stuff with garlic, lemon zest and ham. Sprinkle the bird liberally with the peppercorns

and a little salt and place in the pot. Cover and cook for 40 minutes in the oven preheated to 200°C (400°F) Gas 6.

4. Turn the chicken, basting with butter. Cook for a further 40 minutes.

5. Uncover the pot, baste the chicken with juices and leave breast upwards to brown for 15 minutes.

6. Pour the juices into a saucepan. Keep the chicken in the pot or casserole somewhere warm.

7. Warm the brandy, set it alight and pour into the saucepan. When the flames have died down, boil the juices hard to emulsify.

8. Remove the chicken from the pot, garnish with the ham from the cavity and the remaining fresh bay leaves. Pour sauce around and serve immediately.

Noisettes of Lamb with Cumin and Garlic   WOBR
SERVES 3–4

1 best end of neck, boned and cut into 6–8 noisettes
2 teaspoons finely chopped fresh ginger
3–4 garlic cloves, peeled and crushed
2 tablespoons ground cumin
3 tablespoons olive oil
salt and freshly ground pepper

Garnish
pomegranate seeds
cooked couscous or burgul, studded with raisins
chopped chives

1. Combine the ginger, garlic, cumin, oil and seasonings in a bowl and coat the lamb in this on all sides. Marinate in fridge for up to 3 hours.

2. Place the noisettes on a roasting rack and roast in the oven preheated to 200°C (400°F) Gas 6 for 15–25 minutes depending on size, until brown on the outside but still pink in the centre.

3. Serve the noisettes with pomegranate seeds and raisin-studded couscous or burgul (cracked wheat). Garnish with chives.

Fragrant Lamb   WOBR
SERVES 6

2–3lb (1–1.5kg) fillet end of leg of lamb
3 tablespoons sesame oil
1 clove garlic, chopped
1cm (¹/₂ inch) piece root ginger, chopped
1 spring onion
1–2 tablespoons light soy sauce
2 tablespoons brandy
3 tablespoons white wine
freshly ground black pepper
1 teaspoon cornflour
fresh coriander

1. Seal the lamb briefly in the hot sesame oil.
2. Remove and place in a pressure cooker with the sesame oil, garlic, ginger, spring onion, soy sauce, brandy and white wine, and season with black pepper.
3. Close the pressure cooker and bring to the boil. Lower the heat and cook for 35 minutes. Alternatively, place the ingredients plus 150ml (¹/₄ pint) water in a covered dish and bake for about 1¹/₂–2 hours at 180°C (350°F) Gas 4; check liquid during cooking, adding water if needed.
4. Remove the pressure cooker from the heat and cool under running water. Place the leg of lamb on a chopping board and slice. Arrange on a serving dish, cover loosely with foil and keep warm while preparing the sauce.
5. Drain the meat juices from the pressure cooker or dish, strain into a clean pan and mix with the cornflour. Over a moderate heat thicken the sauce, stirring constantly.
6. Remove the lamb from the oven, and pour the sauce over it. Decorate with fresh coriander and serve immediately.

Liver Pâté OBR
SERVES 4–6

225g (8oz) lambs' liver, cut into small pieces
slices of streaky bacon sufficient to line tin
50g (2oz) butter
1 small onion, peeled and chopped
100g (4oz) streaky bacon, chopped
2 level teaspoons plain flour
4 tablespoons milk
1 thick slice white bread or 40g (1¹/₂oz) breadcrumbs
salt and freshly ground pepper
garlic salt (optional) or 1 clove garlic, peeled and crushed

1. Remove the rind from the lining bacon slices, then stretch and use to line a small bread tin or a 600ml (1 pint) ovenproof dish.
2. Melt the butter, and fry the onion and chopped bacon gently for 5 minutes.
3. Put the onion, bacon and liver into the liquidizer.
4. Stir the flour into the remaining fat to make a roux, then slowly whisk in the milk to make a sauce.
5. Add this sauce and the breadcrumbs to the mixture in liquidizer, and blend for 30 seconds. Season with salt, pepper and garlic.
6. Place in the prepared bacon-lined container. Put into a bain-marie containing 2cm (³/₄ inch) cold water. Cook in the centre of the oven preheated to 180°C (350°F) Gas 4 for 40 minutes. Leave in the tin to cool.
7. Turn out when cold. Garnish with salad ingredients, olives or gherkins and serve with slices of hot toast.

CHEESE AND VEGETABLES

Cheese Pots   WOBR
SERVES 2

1 pear, diced
1 apple, diced
1 celery stick, chopped
finely chopped chives
2 teaspoons lemon juice
225g (8oz) Lancashire cheese
paprika
chopped parsley

1. Mix together the pear, apple, celery and chives.
2. Toss in the lemon juice.
3. Divide between 2 individual dishes, and crumble the cheese over the fruit.
4. Place under a hot grill for 5–10 minutes until golden brown.
5. Sprinkle with paprika and chopped parsley.

Chickpea Dips   WOBR
SERVES 8

2 x 425g (15oz) cans chickpeas, drained and rinsed
1 garlic clove, peeled and crushed
1 tablespoon fresh lemon juice
25ml (1 fl oz) olive oil
175ml (6 fl oz) Greek plain yoghurt
freshly ground black pepper
4 teaspoons freshly chopped parsley
2 teaspoons tomato purée

To garnish and serve
sprigs of parsley
strips of red pepper
pieces of sliced lemon
a selection of raw vegetables (peppers, radishes, carrots, celery and cucumber)

1. Place the chickpeas in a blender or food processor and blend until smooth.
2. Add the garlic, lemon juice, olive oil and yoghurt and mix well. Add black pepper to taste.
3. Transfer one-third of the mixture to a small serving bowl – this will remain plain. Divide the rest between another 2 small mixing bowls.
4. Add the chopped parsley to one of these, stir well and transfer to a small serving bowl.
5. Add the tomato purée to the other, stir well and transfer to a small serving bowl. Adjust the seasoning if necessary.
6. Garnish the herb dip with sprigs of parsley, the tomato dip with red pepper and the plain dip with pieces of lemon.
7. Chop the raw vegetables into sticks. Arrange on a serving dish around the dips.

Stir-fry Vegetables   WOBR

There are many different combinations of vegetable in season that can be used for stir-frying. You can use six or seven different vegetables, or only two or three. To obtain the best results, stir-fry vegetables should be cooked with the minimum oil at a high heat, as rapid cooking seals in the flavour.

There are many nice last-minute additions to your stir-fry. Experiment to find your favourite seasoning and flavouring. Less well-known ingredients are available from healthfood shops.

Seasonings
Salt, pepper, chilli, grated ginger, five-spice powder (use very moderately), sesame seeds (ground), fenugreek (ground), turmeric, coriander, paprika, nori seaweed (toasted and crumbled).

Flavourings
Shoyu/tamari, miso, soy sauce (all Japanese/Chinese condiments made from soya beans), sesame oil, tahini (sesame seed butter), sherry, vermouth, lemon juice.

SERVES 4 WITH NOODLES OR RICE

450g (1lb) fresh broccoli
225g (8oz) cauliflower
1 tablespoon oil
2.5cm (1 inch) fresh root ginger, sliced and finely shredded
2 large carrots, peeled and sliced
1/2 teaspoon sesame oil
225g (8oz) fresh beansprouts
225g (8oz) Chinese leaves or white cabbage, shredded
1/2 teaspoon salt

1. Separate the broccoli heads into small florets and peel and slice the stems. Separate the cauliflower florets and slice stems.
2. Heat the oil in a large wok or frying pan. When it is moderately hot add ginger shreds. Stir-fry for a few seconds.
3. Add the carrots, cauliflower and broccoli and stir-fry for 2–3 minutes, then add the sesame oil, beansprouts and Chinese leaves or white cabbage. Stir-fry for further 2–3 minutes.
4. Season to taste, and serve at once.

Garlic can be substituted for ginger, and soy sauce can be added in final stage of frying before serving.

Crispy Fried Vegetables with Garlic Mayonnaise
WOBR

SERVES 4

500g (1lb) vegetables (aubergine, celeriac, courgettes,
cauliflower florets, Jerusalem artichokes, fennel, mushrooms,
parsnip etc.)
vegetable oil for deep frying

Batter
2 eggs, separated
300ml (1/2 a pint) ale
25g (1oz) butter, melted
175g (6oz) corn or rice flour
freshly ground pepper
1 teaspoon dry mustard

Garlic Mayonnaise
150ml (1/4 pint) mayonnaise
2 tablespoons double cream
2 cloves garlic, peeled and crushed
1 tablespoon chopped mixed herbs
freshly ground pepper

1. Use the courgette and mushrooms raw. Prepare the other vegetables as appropriate, then steam or boil until half cooked. Cut into pieces the size of medium mushrooms.
2. Mix the egg yolks and ale together, add the butter, and beat until smooth.
3. Gradually beat in the flour and seasonings, then fold in the egg whites, beaten until stiff.
4. Dip each vegetable into the batter and fry in hot oil until golden and crisp. Drain on kitchen paper and serve hot.
5. Mix all the ingredients for the mayonnaise together and spoon into a serving dish.

Brown Lentil Scotch Eggs   WOBR
SERVES 4

1½ tablespoons sunflower oil
2 large onions, peeled and finely chopped
1 garlic clove, peeled and crushed
175g (6oz) brown lentils, cooked and drained well
1 tablespoon dried oregano
1 tablespoon basil
1 tablespoon lemon juice
freshly ground black pepper to taste
1 egg, beaten
4 small eggs, hard-boiled and shelled
1 tablespoon sesame seeds

1. Heat half the oil in a frying pan and gently fry the onions for 6–8 minutes.
2. Add the garlic, lentils, oregano, basil, lemon juice and black pepper, and mix well with a fork until the mixture binds together. If necessary, add some of the beaten egg.
3. Dip each boiled egg into the beaten egg mixture and cover with one quarter of the lentil mixture. Brush again with beaten egg and roll in seeds. Repeat this procedure with each egg.
4. Cut 4 squares of foil, large enough to wrap each egg in. Brush each of these squares with the remaining oil, then wrap around the eggs. Place on a baking tray and bake in the preheated oven at 180°C (350°F) Gas 4 for 15 minutes.
5. Remove the foil carefully and serve the eggs hot or cold.

Nutty Quorn Risotto WOBR
SERVES 4

225g (8oz) brown rice
1 tablespoon sunflower oil
1 medium onion, peeled and chopped
1 garlic clove, peeled and crushed
1 red pepper, seeded and sliced
1 green pepper, seeded and sliced
50g (2oz) green beans
100g (4oz) carrots, cut into matchsticks
100g (4oz) courgettes, thinly sliced
100g (4oz) broccoli, broken into florets and stalk sliced
225g (8oz) Quorn, chopped
1 small seedless orange, peeled and segmented
1 tablespoon flaked almonds
1 tablespoon fresh chopped parsley

1. Cook the rice as directed on the packet and put to one side.
2. Heat the oil in a large frying pan and add the onion, garlic, red and green peppers and fry gently for 2–3 minutes.
3. Steam the beans, carrots, courgettes, and broccoli over a pan of boiling water for 5 minutes (alternatively miss the steaming if you like your vegetables crunchy). Add to the other ingredients in the frying pan.
4. Add the Quorn, orange segments, flaked almonds, parsley and rice and heat through until all the ingredients are hot. Serve immediately.

Bean and Tomato Hotpot   WOBR
SERVES 4

2 tablespoons sunflower oil
2 onions, peeled and sliced
3 carrots, sliced
2 celery sticks, sliced
1 large leek, sliced
2 garlic cloves, peeled and crushed
1 x 425g (15oz) can red kidney beans, drained
1 x 400g (14oz) can tomatoes
300ml (¹/₂ pint) stock
1 tablespoon yeast extract
freshly ground black pepper
675 (1¹/₂lb) potatoes, peeled and thinly sliced
15g (¹/₂oz) margarine

1. Heat the oil in a flameproof casserole, add the onions and fry
   for 5 minutes. Add the carrots, celery, leek and garlic and fry
   for a further 5 minutes.
2. Add the kidney beans, tomatoes with their juices, stock,
   yeast extract and pepper to taste. Mix well.
3. Arrange the potatoes neatly on top, sprinkling pepper
   between each layer. Dot with the margarine, cover and cook
   in the oven preheated to 180°C (350°F) Gas 4 for 2 hours.
4. Remove the lid 30 minutes before the end of cooking to
   allow the potatoes to brown.

Oaty Cheese Quiche

BR

SERVES 4–6

Pastry
75g (3oz) self-raising flour
150g (5oz) fine oatmeal
freshly ground black pepper
100g (4oz) vegetable margarine

Filling
350g (12oz) cottage cheese, sieved
2 tablespoons natural yoghurt
6 celery sticks, chopped
75g (3oz) shelled hazelnuts, chopped
a pinch of curry powder.

Garnish
a pinch of paprika
tomato slices
parsley sprigs

1. To make the pastry, mix the flour and oatmeal together with freshly ground pepper to taste. Cut in the margarine and rub in until the mixture resembles breadcrumbs. Stir in enough water to make a fairly stiff pastry and knead together lightly.
2. Turn on to a floured surface, roll out and use to line a 23 cm (9 inch) flan tin. Cover the base with greaseproof paper and fill with dried beans. Bake 'blind' in the preheated oven at 200°C (400°F) Gas 6 for 20 minutes. Remove the paper and beans and return the flan to the oven for 5 minutes. Allow to cool.
3. Mix the cheese, yoghurt, celery, nuts and curry powder together and pile into the flan case. Sprinkle with paprika and garnish with tomato and parsley.

Vegetable Lasagne   OBR
SERVES 6

1 carrot, peeled and chopped
1 large onion, peeled and sliced
1 red pepper, seeded and chopped
1 green pepper, seeded and chopped
1 large aubergine, cut into chunks
225g (8oz) button mushrooms, sliced
1 large courgette, sliced
2 tablespoons olive oil
1 garlic clove, peeled and crushed
1 tablespoon paprika
2 teaspoons dried marjoram
2 x 400g (14oz) cans chopped tomatoes
2 tablespoons tomato purée
2 bay leaves
freshly ground black pepper
350g (12oz) fresh lasagne
900ml (1 1/2 pints) béchamel sauce (see page 262)
3 tablespoons freshly grated Parmesan or Cheddar cheese
  (optional)

1. Heat the oil in saucepan. Add the garlic, carrot, onion and peppers and fry for 1–2 minutes. Add paprika, marjoram and aubergine. Fry for 1– 2 minutes.
2. Add the mushrooms and courgette to the pan with the tomatoes and juices, tomato purée, bay leaves and black pepper. Bring to the boil, reduce the heat, cover and simmer for 30 minutes.
3. Spread a small amount of the tomato sauce in the base of a 3 litre (5 pint) ovenproof dish. Cover with a layer of lasagne and top with a layer of béchamel sauce. Repeat these layers once more, finishing off with a layer of béchamel sauce.
4. Sprinkle with the cheese if using. Bake in the preheated oven at 190°C (375°F) Gas 5 for 45–50 minutes until well browned.

Nut and Vegetable Loaf   WOBR
SERVES 4–6

2 teaspoons sunflower oil
1 small onion, peeled and chopped
1 small carrot, chopped
1 celery stick, chopped
1 tablespoon tomato purée
225g (8oz) tomatoes, skinned and chopped
2 eggs
1 tablespoon chopped parsley
freshly ground black pepper
225 (8oz) shelled nuts, finely chopped or minced

Garnish
onion rings
parsley sprigs

1. Heat the oil in a pan, and cook the onion, carrot and celery until softened. Add the tomato purée and tomatoes and cook for 5 minutes.
2. Put the eggs, parsley and pepper to taste in a bowl and beat well. Stir in the nuts and vegetables.
3. Transfer to a greased 900ml (1½ pint) ovenproof dish and bake in the oven preheated to 220°C (425°F) Gas 7 for 30–35 minutes.
4. Turn out and decorate with onion rings and parsley. Serve hot with vegetables and the following mustard sauce, or cold with salad.

Mustard Sauce   WOBR
SERVES 4–6

If you use only the margarine, cornflour (or ordinary flour if you are not avoiding grains) milk and seasonings, you will have a béchamel sauce to use in the lasagne on page 260.

1 tablespoon margarine
1 garlic clove, peeled and crushed
1¹/₂ tablespoons cornflour
freshly ground black pepper to taste
300ml (¹/₂ pint) milk
1 tablespoon prepared French or German mustard
1 tablespoon lemon juice

1. Melt the margarine in a saucepan over a moderate heat. Add the garlic and cook for 4 minutes.
2. Remove the pan from the heat and stir in the cornflour with a wooden spoon. Add the pepper and make into a smooth paste. Gradually stir in the milk, beating well to avoid lumps.
3. Stir in the mustard thoroughly.
4. Return the sauce to a low heat and cook for 3–4 minutes until it has thickened. Do not let the sauce boil.
5. Remove the pan from the heat and stir in the lemon juice. Pour into a sauce boat and serve immediately.

Tofu, Bean and Herb Stir-fry   WOBR
SERVES 4

2 tablespoons vegetable oil
275g (10oz) tofu (bean curd) drained, dried and cut into cubes
2 garlic cloves, peeled and crushed
350g (12oz) green beans
3 tablespoons chopped fresh herbs (thyme, parsley, chervil and chives)
4 spring onions, thinly sliced
2 tablespoons soy sauce

1. Heat 1 tablespoon of oil in a wok or frying pan. When hot, add the tofu and garlic and stir-fry for 2 minutes. Lift out with slotted spoon and drain.
2. Heat the remaining oil in the pan and when hot add the green beans and stir-fry gently for 4–5 minutes.
3. Add the herbs, spring onions and soy sauce, and stir-fry for a further minute.
4. Return the tofu to the pan and heat through for 1 minute, then serve immediately.

Herb Tofu   WOBR
SERVES 2

1 dessertspoon vegetable oil
1 small red pepper, seeded and thinly sliced
1 garlic clove, peeled and crushed
175g (6oz) tofu, cubed
1/2 tablespoon chopped parsley

1. Heat the oil in a frying pan. Add the red pepper and garlic, and fry for 2–3 minutes.
2. Add the tofu and parsley and continue to stir-fry until the tofu is heated through. Serve immediately.

Red Lentil and Coconut Smoothy   WOBR
SERVES 4

225g (8oz) red split lentils
100g (4oz) carrots, sliced
1 medium onion, peeled and finely chopped
1 garlic clove, peeled and crushed
1 teaspoon paprika
1/2 teaspoon ground ginger
1 bay leaf
1/2oz (15g) creamed coconut, finely chopped
2 tablespoons lemon juice
freshly ground black pepper to taste

1. Wash the lentils and put in a large saucepan with the carrot, onion, garlic, paprika, ginger, bay leaf and 600ml (1 pint) water. Bring to the boil and remove any scum. Cover the pan and simmer for 25–30 minutes until the water has been absorbed.
2. Remove the bay leaf and mash the mixture into a smooth paste with a fork. Add the coconut, lemon juice and black pepper.
3. Serve hot with vegetables and rice.

DESSERTS

Pancakes with Lemon and Sugar   OBR
SERVES 4

100g (4oz) wholemeal (wholewheat or buckwheat) flour
1 egg, size 3
300ml (¹/₂ pint) skimmed milk
sunflower oil

To serve
caster sugar
lemon juice

1. Make a thin batter with the flour, egg and milk.
2. Grease a small frying pan lightly with oil, and put in 2 tablespoons of batter at a time. Swirl the pan around so the batter covers the entire bottom of the pan.
3. Cook until golden, then flip over with a spatula, and cook the other side for a few seconds.
4. Keep warm in a folded teatowel while you make the remaining 7 pancakes.
5. Sprinkle each pancake with sugar and lemon juice and roll up.

Alternative fillings
Put 1 teaspoon low-calorie jam or 1 tablespoon stewed fruit or dried fruit conserve (see page 271), in the centre of each pancake, and roll up.

Corn and Rice Pancakes WOBR
SERVES 4

50g (2oz) cornflour
50g (2oz) rice flour
300ml (¹/₂ pint) milk
1 egg
vegetable oil

1. Blend the flours, milk and egg in the liquidizer.
2. Grease a griddle or frying pan with a little oil and fry pancakes as described in the recipe on page 264.

Rhubarb and Oat Crumble WBR
SERVES 4–6

900g (2 lb) fresh rhubarb
100g (4oz) brown sugar
50g (2oz) butter
100g (4oz) rolled oats
25g (1oz) sunflower seeds
25g (1oz) mixed chopped nuts
1 teaspoon mixed spice
1 teaspoon ground cinnamon

1. Peel and chop the rhubarb, and cook in a saucepan with 75g (3oz) of the sugar until tender. Place in a suitable ovenproof dish.
2. Rub together the butter and oats, then mix in the remaining sugar, sunflower seeds and mixed nuts. Sprinkle over the rhubarb.
3. Bake in the preheated oven at 180°C (350°F) Gas 4 for 20 minutes, or until golden brown on the top. Serve hot, with fresh cream or yoghurt.

Cinnamon Rhubarb   WOBR
SERVES 2

300g (11oz) rhubarb
4 tablespoons water
a pinch of ground cinnamon
40–50g (1¹/₂–2oz) granulated or muscavado sugar

1. Peel and chop the rhubarb, and put in a saucepan with the water, cinnamon and sugar, and stew until the rhubarb is tender.
2. Spoon into dishes and serve.

Fruit Compote   WOBR
SERVES 6

175g (6oz) dried apricots
100g (4oz) dried prunes
100g (4oz) dried figs
100g (4oz) dried apples
600ml (1 pint) apple juice
¹/₂ teaspoon mixed spice
25g (1oz) coarsely chopped walnuts

1. Place the dried fruits in a bowl with apple juice and mixed spice and leave to soak overnight.
2. Transfer to a saucepan and simmer for 15 minutes. Divide between 4 separate dishes and sprinkle with walnuts.
3. Serve hot or cold with cream or yoghurt.

Fresh Fruit Salad WOBR
SERVES 4

1 dessert apple, peeled, cored and sliced
1 banana, peeled and sliced
4 tablespoons lemon juice
1 orange, peeled and segmented
1 grapefruit, peeled and segmented
100g (4oz) seedless grapes
2 kiwi fruits, peeled and sliced
2 tablespoons orange juice
4 sprigs fresh mint

1. Toss the apple and banana in the lemon juice. This will prevent discoloration.
2. Combine all the fruits in a serving bowl. Serve chilled and decorated with the sprigs of mint.

Rhubarb Fool WOBR
SERVES 2

225g (8oz) rhubarb
25g (1oz) margarine
15–25g (¹/₂–1oz) brown sugar
200g (7oz) natural yoghurt

1. Peel and chop the rhubarb.
2. Melt margarine in a pan, add the rhubarb and sugar, and cook until tender. Cool.
3. Purée the rhubarb and yoghurt together in a blender. Chill before serving.

Rhubarb and Ginger Mousse WOBR

SERVES 4

450g (1 lb) rhubarb
juice and grated rind of 1/2 orange
3 tablespoons clear honey
1/4 teaspoon ground ginger
2 teaspoons gelatine powder
2 tablespoons water
2 egg whites

1. Peel the rhubarb and chop into 2.5cm (1 inch) pieces. Put into a pan with the orange juice, rind, honey and ginger and simmer gently until the fruit is soft.
2. Dissolve the gelatine in the water, in a bowl standing in hot water. Stir until the gelatine is dissolved.
3. Add the gelatine to the fruit and beat until smooth. Cool until the mixture is half set.
4. Whisk the egg whites until stiff and fold them lightly into the half set rhubarb mixture.
5. Spoon into decorative glasses and chill until set.

Banana and Tofu Cream WOBR

SERVES 4

200g (7oz) firm tofu
200g (7oz) bananas, peeled and sliced
75g (3oz) ground almonds
a pinch of ground cinnamon
2 teaspoons almond flakes

1. Blend or process the tofu and bananas together. To obtain a creamy texture the mixture may need to be put through a sieve or food mill.
2. Add the ground almonds and mix well.
3. Spoon into 4 bowls or glasses, and sprinkle lightly with cinnamon and a few almond flakes.

Pistachio Cream

WOBR

SERVES 6–8

350g (12oz) unsalted pistachio nuts, shelled
7 egg yolks
65g (2¹/₂oz) caster sugar
a pinch of salt
500ml (17 fl oz) milk
a drop of vanilla essence

1. Boil the pistachios in water for 2–3 minutes, then drain and refresh in cold water. Dry well, and then peel off the skins.
2. Beat the egg yolks, sugar and salt together in a bowl until thick and pale. Scald the milk with the vanilla essence (i.e. bring it just up to the boil).
3. Pour the hot milk into the egg yolk mixture, mix thoroughly, then transfer to a clean saucepan. Stir gently over a gentle heat – do not boil – until the custard coats the back of a wooden spoon.
4. Pour into the food processor, add the pistachios, and process until smooth. Chill until required.

Caramel Custard   WOBR
SERVES 4

Caramel
100g (4oz) granulated sugar
6 tablespoons water
1 tablespoon hot water

Custard
4 eggs
1 tablespoon caster sugar
450ml (3/4 pint) milk
2–3 drops vanilla essence

1. Put the sugar and water for the caramel into a small saucepan. Dissolve the sugar over a gentle heat, stirring occasionally. *Do not boil.*
2. Wrap a folded tea-towel round a 600ml (1 pint) soufflé dish to protect the hands.
3. When all the sugar has dissolved, boil the syrup until it turns a rich brown. At once add the hot water and pour it into the dish. Turn the dish round slowly to coat the base and sides with caramel. Leave to become cold.
4. Beat the eggs and sugar together. Warm the milk until it steams. Stir the heated milk into the beaten egg, add the vanilla. Strain the custard into the soufflé dish.
5. Cover with a piece of greased greaseproof paper and put into a bain-marie. Bake in the preheated oven at 160°C (325°F) Gas 3 for about 1 hour. Test for set with a knife. When set remove from the oven, and allow to become cold.
6. To turn out, loosen the top edge all round with a finger, then tilt the bowl to let the custard draw away from the sides. Invert the serving dish over the custard then turn out on to the dish. Lift the soufflé dish off carefully.

Dried Fruit Conserve

WOBR

SERVES 2

200g (7oz) dried apricots
apple juice

Flavourings
1 teaspoon orange-flower water
or
1 teaspoon grated orange peel
or
50g (2oz) flaked almonds

1. Soak the apricots overnight in apple juice.
2. Put the apricots into a saucepan and just cover them with apple juice, using the minimum amount to ensure a thick purée. Simmer them, uncovered, for about 30 minutes or until they are thoroughly cooked and soft.
3. Cool and thoroughly blend or sieve them until they have a smooth, thick consistency.
4. Add one of the flavourings.
5. The purée will keep in the refrigerator for about 10 days.

Rum and Raisin Cheesecake OBR
SERVES 8

Base
100g (4oz) flour (or rice flour or banana flour if avoiding grains)
50g (2oz) margarine or butter
25g (1oz) ground almonds
25g (1oz) sugar
a pinch of salt
1 egg
2 tablespoons milk

Filling
50g (2oz) raisins
1 tablespoon rum
225g (8oz) Philadelphia or curd cheese
40g (1¹/₂oz) butter or margarine
20g (³/₄oz) ground almonds
2 eggs
70g (2¹/₂oz) sugar
1 egg to glaze

1. Rub the fat into the flour, then add the ground almonds, sugar and salt. Bind with the egg and milk.
2. Knead lightly, roll out and use to line a 23 cm (9 inch) flan tin or sandwich tin. Line with foil and baking beans. Save the pastry trimmings.
3. Bake in the preheated oven at 180°C (350°F) Gas 4 until golden and crisp, about 15 minutes. Remove foil and beans and bake for a further 5– 10 minutes.
4. Soak the raisins in rum while the pastry is baking and the rest of filling is being made.
5. Combine the cheese, butter, almonds, egg and sugar in a liquidizer, then fold in the rum and raisins.
6. Fill the pastry case with the cheese mixture. Use the pastry trimmings to make a lattice pattern across the top.
7. Bake for 20 minutes at 190°C (375°F) Gas 5. Brush entire surface with beaten egg and bake for 10 minutes longer until golden brown.

Walnut Cheesecake   WOBR
SERVES 8

675g (1¹/₂lb) curd cheese
75g (3oz) soft brown sugar
3 eggs, lightly beaten
100g (4oz) shelled walnuts, finely chopped
2 tablespoons rice flour

Decoration
walnut halves
icing sugar
mint leaves

1. Line a 23cm (9 inch) spring-release cake tin with silicone paper.
2. Put the curd cheese, sugar, eggs, walnuts and flour into a bowl and mix until smooth and creamy.
3. Pour into the prepared tin, level the top and bake for 40 minutes in the oven preheated to 180°C (350°F) Gas 4 until set and lightly browned. Leave in the tin until cold.
4. Remove from the tin carefully and decorate with walnut halves, icing sugar and mint leaves. Serve with melba or fruit sauce if you like.

Walnut, Apple and Brandy Roulade   WOBR
SERVES 4–6

4 eggs, separated
100g (4oz) caster sugar
225g (8oz) shelled walnuts, finely chopped

Filling
15g (¹/₂oz) unsalted butter
1 cooking apple, peeled, cored and sliced
15g (¹/₂oz) caster sugar
a pinch of ground cinnamon
200ml (7 fl oz) double cream
brandy

1. Line a Swiss roll tin with silicone paper, and preheat the oven to 190°C (375°F) Gas 5.
2. Whisk the egg whites until stiff, then fold in the egg yolks, caster sugar and chopped nuts. Spread the mixture into the Swiss roll tin evenly. Bake for 20 minutes until firm and golden. Allow to cool before filling and rolling.
3. For the filling, melt the butter in a saucepan, stir in the apple, sugar and cinnamon and cook, stirring from time to time, until the apples are just transparent. Set aside and cool.
4. Whip the cream until thick. Flavour with brandy to taste.
5. Turn the roulade base out on to sugared greaseproof paper, and gently peel off the baked silicone. Release the sides first so as not to break them. Spread the brandy cream evenly over the sponge leaving a 2.5 cm (1 inch) border clear at either end.
6. Now spread the apple mixture over the top and using the greaseproof as support, carefully roll up the roulade. Set aside in the fridge before serving in thick slices.

BREAD AND CAKES

Buckwheat and Rice Bread   OBR
MAKES 2 LOAVES

This makes brown bread which is crisp on the outside and soft on the inside.

350g (12oz) buckwheat flour
175g (6oz) brown rice flour
1¹/₂ packets easy-blend yeast
1 teaspoon sugar
1 tablespoon vegetable oil
¹/₂–1 teaspoon salt
300–350ml (10–12 fl oz) hand-hot water

1. Mix together the flours and the easy-blend yeast.
2. Add the sugar, oil and salt and mix to a thick batter with the hand-hot water.

3. Grease and flour 2 x 450g (1 lb) loaf tins. Divide the mixture between the two tins, cover and leave to rise in a warm place for 20–30 minutes.

4. Bake the loaves in the preheated oven at 230°C (450°F) Gas 8 for 35–40 minutes. The bread will slightly contract from the side of the tins when it is cooked.

5. Cool for 5 minutes in the tins and then turn out on to a wire rack. Slice when cold.

Potato and Rice Bread   WOBR
MAKES 2 LOAVES

This is a white bread which is delicious when freshly baked and subsequently makes very nice toast. It tastes rather like crumpets.

275g (10oz) potato flour
225g (8oz) brown rice flour
1¹/₂ packets easy-blend yeast
1 teaspoon sugar
1 tablespoon oil
¹/₂–1 teaspoon salt
300-350ml (10–12 fl oz) hand-hot water

1. Mix, prove, bake and cool in exactly the same way as the buckwheat and rice bread above.

Potato Shortbread   WOBR
MAKES 8 SLICES

175g (6oz) potato flour
100g (4oz) margarine
50g (2oz) sugar
75g (3oz) ground almonds

1. Put all the ingredients into a food processor and beat together for 5–6 seconds. Scrape the bowl and repeat the process until a ball of dough is formed.

2. Put the dough in a greased 17.5–20cm (7–8 inch) round sandwich tin and press down evenly.
3. Mark out portions with a knife, prick all over and bake in the preheated oven at 180°C (350°F) Gas 4 for 35–40 minutes.
4. Cut into wedges and leave to cool in the tin.

Carrot and Date Cake   OBR
MAKES ABOUT 16 SLICES

100g (4oz) carrots, peeled
100g (4oz) dates, stoned
¹/₄teaspoon sunflower oil
50g (2oz) low-calorie margarine
6 tablespoons honey
175g (6oz) plain granary flour
1 level teaspoon bicarbonate of soda
¹/₂ level teaspoon baking powder
¹/₂ level teaspoon ground cinnamon
1 egg, size 3
125ml (4 fl oz) skimmed milk
3 tablespoons unsweetened orange juice

1. Line a 15cm (6 inch) square tin with greaseproof paper and brush with a little oil. Preheat the oven to 180°C (350°F) Gas 4.
2. Place the margarine and honey in a small pan and warm until melted.
3. Finely grate the carrots and chop the dates.
4. Mix together the flour, bicarbonate of soda, baking powder and cinnamon.
5. Beat the egg with the milk and orange juice until blended, then add to the honey and margarine mixture.
6. Stir all the ingredients together' gently until thoroughly mixed, then pour into the tin. Bake in the preheated oven for 1 hour. Cool on a wire rack.

Apple and Cinnamon Cake

WOBR

MAKES 8 GOOD-SIZED SLICES

4 large cooking apples
225g (8oz) brown rice flour
4 large eggs
100g (4oz) ground almonds
100g (4oz) caster sugar
100g (4oz) soft margarine
a few drops of almond essence
1 tablespoon ground cinnamon

Garnish
about 16 apple slices
1/2 tablespoon ground cinnamon
1 tablespoon caster sugar

1. Grease a deep 20cm (8 inch) loose-bottomed circular cake tin. Preheat the oven to 150°C (300°F) Gas 2.
2. Peel, core and slice the apples and leave to soak in cold water.
3. Place the flour, eggs, ground almonds, caster sugar, margarine and almond essence in the bowl of a mixer and beat until light and fluffy.
4. Line the cake tin with approximately 1½in (3.75cm) of mixture. Place most of the garnish apples in the tin and sprinkle with cinnamon and sugar. Spread the additional mixture on to the top of the apples and smooth off the top ready for decoration.
5. Gently push the remaining apple slices into the top of the cake in a circle and sprinkle with cinnamon and sugar.
6. Bake in the preheated oven for at least 1 hour until cooked through. Cool briefly, then gently ease the cake out of the tin and on to a plate.
7. Serve hot as a pudding or cold as a cake with whipped or pouring cream.

Almond Macaroons   WOBR
MAKES 18

2 large egg whites
175g (6oz) ground almonds
75g (3oz) caster sugar
18 almond halves

1. Put the unbeaten egg whites into a bowl with the ground almonds and beat well, adding the caster sugar 1 tablespoon at a time.
2. Line biscuit trays with greaseproof paper. With moist hands roll the mixture into balls and flatten with the palm of your hand.
3. Lay the flattened biscuits carefully on to the trays and place an almond half in the middle of each biscuit.
4. Bake in the oven preheated at 180°C (350°F) Gas 4 for 25 minutes or until golden brown.
5. Keep in an airtight tin or freeze.

Coconut Pyramids   WOBR
MAKES ABOUT 24

4 egg yolks or 2 whole eggs
75g (3oz) caster sugar
juice and rind of 1/2 lemon
225g (8oz) desiccated coconut

1. Beat the egg yolks and sugar together until creamy.
2. Stir in the lemon juice, rind and coconut.
3. Form into pyramid shapes either with your hands or using a moist egg cup and place on a greased baking tray.
4. Bake in the preheated oven at 190°C (375°F) Gas 5 until the tips are golden brown.
5. Keep in an airtight tin or freeze.

Postscript

As we now live on average to the ripe old age of eighty-three, there is still a lot of living to be done. If you think of the average lifespan in terms of the months of the year, you are, roughly speaking, currently experiencing 'the summer of your life'. Put in those terms it doesn't sound so bad. Although you may have had your share of 'cloudy' days, the chances are that you will soon emerge from the tunnel, feeling healthier, mentally stronger and physically fitter than you have for years.

Life is about give and take – no doubt you have come to realize that by now – and the same applies at the time of the menopause. There are swings and roundabouts; and what you lose on the youth and beauty stakes you gain with the wisdom of your years and in terms of freedom.

Going through 'the change' is nature's way of helping you to adjust, both physically and mentally. Time always allows us to acclimatize to changes. The menopause is a time for reflection and consideration of what you intend to do with the rest of your life. Having dedicated yourself to others' needs, both at home and at work, it may feel somewhat unrealistic to suddenly think about your own. Well, it is the 'change', isn't it?

These are *your* years and they stretch out before you. This is new territory for women and it's up to you to set the scene both for yourself and for future generations.

Having the privilege to reach your fifties, you can now contemplate your future with optimistic expectation. You need to give considerable thought to what you would like to achieve. Many options will present themselves, bringing with them new horizons. At the time of the menopause, after careful evaluation, women boldly make changes: they go back to college to study

279

subjects they had never dreamed about, they make work and lifestyle changes, become volunteers or start new careers. The common denominator is that they have all focused on a direction that appeals to them, rather than going through the motions to please others. These are years of new-found freedom and independence: your future is what you make it.

If you choose a 'natural' menopause you will undoubtedly feel that you are in the driving seat. As a result, you will feel a great sense of achievement for having made the journey without swallowing remedies from the pharmaceutical industry. But it's your menopause and it's up to you to decide whether you want to help yourself by following the natural approach or whether you want a little extra hormonal help in the short-term.

In our experience postmenopausal women become a force to be reckoned with. With new strength and spirit they unknowingly become respected and admired 'towers' in society. They manage to find themselves again after years of being absent. Be as positive as you can while you are making your voyage. Make time for regular rest, relaxation, exercise and most of all time to reflect about what you are aiming for in life. If you are in good physical and spiritual shape, it's yours for the making.

Good luck.

APPENDICES

Appendix 1

Further Help and Telephone Advice Lines

If you would like to attend one of the WNAS clinics or need further details about our telephone and postal courses of treatment, you can write to the WNAS at the address below with a large self-addressed envelope and four separate first-class stamps. Please state clearly that you require information about our menopause services, as we help women with all sorts of other problems.

I should also be interested to hear about your success using the recommendations in this book.

The address to write to is:

Women's Nutritional Advisory Service
PO Box 268
Lewes
East Sussex BN7 2QN

All clinic appointments are booked on 0273–487366.

We also have a number of advice lines you may be interested in listening to:

Overcome Menopause Naturally	0839 556602
The Menopause Diet Line	0839 556603
Overcome PMS Naturally	0839 556600
The PMS Diet Line	0839 556601
Beat Sugar Craving	0839 556604
The Vitality Diet Line	0839 556605
Overcoming Breast Tenderness	0389 556606

Overcome Period Pains Naturally	0839 556607
Get Fit for Pregnancy and Breastfeeding	0839 556608
Skin, Nail & Hair Signs of Deficiency	0839 556609
Improve Libido Naturally	0839 556610
Beat Irritable Bowel Syndrome	0839 556611
Overcome Fatigue	0839 556612
Beat Migraine Naturally	0839 556613
Overcome Ovulation Pain	0839 556614
Directory	0839 556615

Appendix 2
Dictionary of Terms

ABBREVIATIONS
g = gram, mg = milligram (1000 mg = 1g), mcg = microgram
(1000 mcg = 1 mg), IU = international unit, kj = kilojoule

Abdomen The cavity between the lower ribs and pelvis in which the ovaries and womb are contained

Acute A term applied to a disease with a rapid onset or brief duration

Adrenal glands The adrenal glands are two small glands situated at the top of the kidneys. They produce several different hormones, most of which are steroid hormones. Hormones from the adrenal glands influence the metabolism of sugar, salt and water and several other functions.

Aldactone This is a diuretic drug which helps fluid retention. It inhibits the action of aldosterone, a hormone from the adrenal glands. It is also known as spironolactone

Aldosterone This is a steroid hormone produced by the adrenal glands which is involved in salt and water balance. When it is produced in excess it causes the body to hold water and sodium salt

Allergy An unusual and unexpected sensitivity to a particular substance which causes an adverse reaction. Foods, chemicals and environmental pollutants are common irritants and they may cause a whole range of symptoms including headaches, abdominal bloating and discomfort, skin rashes, eczema and asthma

Antibody A specific form of blood protein able to counteract the effects of bacterial antigens or toxins

Amenorrhoea A complete absence of periods

285

Amino acids   Chains of building blocks which combine together to form the proteins that make living things. There are some twenty or more amino acids, some essential, some non-essential

Anti-depressants   These are drugs used to suppress symptoms of depression

Bone mineral density   Measurement of the mineral density of the bone, usually the neck of the femur or a lumbar vertebra (bone inside back) using specialized X-rays. It is an important assessment of the bone strength and likelihood of fracture

Cancer   A general term to describe malignant growths in tissue, which are not encapsulated but infiltrate into surrounding tissue

Candida albicans   A yeast-like fungus occurring in moist areas of the body such as the skin folds, mouth, respiratory tract and vagina

Carbohydrates   Carbohydrates are the main source of calories (kjs) in almost all diets. Complex carbohydrates are essential nutrients and occur in the form of fruits, vegetables, pulses and grains. They are important energy-giving foods. There are two sorts of complex carbohydrates: the first are digestible, such as the starches, and the second are not digestible and are more commonly known as 'fibre'

Refined carbohydrates   These consist of foods that have been processed and refined. In the process, white or brown sugar and white flour have had many of the vitamins and minerals present in the original plant removed.

Cardiovascular system   The heart, blood vessels and circulation of blood round the body

Cervix   The neck of the womb which projects downwards into the vagina

Cholesterol   A fat present in the blood and tissues used in the production of all sex hormones. An excess from the diet or metabolism contributes to the risk of heart disease.

Climacteric   The menopausal period in women

Collagen   A protein that is the principal constituent of white fibrous connective tissue and is present in bone as the framework on which the minerals are arranged

Conjugated oestrogens Oestrogens in their natural, non-synthetic state are teamed up with other components and are termed conjugated oestrogens

Contraceptive An item or method used to prevent pregnancy

Corpus luteum Literally, a little yellow gland or body. It is the part of the ovary that remains after the egg has left. It produces two hormones – oestrogen and progesterone – during the second half of the menstrual cycle

Cyst A sac or cavity containing liquid or semi-solid matter

Cystitis Inflammation of the lining of the bladder which often causes pain and the need to urinate frequently

Deficiency A lack of an essential substance like a vitamin

Diagnosis Process of determining the nature of a disease

Discharge A substance released from the body

Disease A set of signs and symptoms with a definite pathological process

Diuretics Drugs which cause an increased production of urine by the kidneys. They are used to treat fluid retention

Dopamine A brain chemical which affects mood and has a sedating effect

Dysmenorrhoea Painful periods

Endocrine glands Glands that secrete hormones and regulate other organs in the body. The thyroid and the pituitary are endocrine glands

Endometriosis A condition in which the lining of the uterus begins to grow outside the uterus in the abdominal cavity. It is usually a painful condition and can cause infertility

Endometrial cancer Cancer of the lining of the womb. It can occur if the endometrium is overstimulated by some hormones

Endorphins Hormones from the pituitary gland and fluid in the spine which are believed to help control moods, behaviour and part of the workings of the pituitary itself. They may also have an effect on how sugar is used in the body and on other amounts of hormones released from the pituitary gland and the ovaries. If this is so, the production of oestrogen and progesterone could be affected by endorphins

Essential fatty acids One of the essential groups of foods which we need to remain healthy. These are essential fats that are necessary for normal cell structure and body function. There are two: **linoleic** and **linolenic** acids. They are called 'essential' because they cannot be made by the body but have to be eaten in the diet

Fertilization The impregnation of the female sex cell by a male sex cell

Fibroids A benign tumour of fibrous and muscular tissue which often develops in the womb

Follicle Stimulating Hormone (FSH) A hormone of the pituitary gland which stimulates the growth of the follicles in the ovaries

Follicular phase The first half of the menstrual cycle when an egg is growing in the ovary. The egg is surrounded by cells which produce the hormone oestrogen and which thus prepare the uterus for conception. The egg and surrounding cells are called a follicle

Glucose A form of sugar found in the diet or released by the liver into the blood-stream which is then used by the brain for energy. This is the only source of energy it can use

Graafian follicle A mature egg which is surrounded by a bag of fluid within the ovary

Gynaecologist A person who specializes in diseases and problems of the female reproductive system

Heart attack Sudden damage to the heart muscle due to a blockage in its supply of blood. Sudden severe pains in the chest and possibly arms result. Also known as a coronary thrombosis or myocardial infarction

Hormonal implant A substance inserted into the body

Hormone Replacement Therapy (HRT) Hormones used to treat females suffering symptoms relating to the menopause

Hormones Substances formed chiefly in the endocrine glands which then enter the blood-stream and control the activity of an organ or body function. Adrenalin and insulin are hormones, as are oestrogen and progesterone

Hot flush   A sudden feeling of warmth and usually perspiration of the skin of the face and neck

Hyperhydration – too much water present   A term used to describe water retention in the body

Hypoglycaemia – low blood sugar   A condition in which there is a deficiency of insulin or lack of food. As glucose is required for normal brain function, mental disturbance can occur, as can other symptoms: headaches, weakness, faintness, irritability, palpitations, mood swings, sweating and hunger. One of the most common contributing factors is an excess of refined carbohydrates in the diet

Hypothalamus   The region of the brain controlling temperature, hunger, thirst and the hormones produced by the pituitary gland

Hysterectomy   A surgical procedure to remove the womb and the Fallopian tubes. Sometimes one or both ovaries are also removed

Immunology   The study of the body's immunity to disease

Incontinence   Involuntary lack of control in passing urine

Infertility   Inability for a woman or a man to be able to reproduce

Inflammation   The body's protective response to infection or injury which results in pain, swelling and heat of the affected part

Insomnia   Inability to sleep

Luteal phase   The time after the egg has left the follicle in the ovary and the follicle then becomes a gland known as the corpus luteum. The corpus luteum mainly produces progesterone

Luteinizing Hormone (LH)   The pituitary hormone that fosters the development of the corpus luteum

Mastectomy   Surgical removal of a breast

Menarche   The start of menstruation

Menopause   The time at which the last natural period takes place. It is a *date*, not several months or years

Menstruation   The monthly discharge of blood from the uterus

Menorrhagia   An excessive loss of blood during each period

Menses   The discharge of blood and tissue lining from the uterus which occurs approximately every four weeks between puberty and the menopause

Menstrual cycle   The monthly cycle involving the pituitary gland, ovaries and uterus in which an egg is produced ready for conception. In each cycle an egg in the ovary is released and the lining of the womb develops ready for conception and implantation of the fertilized egg. If this does not occur, the lining of the womb is shed and a period occurs

Menstrual symptomatology diary   A chart which is a daily record of all symptoms that occur throughout the menstrual cycle

Metabolism   The process by which the body maintains life. It is the cycle of nutrients being broken down to produce energy which is then used by the body to build new cells and tissues, provide heat, growth and physical activity. The metabolic rate tends to vary from person to person, depending on their age, sex and lifestyle

Mittelschmerz   Pain associated with ovulation which usually occurs about halfway through the menstrual cycle. Translated, it means 'middle pain'

Nutrition   The British Society for Nutritional Medicine's definition is the 'sum of the processes involved in taking nutrients, assimilating and utilizing them'. In other words, the quality of the diet and the ability of your body to utilize the individual nutrients and so maintain health

Oestrogen   A steroid hormone produced in large quantities by the ovaries and in smaller amounts by the adrenal glands. It's responsible at puberty for the development of breasts and other sexual characteristics. Oestrogen is also responsible for the production of fertile cervical mucus, the opening of the cervix and the building-up of blood in the lining of the uterus as it prepares for a fertilized egg

Omega-3 fatty acids   Essential fatty acids found mainly in oily fish and some vegetable oils

Omega-6 fatty acid   Essential fatty acid found in some vegetable oils. Commonest type known as linoleic acid. Evening primrose oil contains a very specialized omega-6 essential fatty acid

Oophorectomy   Surgical removal of an ovary

Oral contraceptives   Medication taken orally to prevent pregnancy

Osteoporosis   Thinning of the bones which leads to their brittleness and weakness

Ovaries   A pair of glands on either side of the uterus in which eggs and sex hormones, including oestrogen, are produced

Ovulation   The release of the ripe egg (ovum) from the ovary. The two ovaries ovulate alternately every month. Occasionally, the two ovaries ovulate simultaneously, in which case the result may be twins

Ovum   The egg which is released from the ovary at the time of ovulation

Palpitations   The heart beating too fast and sometimes irregularly

Pelvic Inflammatory Disease (PID)   Inflammation or infection of the internal female genital organs

Perimenopausal   The time around the menopause especially the time leading up to it

Pituitary gland   A small gland situated at the base of the brain which produces many hormones, among which are those that stimulate the ovaries and thyroid

Premenstrual   A term used to describe the time before the arrival of a period

Premenstrual syndrome   A collection of mental and physical symptoms that can manifest themselves before the onset of a period

Premenstrual tension   The name first given in 1931 by Dr Frank to the physical and mental symptoms detected before a period. Today the correct name is premenstrual syndrome. However, many women still prefer to call the condition PMT – premenstrual tension

Progesterone   A hormone secreted by the corpus luteum of the ovary during the second half of the menstrual cycle. Progesterone is an important hormone during pregnancy

Progestogens A group of synthetic hormones with actions similar to progesterone

Prolactin The hormone involved in milk production which is secreted by the pituitary gland. It is also known to affect the water and mineral balance in the body and in some women it may play a part in premenstrual changes

Prostaglandins Hormone-like substances found in almost every cell in the body. They are necessary for the normal function of involuntary muscles, including the heart, the uterus, blood vessels, the lungs and the intestines. Sometimes regarded as health-controllers, as they seem to play an important part in controlling many essential body functions. They do not come directly from the diet, but are made in the body itself, so the body relies on a good diet in order to produce them. The special substances the body needs to make prostaglandins are called **essential fatty acids**

Puberty The age at which the male and female reproductive organs begin to function

Serotonin A brain chemical that influences mood

Serum A clear fluid residue of blood

Sterilization A surgical procedure rendering males and females infertile

Steroids Substances which have a particular chemical structure in common. All the sex hormones, such as oestrogen, progesterone and testosterone are steroids. The term 'steroid' is also used in the context of corticosteroids (or cortisone), powerful agents that suppress inflammation and allergic reactions

Symptom An indication of disease such as a feeling, pain or complaint felt by the patient

Testosterone The male sex hormone

Thyroid gland A gland in the neck which produces the hormone thyroxine. The thyroid gland regulates the metabolism

Tranquillizers A group of drugs which artificially sedate the body. They can be useful in the short-term but in the long-term they may have addictive qualities

Urethra The canal through which urine is released from the bladder

Uterus (womb) A sac-like organ located in the abdomen of a woman and designed to hold and nourish a growing child from conception until birth

Vagina The passage that leads from the uterus to the external genital organs

Virus A microscopic organism capable of producing infection

Vulva External female genital organs

Womb The uterus. It is situated at the top of the vagina and receives the eggs, where they can develop into a pregnancy if fertilized

Appendix 3

Recommended Reading

NOTE
UK, USA and A denote the following books are available in Great Britain, the United States of America and Australia.

GENERAL HEALTH
1. *The Food Scandal*
   by Caroline Walker and Geoffrey Cannon
   (published by Century Publishing Co.) UK A
2. *The Migraine Revolution – The New Drug-free Solution*
   by Dr John Mansfield
   (published by Thorsons) UK USA A (Lothian Publishing Co.)
3. *Conquering Cystitis*
   by Dr Patrick Kingsley
   (published by Ebury Press) UK
4. *Candida Albicans: Could Yeast Be Your Problem?*
   by Leon Chaitow
   (published by Thorsons) UK USA A (Lothian Publishing Co.)
5. *Nutritional Medicine*
   by Dr Stephen Davies and Dr Alan Stewart
   (published by Hamlyn) UK A
6. *Y Plan Exercise Book*
   (published by Hamlyn) UK
7. *Bone Boosters – Natural Ways to Beat Osteoporosis*
   by Diana Moran and Helen Franks
   (published by Boxtree Limited) UK
8. *The Migraine Handbook*
   by Jenny Lewis

(published by Vermilion) UK A
9. *Food Allergy and Intolerance*
by Jonathan Bristoff and Linda Gamlin
(published by Bloomsbury) UK A

DIET
1. *The Vitality Diet*
by Maryon Stewart and Dr Alan Stewart
(published by Optima) UK A
2. *The Food Intolerance Diet*
by Elizabeth Workman SRD, Dr Virginia Alun Jones and
Dr John Hunter
(published by Martin Dunitz) UK USA
3. *The Salt-Free Diet Book*
by Dr Graham McGregor
(published by Martin Dunitz) UK USA
4. *The Allergy Diet*
by Elizabeth Workman SRD, Dr John Hunter and Dr
Virginia Alun Jones
(published by Martin Dunitz) US USA

STRESS
1. *Self-Help for Your Nerves*
by Dr Clair Weekes
(published by Angus and Robertson) UK USA (Hawthorn
Publishing Co.)
2. *Stress and Relaxation Self-Help Techniques for Everyone*
by Jane Hadders
(published by Optima) US USA A
3. *Lyn Marshall's Instant Stress Cure*
(published by Optima) UK A
4. *The Book of Massage*
(published by Ebury Press) UK
5. *Do-It-Yourself Shiatsu*
by W. Ohashi
(published by Unwin) UK

6. *The Book of Yoga* (The Sivananda Yoga Centre) (published by Ebury Press) UK A

RECIPE BOOKS
1. *Good Food Gluten Free*
   by Hilda Cherry Hills
   (published by Keats) USA
2. *Gluten-Free Cookery*
   by Rita Greer
   (published by Thorsons)
3. *The Wheat and Gluten Free Cookbook*
   by Joan Noble
   (published by Joan Noble)
4. *The Candida Albicans Yeast-Free Cookbook*
   by Pat Connolly and Associates of the Price Pottenger Nutrition Foundation
   (published by Keats Publishing Inc) UK USA
5. *The Cranks Recipe Book*
   by David Canter, Kay Canter and Daphne Swann
   (published by Granada) UK
6. *Raw Energy*
   by Leslie and Susannah Kenton
   (published by Century Publishing Co.) UK A (Doubleday Publishing Co.)
7. *The Reluctant Vegetarian*
   by Simon Hope
   (published by William Heinemann) UK
8. *Gourmet Vegetarian*
   by Rose Elliot
   (published by Fontana) UK A
9. *Healthy Cooking* from Tesco Stores
10. *The Gluten-free and Wheat-free Bumper Bake Book*
    by Rita Greer
    (published by Bunterbird Ltd) UK

GENERAL
1. *How to Stop Smoking and Stay Stopped for Good*
   by Gillian Riley

(published by Vermilion) UK A
2. *Getting Sober and Loving It*
   by Joan and Derek Taylor
   (published by Vermilion) UK A
3. *Tired all the Time*
   by Dr Alan Stewart
   (published by Optima) UK
4. *Memory Power*
   by Ursula Markham
   (published by Vermilion) UK A
5. *Alternative Health Aromatherapy*
   by Gill Martin
   (published by Optima) UK USA A
6. *Alternative Health Acupuncture*
   by Dr Michael Nightingale
   (published by Optima) UK USA A
7. *Alternative Health Osteopathy*
   by Stephen Sandler
   (published by Optima) UK USA A
8. *Pure, White and Deadly*
   by Professor John Yudkin
   (published by Viking) UK A
9. *Coming off Tranquillizers*
   by Dr Susan Trickett
   (published by Thorsons) UK USA A (Lothian Publishing
   Co.).
10. *Beat Sugar Craving*
    by Maryon Stewart
    (published by Vermilion) UK
11. *The Real Food Shop and Restaurant Guide*
    by Clive Johnson
    (published by Ebury Press) UK

IBS
1. *Beat IBS Through Diet*
   by Maryon Stewart and Dr Alan Stewart
   (published by Vermilion) UK A

EXERCISE
1. *Diana Moran's 3 in 1 Workout*
   video by Diana Moran

PMS
1. *Beat PMS Through Diet*
   by Maryon Stewart
   (published by Vermilion) UK A
2. *Beat PMS Cookbook*
   by Maryon Stewart and Sarah Tooley
   (published by Vermilion) UK A

Appendix 4

Summary of HRT Formulations

Conjugated Natural Oestrogen
Premarin 0.625 and 1.25 mg strengths.
Natural oestrogen from pregnant mares' urine.

Oestradiol
Progynova, Climaval, Zumenon and
Estraderm and Evorel (patches).

Oestrone
Harmogen.

Oestriol, Oestradiol and **Oestrone**
Hormonin.

OPPOSED OR COMBINED OESTROGEN AND PROGESTERONE
PREPARATIONS

Conjugated Natural Oestrogen and Norgestrel
Prempak-C 0.625 and 1.25mg strengths.

Oestradiol and Norethisterone
Climagest 1 and 2mg, Estracombi and Estrapak (patches).

Oestradiol and Levonorgestrel
Cyclo-Progynova 1mg and Nuvelle.

Oestradiol and Norgestrel
Cyclo-Progynova 2mg.

Mestranol and Norethisterone
Menophase.

Oestriol, Oestradiol and Norethisterone
Trisequens and Trisequens Forte.

TOPICAL OESTROGEN AS A CREAM
Ortho Dinoestrol, Ortho-Gynest and Ovestin.

TOPICAL OESTROGEN AS A PESSARY
Ortho-Gynest, Tampovagan and Vagifem.

OTHERS

Tibolone
Livial.

Appendix 5
Useful Addresses

UK

Action against Allergy
23–24 George Street
Richmond
Surrey TW9 1JY

Action on Phobias
c/o Shandy Mathias
8–9 The Avenue
Eastbourne
East Sussex
Letters only enclosing sae

Age Concern
Astral House
1268 London Road
London SW16 4EJ
Tel: 081 679 8000

Alcoholics Anonymous (AA)
General Services Office
PO Box 1
Stonebow House
Stonebow
York Y01 2NJ
Tel: 0904 644026

Amarant Trust
56–60 St John Street
London EC1M 4DT
Tel: 071 490 1644

ASH (Action on Smoking and Health)
109 Gloucester Place
London W1H 3PN
Tel: 071 935 3519

Asset (Exercise Association)
4 Angel Gate
City Road
London EC1V 2PT
Tel: 071 278 0811

British Acupuncture Register and Directory
34 Alderney Street
London SW1V 4UE
Tel: 071 834 1012

The British Homoeopathic Association
27a Devonshire Street
London W1N 1RJ
Tel: 071 935 2163

British School of Osteopathy
Little John House
1 Suffolk Street
London SW1Y 4HG
Tel: 071 930 9254

The Council for Acupuncture
Suite 1
19a Cavendish Square
London W1M 9AD
Tel: 071 409 1440

Endometriosis Society
35 Belgrave Square
London SW1X 8QB
Tel: 071 235 4137

The European School of Osteopathy
Little John House
1–4 Suffolk Street
London SW1 4HG
Tel: 071 930 9254/8

The Faculty of Homoeopathy
The Royal London Homoeopathic Hospital
Great Ormond Street
London WC1N 3HR
Tel: 071 837 3091, Ext. 72/85

Food Watch International
Butts Pond Industrial Estate
Sturminster Newton
Dorset DT10 1AZ
Tel: 0258 73356

Friends of the Earth
26–28 Underwood Street
London N1 7JQ
Tel: 071 490 1555

The Henry Doubleday Research Association
Ryton Gardens
National Centre for Organic Gardening
Ryton on Dunsmore
Coventry CV8 3LG
Tel: 0203 303517

Homoeopathic Development Foundation
19a Cavendish Square
London W1M 9AD
Tel: 071 629 3205

International Federation of Aromatherapists
4 Eastmearn Road
West Dulwich
London SE21 8HA

Migraine Trust
45 Great Ormond Street
London WC1 3HZ
Tel: 071 278 2676

The National Institute of Medical Herbalists
56 Longbrook Street
Exeter EX4 6AN
Tel: 0392 426022

The National Osteoporosis Society
Barton Meade House
PO Box 10
Redstock
Bath BA3 3YB

National Society for Research into Allergy
PO Box 45
Hinkley
Leicestershire LE10 1JY
Tel: 0455 303517

Patients' Association
Room 33
18 Charing Cross Road
London WC2H 0HR
Tel: 071 981 5676

Release
388 Old Street
London EC1V 9LT
Tel: 071 729 9904

The Samaritans
10 The Grove
Slough SL1 1QP
Tel: 0753 532713

The Shiatsu Society
14 Oakdene Road
Redhill
Surrey
Tel: 0730 767896

The Soil Association
86–88 Colston Street
Bristol BS1 5BB
Tel: 0272 290661

The Sports Council
16 Upper Woburn Place
London WC1H 0QP
Tel: 071 388 1277

Tranx Release (Northampton)
Anita Gordon
24 Hazelwood Road
Northampton NN1 1LN
Tel: 0604 250976

Trax (UK) Ltd.
National Tranquillizer Advice Centre
Registered Office
25a Masons Avenue
Wealdstone, Harrow
Middlesex HA3 5AH
Tel: (client line) 081 427 2065
(24 hr answering service 081 427 2827)

Women's Health
52 Featherstone Street
London EC1Y 8RT
Tel: 071 251 6580

The Women's Nutritional Advisory Service
PO Box 268, Lewes
East Sussex BN7 2QN
Tel: 0273 487366

YMCA
112 Great Russell Street
London WC1B 3NQ
Tel: 071 580 2989

AUSTRALIA

Adelaide Women's Community Health
64 Pennington Terrace
Nth Adelaide SA 5006
Tel: 08 267 5366

Blackmores Limited – Women's Health Advisory Service
23 Roseberry Street
Balgowlah
NSW 2093
Tel: 02 949 3177

Liverpool Women's Health Centre
26 Bathurst Street
Liverpool
NSW 2170
Tel: 02 601 3555

Women's Health Advisory Service
155 Eaglecreek Road
Werombi 2570
NSW
Tel: 046 531 445

NEW ZEALAND

Health Alternative for Women
Room 101, Cranmer Centre
PO Box 884
Christchurch
Tel: 796 970

Papakura Women's Centre
4 Opaneke Road
Papakura
Auckland
Tel: 08 267 5366

Tauranga Women's Centre
PO Box 368
Tauranga
Tel: 783 530

West Auckland Women's Centre
PO Box 69116
Glendene
Auckland
Tel: 09 838 6381

Whakatane Women's Collective
PO Box 3049
Ohope
Tel: 076 24757

Women's Health Collective
63 Ponsonby Road
Ponsonby
Auckland
Tel: 764 506

Note: Readers are reminded that from 16 April 1995 all United Kingdom area dialling codes will have a 1 inserted after the leading 0 (e.g. 071 becomes 0171).

Appendix 6
References

2: The Facts of the Menopause

1. Wilbush, J., 'Climacteric Disorders – Historical Perspectives', in *The Menopause*, Eds. Studd, J.W.W., Whitehead, M.I. Blackwell Scientific Publications, Oxford, 1988, pp 1–14.

3: The Menopause is Here

1. Ginsburg, J., 'What determines the age at the menopause?' *The British Medical Journal*, 1991; 302: 1288–9.
2. Mahadevan, K., Murthy, M.S.R., Reddy, P.R., Bhaskaran, S., 'Early Menopause and its Determinants'. *Journal of Biosocial Science* 1982; 14: 473–9.
3. Magos, A.L., Brewster, E., Singh, R., O'Dowd, T., Brincat, M., Studd, J.W.W., 'The effects of norethisterone in post-menopausal women on oestrogen replacement therapy: a model for the premenstrual syndrome'. *British Journal of Obstetrics and Gynaecology*, 1986; 93: 1290–96.
4. Wilcox, L.S. et al, 'Hysterectomy in the United States'. *Obstetrics and Gynecology*, 1994; 83: 549–55.
5. Carlson, K.J., Miller, B.A., Fowler, F.J., 'The Maine Women's Health Study: I. Outcomes of hysterectomy.' *Obstetrics and Gynecology*, 1994; 83: 556–65.
6. Guillebaud, J., 'Contraception for women over 35 years of age'. *British Journal of Family Planning*, 1992; 17: 115–18.

4: The Symptoms of the Menopause

1. Haas, S., Schiff, I., 'Symptoms of Oestrogen Deficiency', in *The Menopause*, Eds. Studd, J.W.W., Whitehead, M.I. Blackwell Scientific Publications, Oxford, 1988, pp 15–23.

2. Sturdee, D., Brincat, M., 'The Hot Flush', in *The Menopause*, Eds. Studd, J.W.W., Whitehead, M.I. Blackwell Scientific Publications, Oxford, 1988, pp 24–42.
3. Brincat, M., Studd, J.W.W., 'Skin and the Menopause', in *The Menopause*, Eds. Studd, J.W.W., Whitehead, M.I. Blackwell Scientific Publications, Oxford, 1988, pp 85–101.
4. Hunter, M., 'Psychological Aspects of the Climacteric and the Postmenopause', in *The Menopause*, Eds. Studd, J.W.W., Whitehead, M.I. Blackwell Scientific Publications, Oxford, 1988, pp 55–64.

5: The Bone Robber: Osteoporosis
1. Law, M.R., Wald, N.J., Meade, T.W., 'Strategies for the prevention of osteoporosis and hip fracture'. *The British Medical Journal*, 1991; 303: 453–9.
2. Compston, J.E., 'Risk factors for osteoporosis'. *Clinical Endocrinology*, 1992; 36: 223–4.
3. Freudenheim, J.L., Johnson, N.E., Smith, E.L., 'Relationships between usual nutrient intake and bone-mineral content of women 35–65 years of age: longitudinal and cross-sectional analysis'. *The American Journal of Clinical Nutrition*, 1986; 44: 863–76.
4. Kanis, J.A. et al, 'Evidence of efficacy of drugs affecting bone metabolism in preventing hip fracture'. *British Medical Journal*, 1992; 305: 1124–8.
5. Storm, T., Thamsborg, G., Steiniche, T., Genant, H.K., Sorensen, O.H., 'Effect of intermittent cyclical etidronate therapy on bone mass and fracture rate in women with postmenopausal osteoporosis'. *The New England Journal of Medicine*, 1990; 322: 1265–71.
6. LaCroix, A.Z., et al, 'Thiazide diuretic agents and the incidence of hip fracture'. *The New England Journal of Medicine*, 1990; 322: 286–90.
7. Ettinger, B., Grady, D., 'The waning effect of postmenopausal estrogen therapy on osteoporosis'. *The New England Journal of Medicine*, 1993; 329: 1192–3.
8. Recker, R.R., 'Calcium absorption and achlorhydria'. *The*

New England Journal of Medicine, 1985; 313: 70–73.

6: HRT – The Choices
1. Wilbush, J., 'Climacteric Disorders – Historical Perspectives', in *The Menopause*, Eds. Studd, J.W.W., Whitehead, M.I. Blackwell Scientific Publications, Oxford, 1988, pp 1–14.
2. Wilson, R.C.D., *Understanding HRT and the Menopause*. Consumers Association, London, 1992.

8 and 9: The Side-effects of HRT
1. *MIMS*, May, 1994. Haymarket Medical Ltd., London.
2. Jacobs, H.S., Loeffler F.E., 'Postmenopausal hormone replacement therapy'. *British Medical Journal*, 1992; 305: 1403–8.
3. Grady, D. et al, 'Hormone Therapy to Prevent Disease and Prolong Life in Postmenopausal Women'. *Annals of Internal Medicine*, 1992; 117: 1016–37.
4. Stampfer, M.J., et al, 'Postmenopausal Estrogen Therapy and Cardiovascular Disease'. *The New England Journal of Medicine*, 1991; 325: 756–62.
5. Barret-Connor, E., Bush T.L., 'Estrogen and Coronary Heart Disease in Women'. *Journal of the American Medical Association*, 1991; 265: 1861–7.
6. Hemminki, E., Sihvo, S., 'A Review of Postmenopausal Hormone Replacement Therapy Recommendations: Potential for Selection Bias'. *Obstetrics and Gynaecology*, 1993; 82: 1021–8.
7. Hunt, K., Vessey, M., McPherson, K., 'Mortality in a Cohort of Long-Term Users of Hormone Replacement Therapy: an Updated Analysis'. *British Journal of Obstetrics and Gynaecology*, 1990; 97: 1080–86.
8. Nabulsi, A.A., et al, 'Association of Hormone-Replacement Therapy with various Cardiovascular Risk factors in Postmenopausal Women'. *The New England Journal of Medicine*, 1993; 328: 1069–75.
9. Lindheim, S.R., et al, 'The Independent Effects of Exercise

and Estrogen on Lipids and Lipoproteins in Postmenopausal Women'. *Obstetrics and Gynaecology*, 1994; 83: 167–72.

10. Ross, D., Stevenson, J., 'HRT and cardiovascular disease'. *British Journal of Sexual Medicine*, 1993; Nov/Dec: 10–13.

11. Rosano, G.M.C., et al, 'Beneficial effect of oestrogen on exercise-induced myocardial ischaemia in women with coronary heart disease'. *The Lancet*, 1993; 342: 133–6.

12. Martin, K.A., Freeman, M.W., 'Postmenopausal Hormone-Replacement Therapy'. *The New England Journal of Medicine*, 1993; 328: 1115–17.

13. Magos, A.L., Brewster, E., Singh, R., O'Dowd, T., Brincat, M., Studd, J.W.W., 'The effects of norethisterone in postmenopausal women on oestrogen replacement therapy: a model for the premenstrual syndrome'. *British Journal of Obstetrics and Gynaecology*, 1986; 93: 1290–96.

14. Coope, J., Thompson, J.M., Poller, L., 'Effects of "natural oestrogen" replacement therapy on menopausal symptoms and blood clotting'. *British Medical Journal*, 1975; 4: 139–43.

15. Wallace, W.A., 'Hormone Replacement Therapy and the Surgeon', in British Menopause Society *Newsletter*, December 1993, pp 19–21.

11: Nutrition and Hormone Function

1. Goldin, B.R., Aldercreutz, H., Dwyer, J.T., Swenson, L., Warram, J.H., Gorbach, S.L., 'Effect of diet on excretion of estrogens in pre- and postmenopausal women'. *Cancer Research*, 1981; 41: 3771–3.

2. Armstrong, B.K., Brown, J.B., Clarke, H.T., Crooke, D.K., Hahnel, R., Masarei, J.R., Ratajczak, T., 'Diet and Reproductive Hormones: A Study of Vegetarian and Non-vegetarian Postmenopausal Women'. *Journal of the National Cancer Institute*, 1981; 67: 761–7.

3. Hill, P., Garabaczewski, L., Helman, P., Huskisson, J., Wynder, E.L., 'Diet, Lifestyle and Menstrual Activity'. *American Journal of Nutrition*, 1980; 33: 1192–8.

4. Davies, S., Stewart, A., *Nutritional Medicine*, Pan Books, London, 1987.
5. McLaren, H.C., 'Vitamin E and the Menopause'. *British Medical Journal*, 1949; Dec 17th: 1378–81.
6. Ford, K.A., LaBarbera, A.R., 'Cationic Modulation of Follicle-Stimulating Hormone Binding to Granulosa Cell Receptor'. *Biology of Reproduction*, 1987; 36: 643–50.
7. Feldman, D., Stathis, P.A., Hirst, M.A., Stover, E.P., Do, Y.S., 'Saccharomyces cervisiae produces a yeast substance that exhibits estrogenic activity in mammalian systems'. *Science*, 1984; 224: 1109–11.
8. Punnonen, R., Lukola, A., 'Oestrogen-like effect of ginseng'. *British Medical Journal*, 1980; 281: 1110.
9. Wilcox, G., Wahlqvist, M.L., Burger, H.G., Medley, G., 'Oestrogenic effects of plant foods in postmenopausal women'. *British Medical Journal*, 1990; 301: 905.

12: The Benefits of Exercise

1. Notelovitz, M., 'The non-hormonal management of the menopause', in *The Menopause*, Eds. Studd, J.W.W., Whitehead, M.I. Blackwell Scientific Publications, Oxford, 1988.
2. Notelovitz, M., 'The non-hormonal management of the menopause', in *The Modern Management of the Menopause*, edited by G. Berg & M. Hammer, Parthenon Publishing, 1994.
3. Cowan, M.M., Gregory, L.W., 'Responses of pre- and postmenopausal females to aerobic conditioning'. *Medical Science, Sports and Exercise*, 1985; 17: 138–43.
4. Morgan, W.P., 'Anxiety reduction following acute physical activity'. *Psychiatry Annals*, 1979; 9: 36–45.
5. Morgan, W.P., et al, 'Facilitation of physical performance by means of cognitive strategy'. *Cognitive Therapy Research*, 1983; 7: 251–64.
6. Penny, G.D., Rust, J.O., 'Effect of walking-jogging programme on personality characteristics of middle-aged females'. *Journal of Sports Medicine*, 1982; 20: 221–6.

7. Gill, A.A., et al, 'A well woman's health maintenance study comparing physical fitness and group support programs'. *Journal of Occupational Therapy and Research*, 1984; 4: 286–308.

8. Greist, J.H., et al, 'Running as treatment for depression'. *Comprehensive Psychiatry*, 1979; 20: 41–53.

9. Goldberg, L., et al, 'Changes in lipid and lipoprotein levels after weight training'. *Journal of American Medical Association*, 1984; 252: 504–6.

10. Martin, A.D., et al, 'Predicting maximal oxygen uptake from treadmill testing in trained and untrained women'. *American Journal of Obstetrics and Gynaecology*, 1989; 161: 127–32.

11. Martin, D., Notelovitz, M., 'Effects of aerobic training on bone mineral density of postmenopausal women'. *Journal of Bone and Mineral Research*, 1993; 8: 931–6.

12. Notelovitz, M., et al, 'Cardiorespiratory fitness evaluation in climacteric women: comparison of two methods'. *American Journal of Obstetrics and Gynaecology*, 1986; 154: 1009–13.

13. Probart, C.K., et al, 'The effect of moderate aerobic exercise on physical fitness among women 70 years and older'. *Maturitas*, 1991; 14: 49–56.

14. Van Dam, S., et al, 'Effect of exercise on glucose metabolism in postmenopausal women'. *American Journal of Obstetrics and Gynaecology*, 1988; 159: 82–6.

15. Spiriduso, W.W., 'Exercise as a factor in aging motor behaviour plasticity in exercise and health', pp 89–100. American Academy of Physical Education Papers 17, Human Kinetics Publishers, Inc., Champaign, Illinois.

16. Spiriduso, W.W., Clifford, P., 'Replication of age and physical activity effects in reaction and movement time'. *Journal of Gerontology*, 1978; 33: 26–30.

Appendix 7
Charts and Diaries

Menopause Symptom Questionnaire

Do you suffer from any of the following? Please ensure each symptom is only ticked *once*.

	*How many times per month	None	Mild	Moderate	Severe
1 Hot/cold flushes*					
2 Facial/body flushing*					
3 Nightsweats*					
4 Palpitations*					
5 Panic attacks*					
6 Generalised aches and pains					
7 Depression					
8 Perspiration					
9 Numbness/skin tingling in arms and legs					
10 Headaches					
11 Backache					
12 Fatigue					
13 Irritability					
14 Anxiety					
15 Nervousness					
16 Loss of confidence					
17 Insomnia					
18 Giddiness/dizziness					
19 Difficulty/frequency in passing water					
20 Water retention					

21 Bloated abdomen				
22 Constipation				
23 Itchy vagina				
24 Dry vagina				
25 Painful intercourse				
26 Decreased sex drive				
27 Loss of concentration				
28 Confusion/Loss of vitality				

Menopause Symptomatology Daily Diary

Grading of symptoms

0 None
1 Mild – present but does not interfere with activities
2 Moderate – present and interferes with activities but not disabling
3 Severe – disabling. Unable to function

Date																												
Hot/cold flushes																												
Facial/body flushing																												
Nightsweats																												
Palpitations																												
Panic attacks																												
Generalised aches and pains																												
Depression																												
Perspiration																												
Numbness/skin tingling in arms and legs																												
Headaches																												
Backache																												
Fatigue																												
Irritability																												
Anxiety																												
Nervousness																												
Loss of confidence																												

Insomnia											
Giddiness/dizziness											
Difficulty/frequency in passing water											
Constipation											
Itchy vagina											
Dry vagina											
Painful intercourse											
Decreased sex drive											
Loss of concentration											
Weight in pounds											

Notes

Please complete on a *daily basis* for all food and drink consumed

	BREAKFAST	LUNCH	DINNER	SNACKS
DAY 1				
DAY 2				
DAY 3				

DAY 4			
DAY 5			
DAY 6			
DAY 7			

Exercise and Relaxation Chart

Type of exercise and time	Time on Monday	Time on Tuesday	Time on Wednesday	Time on Thursday	Time on Friday	Time on Saturday	Time on Sunday

Type of relaxation						

Once you have completed this for the week, pin it up on a noticeboard or on your fridge and tick off the sessions as you do them.

Index of Recipes

324

Index